Contents

Introduction

This new version of the Level 2 NVQ Certificate in Business and Administration aims to reflect the work of administration staff who often work as part of a team and provide information and resources to others. The qualification provides evidence of competence in being able to carry out a supporting role in an office environment. It introduces many of the functional areas and tasks involved in business administration. There is a wide range of units, but the qualification itself is competence-based and has been designed so that students can tackle each part of a unit in systematic chunks.

The Level 2 NVQ Certificate in Business and Administration is part of a broader range of qualifications, all of which have been accredited onto the Qualifications and Credit Framework (QCF). The qualification has also been endorsed by the Council for Administration (CfA).

In order to achieve the Level 2 NVQ Certificate in Business and Administration, students need to complete a minimum of 21 credits at Level 2. This book offers not only the 4 mandatory units but also 5 of the most popular optional units. There are numerous other optional units, offered at Levels 1, 2 and 3, which may be more appropriate to your workplace situation. You will need to complete all 4 of the mandatory units. This will give you 9 credits. The remaining 14 credits can come from any combination of the optional units.

Not all of the units are worth the same number of credits. The mandatory units are:

- 201 – Manage Own Performance in a Business Environment (2 credits)
- 202 – Improve Own Performance in a Business Environment (2 credits)
- 203 – Work in a Business Environment (2 credits)
- 206 – Communicate in a Business Environment (3 credits).

The optional units that have proved to be the most popular over the years are:

- 205 – Work with Other People in a Business Environment (3 credits)
- 212 – Produce Documents in a Business Environment (4 credits)
- 219 – Store and Retrieve Information (3 credits)
- 221 – Use Office Equipment (4 credits)
- 256 – Meet and Welcome Visitors (3 credits).

Probably unlike anything that you have done before, assessors at your centre will make the decision as to whether or not you have met all the requirements for a unit. They will confirm this by signing an evidence record sheet that shows that the assessment process for the unit has been completed. They will agree with you about the best source of evidence for each unit. They will discuss with you the best way to assess you and also confirm the times, dates and places that any assessments will happen. The methods of assessment need to be valid, reliable, safe and suitable to you.

One of the key features of this book is that it identifies the typical type of evidence that you will need for each part of every unit covered. It may not always be possible for you to provide evidence that you have carried out certain types of work. In these cases this book contains a backup set of tasks that you can use to create the evidence that otherwise you may be missing. When you are carrying out these types of tasks, the assessors will observe you and see how you tackle the tasks at hand. Ideally, real work situations are the best way to gather evidence. The case studies in the book are simulations; they have been designed to be just like real work activities. Your centre will have a realistic working environment, with all the necessary resources for you to carry these out if you are a full-time student.

This book aims to cater for candidates who are in full-time work, providing guidance on the type of evidence and an explanation of all the assessment criteria and learning outcomes. For day-release students the book provides not only vital guidance but also tasks and activities to complete in order to bridge any gaps in evidence. For full-time students there is a comprehensive series of tasks and activities that can be carried out in a model office environment, or during work experience.

Features of the book

This book has four main goals:

- to explain what the learning outcomes mean, and what you have to show that you can do or understand to help you meet the assessment criteria
- to check that you actually understand what is involved by providing you with a range of tasks and activities, so that you can practise and fill any gaps in your knowledge
- to provide you with a real work simulation that should give you enough evidence for the assessment criteria. These are designed so that you can plug any gaps in your work evidence
- to explain exactly what type of evidence the assessor is looking for and whether there are any specific things that you should include.

There are five main features included in the book:

Give it a go

these are activities, tasks or questions that are designed to test whether or not you actually understand something. They also give you an opportunity to have an early practice.

Don't forget

these are definitions of key words, phrases or terms that you may not have come across yet, or may not be completely clear as to their meaning.

Over to you

these are bigger activities or sets of tasks that are designed to bring together several different elements. They will help you to begin to show your ability to perform in an administration support role.

Pull it together

these are the major simulations, or assignments. They are a series of tasks and activities that aims to cover the learning outcomes of the unit. They will provide you with the necessary evidence in cases when you cannot provide that evidence yourself from your normal job role.

What is Evidence ?

this feature lists the evidence you need to provide for each of the assessment criteria, as recommended by the Council for Administration. In some cases they will be written pieces of work or examples of work, in other cases they may be records of conversations or question and answer sessions.

The Give it a go, Over to you and Pull it together features are all activities, tasks or questions. They are designed to provide opportunities to create evidence to cover assessment criteria that may not usually form a part of your normal work. As you complete each of these activities your assessor will question you as to how you went about completing it. Your assessor will give written feedback as to your level of understanding of the task and this will form part of your evidence for the assessment criteria.

The book systematically covers each learning outcome in the units and each assessment criterion. Sometimes it is better to consider a number of assessment criteria together, but you will find clear headings for each learning outcome and each assessment criterion. Each of the chapters covering a unit gives you the following:

- a basic introduction, which describes the purpose of the unit
- the assessment requirements, which explain the scope of the unit and the main areas that you will be covering
- a complete coverage of each learning outcome and each assessment criterion
- a series of features to test that you understand things, highlighting key words and terms, and an opportunity to try out some activities
- a clear indication of what evidence the assessor is expecting to see for each of the assessment criteria
- a complete simulated series of exercises and tasks at the end of each unit, should you need to create your own evidence.

Assessment – how it works

As soon as you enrol on this course your centre will carry out an initial assessment which will provide the information needed to plan your learning and to improve your chances of learning effectively. It will identify any competences and knowledge that you already have. It will then focus on the gaps. This is an ideal way of helping you with your choice of units and to understand how you need to go about collecting evidence. It will also identify any units that you may have particular problems with.

Your assessor will plan your assessments with you to help you find the best source of evidence for you to use and the best way of assessing you as an individual. They will indicate to you which tasks in each of the units you will need to complete to gain evidence and help you map the knowledge and understanding within the units. The assessor will also confirm with you when and where any assessments will take place.

The assessor will make all of the necessary assessment decisions. You will need to produce evidence to demonstrate competence when meeting all of the assessment criteria. This will be planned alongside the assessor. As we have seen, the methods of collecting evidence have to be:

- valid – evidence needs to measure your knowledge or skills. You need to know what is required of you and the evidence that you produce needs to do the job of meeting the assessment criteria

- reliable – simply, it needs to show that you consistently meet the criteria because you may be assessed by different people in different places. It also needs to be your own work

- safe and manageable – it should not put any unnecessary demands on you or the organisation that you work for

- suitable – so the majority of the evidence that you collect is part of your normal working week. Collecting evidence should not involve carrying out too many tasks on a one-off basis.

Only approved and qualified assessors will examine your evidence. Evidence generally falls into three different categories:

- it can be an observation by an assessor on how you actually carried out a process

- it can be a work product, such as a document

- it can be an observation by a witness or a statement that confirms you show competence in a particular area of work.

It is a good idea to look at typical ways of collecting evidence. This is summarised in the following table:

What evidence?	Who is allowed to do it?	What does it mean?
Observation	Assessor	The assessor records their observation of you carrying out a task
Questioning	Assessor	The assessor asks you questions to test your knowledge of facts, procedures, principles, theories and processes
Professional discussion	Assessor	This is an in-depth discussion that allows you to present evidence of competence and skills, knowledge and understanding
Witness testimony	Work colleagues/ assessor	This can be a written or verbal statement, where a work colleague provides a list of skills and competences that they have witnessed you performing in the workplace
Personal statements	Yourself/witness/ assessor	You give an account of what you did, backed up by evidence or witnesses, such as log books or diaries. These need to be countersigned
Performance evidence	Yourself	Some physical proof that you can do something, such as a document or a video. It can also be an assessor's observation of you working or a witness statement

All of the evidence that you collect and submit to the assessor needs to meet the requirements of the assessment criteria. This means that there is a wide variety of evidence that you can produce:

- assessor's observation of workplace activities – the assessor provides information based on their observations

- products – reports, letters, memos, printouts, emails, etc. (You should be aware that in the majority of modern offices, memos have been superseded by email.)

- expert witnesses – these are identified and trained by the centre and are used to help fill in any gaps in the competence of assessors. They also handle evidence that may be confidential or sensitive

- witness testimony – statements indicating how you carry out your job

- candidate reports – verbal or written reports that describe activities and processes, such as a work diary

- reflective account – a written account by you of how you carried out part of your job and including a record of events that happened

- recognition of prior learning or achievement – this will be determined by the assessor, who will look at what you have studied in the past, or have achieved already. They will match these to the assessment criteria

- professional discussions – structured and planned in-depth discussions to support observation or products

- verbal or written questions – these are used to fill in gaps only where knowledge is not obvious

- projects – extended pieces of practical or written work involving planning and research

- assignments – practical or written tasks to test your skills, knowledge and understanding

- case studies – these require you to produce a report, identifying problems, analysing issues, discussing and justifying solutions and presenting recommendations

- audio or video recordings – these can be used to support observation or discussions

- simulations and role plays – sets of tasks in a 'realistic working environment'.

You will discover that it is often the case that when you provide evidence for one part of a unit it can also be used as evidence or part-evidence for another unit. This is known as a holistic approach to assessment and your assessor will be able to guide you through this. It makes a great deal of sense to use this approach because it means that you will not have to duplicate evidence. It also means that your evidence will come from a range of activities. It is a far more efficient way of collecting evidence.

■ Organising your evidence

Each unit you study will have an evidence record sheet which links the evidence to the assessment criteria. You will give each piece of evidence a reference or location and identify the assessment method used and the assessment criteria covered. Your assessor will be able to provide you with feedback to help you complete your evidence reference sheet and identify which criteria have been covered. The assessment record sheet needs to be signed by you and, after it has been checked, signed by the assessor. In due course it may also be counter-signed by the internal verifier, who monitors and samples the assessment decisions of assessors.

This means that your portfolio of work can be a combination of written material, observation records, witness statements, or a mix of some or all of the different types of evidence that we have looked at. Wherever possible, real work evidence is best, even if this means evidence that comes from your working on a voluntary basis or during work experience. Simulations are acceptable and these can be carried out in a realistic working environment at your centre. They tend to be used only when you cannot complete the units because you do not have the opportunity to practise them in a real work environment.

■ Managing the evidence

This is a business and administration course and a basic piece of advice is to start as you mean to go on. This means from the very beginning organising your evidence. It needs to be kept safe, logged and given reference numbers and you need to be absolutely clear about its location if it is not in your portfolio of evidence.

By systematically completing the evidence record sheets and then the evidence summary sheets, you will be able to identify each piece of evidence, and which units, learning outcomes and assessment criteria it relates to. Much of the evidence you generate for your optional units will also provide evidence for the madatory units. This will make the job of assessment much easier. It also means that you can quickly identify gaps and particular assessment criteria that are proving to be a problem. Discuss these problem areas with your assessor and they will be able to suggest solutions.

Acknowledgments

The authors and publishers would like to thank the following for permission to reproduce material in this book:

Figure 201.1 Fotolia.com; Figure 201.4 microimages / Fotolia.com; Figure 201.5 Image State Media; Figure 203.1 Yuri Arcurs / Fotolia.com; Figure 203.2 Sergey Tumanov / Fotolia.com; Figure 203.6 Bill Howe / Fotolia.com; Figure 205.1 Nick Cunard / Alamy; Figure 205.2 George Wada / Fotolia.com; Figure 205.7 Sly / Fotolia.com; Figure 206.1 Zsolt Nyulaszi / Fotolia.com; Figure 212.2 Art Directors & TRIP / Alamy; Figure 212.3 mediablitzimages (UK) Limited / Alamy; Figure 221.1 Bogdan Dumitru / Fotolia.com; Figure 256.1 Marcel Mooij / Fotolia.com

Every effort has been made to obtain necessary permission with reference to copyright material. The publishers apologise if inadvertently any sources remain unacknowledged and will be glad to make the necessary arrangements at the earliest opportunity.

Unit 201

Manage Own Performance in a Business Environment

■ Purpose of the unit

This unit is about being able to manage your own work and be accountable for it.

■ Assessment requirements

There are four parts to this unit. The first two parts introduce planning and work and behaving in a way that supports effective working. The four parts are:

1 Understand how to plan, work and be accountable to others – guidelines, procedures and codes of practice, planning work and being accountable, purpose of realistic targets and how to agree them, planning work to meet deadlines, keeping others informed about progress, letting others know about work plans needing to be changed, problems that may occur during work, seeking guidance to resolve problems and recognising and learning from mistakes.

2 Understand how to behave in a way that supports effective working – purpose and ways of setting high standards for own work, taking on new challenges, adapting to change, treating others with honesty, respect and consideration, workplace behaviour.

3 Be able to plan and be responsible for own work supported by others – agreeing realistic targets and achievable timescales, planning work tasks, confirming effective working methods, identifying and reporting problems, keeping others informed about progress, completing tasks to agreed deadlines, taking responsibility for own work and any mistakes made, following agreed work guidelines, procedures and codes of practice.

4 Behave in a way that supports effective working – setting high standards and showing commitment, taking on new challenges, adapting to new ways of working, treating others with honesty, respect and consideration, providing help and support to others.

■ 1. Understand how to plan, work and be accountable to others

1.1 Outline guidelines, procedures and codes of practice relevant to personal work
1.2 Explain the purpose of planning work, and being accountable to others for own work

Guidelines are preferred ways in which businesses want documents and other forms of communication to take place. Procedures are preferred ways in which work is carried out. Codes of practice are minimum standards that are either set by the business or organisation, or are legal requirements.

All organisations work in different ways and have different systems and procedures with which their employees are expected to comply in the course of their duties. The running of an organisation requires an organised approach if it is to be efficient and effective. Administration plays a vital role in this approach. Administration is the means by which the organisation is able to operate as a whole.

The administrative systems which the organisation has in place should aim to establish a means by which the operations it carries out can be assessed and amended if necessary. They require continued monitoring to ensure efficiency and effectiveness. They should also be flexible enough to be able to respond to any changes that take place within the organisation.

When we use the term 'administrative systems', we are considering those set up to:

- gather information

- store information

- coordinate information

- retrieve information

- disseminate (pass on) information

- process information.

These administrative tasks will be carried out at all levels of the organisation. In larger organisations there may be an administration department designed specifically for this task. Administrative systems are in place to:

- allow the activities of the managers to determine the aims and policies of the organisation

- control the day-to-day running of the business

- provide support systems for all resources used by the organisation (human, physical and financial)

- keep records relating to the activities of the organisation
- monitor the performance of the business's activities.

At departmental level there are administration considerations too, including:

- receiving and distributing internal mail (mail which has come from inside the business)
- receiving and distributing external mail (mail which has come from outside the business)
- sending mail out of the department
- sending faxes
- sending email messages
- filing paperwork
- storing computer files
- answering the telephone and taking messages
- preparing paperwork for a meeting
- preparing and responding to memos
- writing business letters
- preparing articles, notices, leaflets and newsletters
- preparing advertisements.

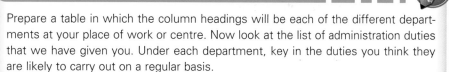

Give it a go

Prepare a table in which the column headings will be each of the different departments at your place of work or centre. Now look at the list of administration duties that we have given you. Under each department, key in the duties you think they are likely to carry out on a regular basis.

One of the most frustrating aspects of work, no matter what your role, is the feeling that you are constantly working hard just to cope with the flow of work passing across your desk. Being effective in any role requires a degree of planning. You also need to prioritise the work which is presented to you.

There are many ways of achieving effective planning, but this is only part of being effective in your job. You will be required to provide information and carry out work according to the timetable of others, as they may need what you are doing by a particular date. You will also need to be careful with the information which you receive, as it may be confidential.

Most senior members of staff who ask you to carry out work on their behalf will wish to be updated and kept informed of your progress. There are many

Figure 201.1

things to remember, many different demands on your time, and in this part of the unit we will be examining methods of doing this.

Action planning is an important part of objective, target and goal setting and problem solving. Action planning can assist a business to plan for the future, ensuring that as situations change they can be controlled. It converts the goals or objectives into a series of steps, in order to decide what has to be done, by whom and by when. It involves the following steps:

1 Decide a goal or objective.

2 Identify the actions required to achieve this objective or goal.

3 Amend the plan by identifying where it may go wrong.

4 Having identified what may go wrong, make another plan or decide on more actions to deal with these problems.

The action plan should describe in detail how the business gets from where it is now to where it wishes to be, describing in detail how the business proposes to do this.

Effective action planning requires all those involved to be aware of their role in the process and involves:

1 Development of the rough action plan – this will combine the work of all individuals involved. It will list their proposed activities to reach the goal. Once this has been completed, all of the activities are then discussed and the most appropriate ones are chosen. These then need to be arranged in the correct order to make sure the tasks are completed by the time they are needed.

2   Each step in the action plan needs to be detailed in terms of what, when and who.

3   Constant checks are necessary to make sure the skills, time, finance and materials involved will be available when required. Those involved also need to consider how problems may be dealt with if an unexpected problem arises.

The importance of planning cannot be stressed enough. Good planning skills mean you should be able to:

●   waste less time

●   make fewer mistakes

●   stick to deadlines

●   not have to start tasks again

●   get more job satisfaction out of your work

●   generally work better

●   have the opportunity to take on more challenging work

●   be valued by others for your abilities.

Each task or project is given to you or a team on the assumption that it will be completed. You therefore need to make the best use of your time and resources in order to achieve a successful outcome, by the date on which the work is required.

At the outset you should have a clear idea as to how, when and why you are undertaking particular work. You also need to know precisely what the person who has allocated the work to you wants. If you are unclear about any of these issues, you should clarify this before you get started on the work. Only by knowing what is required of you will you know what it is you have to produce or complete.

You need to know precisely what is wanted, who wants it, when they want it and, above all, how you are going to do it. You could create a task log sheet on which you could write the necessary information regarding any task which has been set. You may wish to use a log sheet such as this, or perhaps amend it so that it has sections covering the following:

●   what is the required outcome (what does the person who set you the task expect of you?)

●   tasks needed to achieve the required outcome (break down complex tasks or projects into manageable chunks which can be dealt with stage by stage, otherwise tackling the whole project in one huge chunk may prove too daunting and complicated)

●   appropriate methods to be used (how exactly are you going to go about doing the task? What will it involve you having to find out and where is that information? Do you have access to or knowledge of the methods which are the most appropriate?)

- timescale (the first real question is whether the timescale is reasonable. Is it possible for you to meet the deadline which has been set? If you have any doubts about meeting the deadline, you should say so as soon as possible)

- resources required (note down any people, equipment or materials which you will need in order to complete the task).

You will need to learn to juggle the various demands placed upon your time. Experience will gradually tell you what is truly urgent and what is really important. Remember that your priorities may not be shared by those who give you the tasks. Neither will your priorities necessarily be the same as those of the people with whom you may have to work to complete the tasks.

Prioritising is therefore a matter of personal judgement, but also negotiation with the task setter and other members of staff on whom you will need to rely to get the job done.

Organisational skills are very important to anybody who works in adminis-tration. They are also important to anybody who is undertaking a programme of study and you will know this from your experiences at school and college. In the business world, disorganisation can lead to time wastage and mistakes, some of which may potentially damage the business. Organisational skills include the following:

- being neat and tidy in your desk area

- keeping a diary of dates and times when meetings should be attended. You should also keep a record of any expected visitors (who may be customers or prospective customers) to the organisation

- having an efficient way of storing and retrieving documents, whether this is paper-based or on a computer system

- having a follow-up procedure in place so that documents are always available at the correct date and time

- managing time efficiently. Time management does not apply just to those people who are in authority and have many responsibilities at work. It is important for everyone to monitor how they use their time at work

- having a 'to do' list. This list can be weekly and/or daily and should list the duties that have to be carried out. Prioritising duties or tasks and then ticking off those completed is very satisfying and a finished list is a nice way to end the day.

Planning does not just involve daily or even weekly routines – sometimes you may have to plan weeks or months in advance. The simplest way of achieving this is to put a wall chart or planner in the office. You can then either write

Figure 201.2

deadlines onto this chart or use a variety of stick-on symbols to alert you to particularly important dates in the future.

Increasingly, people use personal digital assistants (PDAs). These are mini-computers which have a function which allows you to enter information regarding deadlines and will alert you to the fact that deadlines are coming up. They can also alert you to the fact that you need to be in a particular place, at a particular time, so that you do not miss meetings or appointments.

As an alternative to the usual form of diary, some organisations may use an electronic diary method of logging appointments and meetings. This information can be stored on the main computer system, or on a laptop or in a personal organiser. The electronic diary enables the user to scroll forwards or backwards by day, month or year. It can store around five years' worth of days and dates. You can therefore store provisional or confirmed appointments, mark out holiday periods and set reminders for particular days, weeks or months in the future. The electronic diary can also be used to detail appointments and cross-reference appointments or tasks.

Give it a go

Design a simple questionnaire that allows you to find out how other people you work with keep track of what they have to do. Ask at least 20 of your colleagues what it is that they use. Get them to tell you what else they have tried and, if appropriate, why they stopped using this method and moved on to another.

There are very few people who are well organised all the time. The organised ones are self-disciplined and keep their work area neat and tidy and have lists of things which are waiting to be completed. They carry out tasks in a strict order, rather than concentrating on work which they enjoy doing. Without some organisation, work can become chaotic and put unnecessary pressure on you. It is therefore important to become organised at work in order to:

- be able to find what you need
- not keep everything in your head but on paper, where you can use it to remind you
- make the best use of your time
- finish jobs quicker
- be more confident
- be less stressed
- be more efficient.

Becoming organised begins with your own work area. We have all seen desks littered with papers; reports, memos, letters and scrap paper all randomly poking out of the piles. There is always the problem of finding a pen, knowing where you left that ruler, having to move vast piles of things in order to reach the keyboard.

Most desks have filing trays, or little trays to put your pens, paperclips and stapler. But the natural thing to do is to say to yourself that you'll put that work away once you have a chance. That chance very often never arrives and before long your desk is a mountain of part-finished work.

You need to use the area which you have been given to its best effect. It is easy to move things from your area to someone else's once yours is full. Cleaning up after yourself is not always possible, but by putting things away in the right place you have a much better chance of finding them next time.

Things which you use on a daily basis should be on your desk. Things that you do not use very often should be put away in drawers. Stationery items and files and any other spare paperwork or equipment can also be placed in drawers. This means that what is on your desk should be what you are working on, together with any equipment you need to do that work. It probably takes far less time to put something away where it belongs than the time you will spend trying to find it if you have abandoned it somewhere else.

Many people use a series of trays on their desk. One of the trays will be for information or work which has just arrived – this is known as an in-tray. Work that has been completed and needs to be passed on is placed in the out-tray. Work that is partly finished and may need extra work by you later is placed in a pending tray, and any information which you have taken from the records or work which can now be put into the records is placed in a filing tray.

Over to you

How well organised are you? Try to answer these questions as honestly as possible:

1 How messy is your bedroom at home?

2 If you have a work area at home, or at work or college, just how much have you managed to push into your desk drawers?

3 How forgetful are you? Do you rely on trying to remember things rather than writing down what you have to do?

4 If you had to go shopping for various items, would you write a list or would you try to remember what it is you have gone out to buy?

5 Have you got a clear idea about what you have to do each day?

6 How do you prefer to pass on messages to people?

7 When was the last time you lost something important?

8 How often do you have to search for clean or uncrumpled clothes in the morning when you are getting dressed?

9 When was the last time you failed to get a piece of coursework in on time?

10 Would you know where to find your National Insurance number if you needed it immediately?

1.3 Explain the purpose and benefits of agreeing realistic targets for work
1.4 Explain how to agree realistic targets
1.5 Describe ways of planning work to meet agreed deadlines

It is important to agree realistic targets for particular tasks. This is sometimes difficult, as you will often have routine jobs to complete as part of your workflow, as well as new or specific tasks assigned to you. Setting a realistic target is always a matter of judgement. You need to be sure that whatever target you agree takes into account the rest of your workflow. However, it may also be the case that you will need to give a particular task priority, which will have an impact on the rest of your work. Setting a realistic target is best achieved by negotiation. You can give a reasonably realistic estimate of how long a particular task may take. This needs to take into consideration when the work is needed. The purpose of this is for both the task setter and the task completer to know what has been agreed and when the work can be expected. The benefits are to be able to plan for the task to be completed by a specific date, for the task setter to know when the work will be ready and for there to be agreement as to the priority of that task.

It is always the best policy to make sure you know precisely what is expected of you. It is not always clear exactly what your role or responsibility may be in a team, or what your tasks are and how they relate to the work as a whole. Basic things to check are:

- What is my role in the team?
- What am I expected to do?
- When do I need to do this?
- How long do I have to do this?
- Who do I report to?
- Where can I receive help?
- What do I do if I get stuck or do not understand?

Some tasks and responsibilities may be obvious and do not require you to have to confirm your responsibilities with anyone. But many job roles within a team can become confused and will change over time. The term 'working arrangements' may mean a variety of things. These could include:

- start and finish times of the day
- days of the week to be worked
- times of breaks, including lunch
- who is in charge if the team leader or manager is not available
- when work and progress will be reviewed
- who has the right to instruct the team
- where the team goes about getting additional resources when they need them.

Give it a go

Allocating time off for members of a team which needs to cover the work at all times can be difficult. Here is a typical problem.

It is the beginning of the summer and three members of the team have already booked off time over June, July and August. Three more want time off, but you need to have five people available to cover the work at all times:

June	Week 1	Justine Off
	Week 2	Justine Off
	Week 3	Pete Off
	Week 4	Pete Off

July	Week 1	Sylvia Off
	Week 2	Sylvia Off
	Week 3	Sylvia Off
	Week 4	Sylvia Off
August	Week 1	
	Week 2	
	Week 3	
	Week 4	

Liz wants to book three weeks, hopefully in July, but part of August would be OK. Seamus wants a week off in June, one in July and two in August. Tariq wants three weeks in August. You have yourself, although you do not want to take a holiday until September, and Mike, who has already taken all of his holiday.

Work out a rota for the summer break, making sure you try to have five staff available. It may not be possible! If this is the case, say what you will do to overcome the problem.

Targets need to be realistic and achievable. There is much more about target setting in *Unit 205: Work with Other People in a Business Environment*.

The key to realistic target setting is to ensure that each target is specific. This means knowing exactly what is required. Each target also has to be measurable, meaning that you know the limits or requirements. It has to be achievable, so the task should not be beyond your abilities. It has to be realistic, so this means that setting unreasonable targets to complete certain tasks is not very helpful. The target also needs to be timely, which simply means knowing the deadline by which the target has to be achieved.

As far as deadlines are concerned, it is useful to think about three different sets of timescales which could apply to a task or an objective:

● short term – this really means that the activity has to be done immediately or certainly over the next few days

● medium term – possibly a couple of weeks or perhaps months, but certainly not immediately or some vague time in the future

● long term – probably reserved for really major objectives, perhaps as long as a year, but certainly several months.

Working with resources and to a timescale involves a degree of planning and forward thinking. The more complicated an objective, the more resources may be needed and the longer the timescale may be. It is always valuable to think about complicated tasks or objectives as a series of mini-tasks or mini-objectives. This means that it is useful to break down the major job into manageable chunks. You need to know what has to be done first before you can get on with the next phase of the work.

In business, breaking down large tasks and objectives (sometimes referred to as projects) is known as setting up milestones. This means you identify key things which have to be done on your route to completing the main objective. It also means that you can tell when you need your resources and how long each of the milestones is likely to take you as a team. Here is an example:

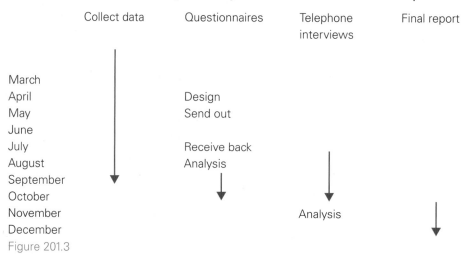

Figure 201.3

Using this kind of table, the team would be able to work out where they would need resources and when the most work would have to be done.

Give it a go

Look at the milestone diagram and answer the following questions:

1 When would the team need to have a stock of envelopes and stamps ready?
2 When would the team need to be using the telephones for the interviews?
3 What months could be used to analyse the information they have collected?
4 What is the overall length of the task?
5 When must the final report be ready?

Timescales refer to both the time that you have been given to complete a task and the deadline you have been given. This means that any task needs to be prioritised in terms of its importance. Broadly speaking, tasks can be divided into the following categories as far as priorities are concerned:

● urgent and important tasks

● urgent but not important tasks

● important but not urgent tasks

● not urgent or important tasks.

The natural thing is to concentrate on the first two priorities and to put the other two to the side. The problem is that they are often forgotten.

Give it a go

Using the four different sets of priorities in the above list, try to categorise your immediate workload either at college or at work. Where do most of the tasks or jobs you have to do fall? If there are many tasks in the higher priority categories, how do you prioritise them?

Let's look at timescales and priorities in a little more detail:

● Firstly, you will have a series of fairly routine tasks to complete (these would include filing, answering the telephone and photocopying, for example).

● Secondly, you will have large tasks to complete (such as checking and ordering the stationery or keeping a track of the petty cash).

● Thirdly, you may have sets of tasks which do not occur that often (such as preparing for the end-of-year accounts, clearing out the stock cupboard or sending out a mailshot to customers).

● Fourthly, you will have small tasks which tend to crop up when you least expect them to (such as carrying out a job for a senior member of staff or dealing with something because someone else is not available).

Broadly speaking, all of these tasks can still be considered to be either:

● important or not important

● urgent or non-urgent.

At the end of the day, only you can decide whether a job is important and urgent enough to drop everything else and get on with it. You probably need to think about the following points before making up your mind:

● What will happen if you don't manage to meet the deadlines you have been set?

● Who actually gave you the work? How senior are they in the organisation?

● How long will the job really take to do if you concentrate on it (assuming that you can)?

● Can the deadline be altered?

Give it a go

Have another look at the list of tasks which you prioritised in the last activity. Which of the tasks could be set aside for now? Which of the tasks could have their deadlines renegotiated? Have you prioritised your tasks because some of them have been demanded by senior or important people?

1.6 Explain the purpose of keeping other people informed about progress

By keeping others informed about progress you can warn them at the earliest possible date if you are experiencing problems in meeting their deadline. You can then ask for additional help, or time. It also means that the person waiting for the work can factor in these delays and change their own plans accordingly.

Deadlines state the latest date by which a particular task must be achieved. Some people actually respond well to having a series of deadlines as they are challenged by the prospect of having to complete jobs by a particular date. At the earliest stage possible, it is important that you begin to take account of deadlines and work towards the completion of tasks by the time you are required to complete them. This becomes all the more difficult if you have to rely on others in the team to contribute towards the completion of work.

What happens when it becomes obvious that the deadline is not going to be met for whatever reason? It would be rare in working for a business that you will ever enjoy the opportunity to work on one task, finish it and then start on another. Work is never quite that simple. Therefore, as we have seen, prioritising jobs is the only real way forward.

Each deadline and task needs to be looked at on an individual basis. The best policy, however, is that as soon as it becomes obvious to you and the team that a deadline will not be met, you should inform your team leader or the individual who has set you the task. There may well be room for renegotiation of the deadline (pushing the deadline back) or for work that is not a priority to be put aside so that you can concentrate on the most important deadline. Unexpected problems which could lead to a deadline becoming difficult or impossible to meet could include the following:

- staff shortages (either not enough staff or staff off sick or on holiday leave)
- other work piling up which has the same degree of priority
- difficulty in collecting information to do the task
- difficulty in contacting individuals you need to communicate with to complete the task.

In many cases, difficult deadlines and unexpected problems arise out of not having thought about the task and its implications in enough detail at the very beginning.

Give it a go

Managing your day and the workload is a difficult task in itself. You will always have several people and several tasks wanting to take up your time. Here is a typical day's work, with the times (deadlines) needed for each of the tasks. Order the work so that you can attempt to get all of the tasks completed as close to the deadlines as possible.

1 You work flexi-time, so you could start at 0800 or 0900 and finish at either 1600 or 1700.

2 Call Mr Peters by 1000 (duration 10 minutes).

3 Call Mrs Jones (duration 10 minutes).

4 Photocopy 100 copies of the sales price list by 1200 (duration 45 minutes, needs collating).

5 Type up minutes of yesterday's meeting (45 minutes).

6 Distribute copies of yesterday's meeting (20 copies) (duration 30 minutes) by 1200.

7 Attend sales meeting at 1400 (duration 1 hour).

8 Check and reorder stationery (30 minutes) – order needs to be with the supplier by 1600 to ensure next-day delivery (call duration 10 minutes).

9 Call Ms Smith at 1530 (duration 10 minutes).

1.7 Explain the purpose and benefits of letting other people know work plans need to be changed
1.8 Describe types of problems that may occur during work
1.9 Describe ways of seeking assistance with getting help to resolve problems

One quality that many employers are looking for is flexibility from their employees. This means not necessarily doing things which you are not trained to do but rather being prepared to help or adapt what you do to make sure that jobs are completed as soon as possible. The more multi-skilled you become through your experience of doing different types of work, the more valuable you will become to your employer.

Flexibility is important as you need to put aside any fears of not knowing precisely what to do in a new situation. You need to show that you have a desire to learn new things. Flexibility cuts across nearly all work and, as we will see, it is often impossible to set your mind to carry out a task in a particular way, on a particular day, without either being interrupted or having to change your plans.

Once you have planned a job and have a clear understanding as to what is required of you, you are then in a position to actually begin work. Team leaders, supervisors and managers may want progress reports. So it is important that you know where you are, how much you have done and when you are likely to finish.

With other work and activities going on around you which may drag you away from the task at hand, it is vital that you remember where you are. When you return to the work you can then pick it up from where you left it. As your work on the task continues, you may foresee some difficulties – perhaps a vital piece of information is missing or you discover that there are insufficient envelopes or paper. Anything could happen. Rather than waiting until the problem stops you from working, you should try to make sure that whatever the difficulty is has been dealt with before you reach that point. If you realise that information is missing and that you will need it before the end of the week, take steps to acquire it immediately. In the case of the missing envelopes, a timely order to the stationery supplier would solve this potential difficulty.

It is rare to work in a business where things do not change. Workloads change, priorities change, the availability of staff changes with sickness and holiday leave. Sometimes the business is busier for no apparent reason and there may be pressures on you to carry out other duties which take you away from the tasks which you had expected to be doing. If you are aware of where you are with a task and you know where all the information is because it is filed away safely, you can return to it as soon as you have a chance.

If you are working with several other people, or carrying out work for various supervisors or managers, they will not necessarily know that you have had to abandon the work you were doing for them. Contingencies are situations which arise that could affect your ability to continue working on a particular task. What this means is that you will have to think about what is necessary in order to complete the task if you cannot spend the amount of time on it that you expected. If the task is not completed, who will be affected? What will happen if you cannot meet the deadlines? Providing the person who has set you the work knows what your alternative plans are, they may be happy for you to reschedule the work and delay its completion.

Some work cannot be rescheduled, however, because it is important and urgent. In order to think about how to handle this, you should set aside a short period of time and think through the implications of not finishing the work before you decide that you must put it aside. At all times you must contact the person who has set you the work, or the person who is relying on you to finish the work. They must be aware and then they can put their own contingency plans in action.

Give it a go

In the following situations, suggest whether you could take action yourself to solve these problems or whether you should refer the problem to a colleague, a supervisor or a manager.

1 Yesterday you and a colleague were working late to finish a report which needed to be completed for a meeting this afternoon. You both agreed to come in early this morning and on your voicemail you have just listened to a message from your colleague. She will not be in today because she is ill. You will not get the work completed alone.

2 You have spent the morning calling the various sales representatives, asking them for their sales figures for the week. You have entered everything onto a

spreadsheet and have shown a draft to the sales manager. He noticed that you have forgotten to put in the figures for the Bristol sales rep. You tell him that you will call the rep now, but you discover that his mobile phone is switched off.

3 You work in the human resources department. It is Friday afternoon and you are just completing a series of induction packs for five new employees who are starting on Monday morning. All of the documents are neatly stacked on your desk and you go to the stationery cupboard to find folders to put the packs in. When you return the cleaner has put your induction packs into the recycling bin.

1.10 Explain the purpose and benefits of recognising and learning from mistakes

It is always a good policy to admit that you have made a mistake and to then apologise. This avoids unnecessary workplace friction. In order to learn from that mistake you need to work out what went wrong. Once you have identified this you can then try to improve on that area of your work. You can learn from others in this way. They may be able to suggest solutions to common mistakes. If, for example, you are consistently missing deadlines you may want to use either a 'to do' list, with dates and prioritise the work you have, or to use post-it note reminders of particular deadlines.

There will be occasions when there is no one to ask for assistance or guidance and it will be left to you to decide whether to carry on with a task or to wait. Unfortunately, putting off doing work just because you cannot gain help is not always an option. Therefore you need to make a judgement as to whether you can proceed with the work or not. You must use what is known as your own initiative (or judgement) in these situations. There may well be an answer to your questions without having to wait and ask someone.

It is also the case that you will be expected to show your initiative and not ask for assistance every time there is a problem which you cannot immediately solve yourself. Gradually, as you become more experienced, you will be able to make these judgements as to whether to continue or whether you really do need to wait for help.

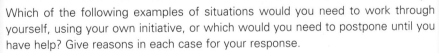

Give it a go

Which of the following examples of situations would you need to work through yourself, using your own initiative, or which would you need to postpone until you have help? Give reasons in each case for your response.

1 The photocopier is jammed. You open it up and see the paper trapped and torn inside.

2 The stapler will not work; it keeps jamming inside.

3 A customer wants a price on a product now. No one else is around and you will need 10 minutes to look up the price.

4 There are three wasps in the office and they keep coming near you.

5 You left a £5 note on the top of your computer and now it is gone.

It is inevitable that no matter what stage of your career, you will encounter situations where you made the wrong choice. This could be a question of doing something wrong or maybe failing to remember a task deadline. In recognising and then learning from such mistakes you can improve your overall administrative abilities. It also helps to prove the fact that planning is extremely important and that the value of very simple tools such as to-do lists is huge.

What is Evidence ?

Evidence can be reports, accounts, discussions and questioning.

■ 2. Understand how to behave in a way that supports effective working

2.1 Explain the purpose and benefits of agreeing and setting high standards for own work
2.2 Describe ways of setting high standards for work

In a busy office there are literally dozens of things which could prevent you from concentrating on a job, or being able to do that job to the best of your ability. Offices are usually busy and noisy places, with frequent comings and goings, phones ringing, people talking across the office to one another and visitors appearing when you least need to see them.

The key benefits of setting high standards for your own work are that they establish you as a valued team member whose work is always consistently good. This can lead to your being given more challenging tasks, as you will have proven your ability to cope and to produce consistently high levels of work. This in turn means that you will have a far more varied, interesting, and rewarding job role.

Concentration is not always possible. There is often little opportunity to confirm what it is someone is asking you to do and, above all, it is often the case that the person you need to speak to is either busy or unavailable. All of these factors and many more can impact upon both your ability to meet high standards and the efficiency of others in the office. There are a number of different ways in which you can reduce the negative impact on meeting high standards, including the following:

● Listen carefully to instructions which are being given to you. Ask the appropriate questions to confirm what it is you need to do and if necessary, write down the instructions on a task log sheet. This can serve as a useful reminder.

● Make sure you follow the instructions given to you. If you have any problems, remember to report them to the right person.

- Try to use your time as efficiently as possible by not getting sidetracked. If you do not use your time efficiently then you will be putting yourself under unnecessary pressure. If you are doing work in cooperation with others, you will be wasting their time if you have not completed the tasks which they are waiting for in order to get on with their own work.

- Don't allow other people to distract you. Other employees, or visitors, may have time to chat because their workload is not as heavy as yours or because they have finished their tasks. Don't be tempted to chat until all your work is completed.

- If you need to concentrate and the office is particularly noisy or busy, if possible take yourself off to a quiet area to work. Make sure you tell someone where you have gone and why.

- Since your time and the time of others may be precious, it is important to make the best use of any chance you have to communicate with them. Effective communication means giving or receiving information in an easy-to-understand and clear way. It also means receiving information at the right time.

- The organisation will have set procedures for its employees to follow because it has discovered that this increases their efficiency. Make sure you follow these procedures and that those working with you do the same.

Figure 201.4

Although standards need to be high, they should not be unrealistic. It is often said that if you set standards too high then everyone will fail because they are unable to reach these high expectations. The standards need to be set by the organisation, reinforced by team leaders and supervisors and then taken on by all members of the team. This sets an acceptable level of performance. It also reminds team members what an acceptable level is. It will make things difficult in the short term but improve everything in the longer term.

By setting the bar too low in terms of standards, the work output will be poor. It is not usually helpful to compare the work of one team with that of another. The team needs to set its own standards for work, whether this is completing work ahead of schedule or being able to perform work tasks consistently and efficiently.

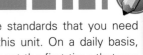

Give it a go

Your tutor or assessor will have a clear idea as to the standards that you need to achieve in order to provide sufficient evidence for this unit. On a daily basis, however, you are carrying out a series of tasks. Think about the first time that you were shown how to carry out these tasks. Were you:

- Told what the task meant?
- Shown where it fits into the broader picture?
- Shown how the work was done by others before you?
- Shown any procedures or policies that should be adopted?
- Shown a standardised way of performing the task?
- Given feedback on your first, second or third attempt at carrying out the task?
- Able to respond and change how you did the task as a result?
- Able to set your own new standards for doing the tasks?

2.3 Explain the purpose and benefits of taking on new challenges if they arise
2.4 Explain the purpose and benefits of adapting to change

Being prepared to take on new challenges and changes highlights you as an individual who is adaptable, competent and reliable. This can mean that you will be given more challenging work and, ultimately, your work will be far more interesting and varied.

Many employees have faced changes in their working conditions as a result of their employer's drive to beat off the competition. Many retail employees now find themselves in a position where they have to work across the whole weekend. Other employees may find that their employer wishes to change their working hours. Many manufacturers or factories wish to run their machinery for 24 hours a day, 365 days of the year. This means that a proportion of their employees will work regular hours during the day, while others will get into work very early and leave at lunchtime; others will start in the evening and finish in the early hours of the morning.

Sometimes these changes in arrangements actually suit employees and there has been a trend for employers to bring in what is known as a compressed working week. If, for example, an employee had to work 42 hours per week, instead of spreading out those hours over 5 days they would work just 3½ days. Each of the days would consist of 12 hours and the half-day would consist of 6 hours. This would mean that the employee, although they were working for longer hours in a single day, would have 3½ days' leave per week.

It is not just the pattern of when an employee works that could affect their working conditions, there may be changes in the way the employee actually carries out their work. Perhaps the introduction of new technology would change what may have been a paper-based job to an electronic-based series of duties. Jobs also change in manufacturing as new machinery and equipment are developed, making the jobs far more to do with checking and monitoring machinery than actual physical work.

When employers expect their employees to change the very nature of their jobs they usually provide re-training and assistance in order to help their employees make the transition.

Employers are increasingly looking for people with skills that they can transfer to any job. For example:

- a willingness to learn
- good verbal and written communication skills
- self-motivation
- team work
- commitment
- energy and enthusiasm
- reliability and honesty
- problem-solving and analytical ability
- organisational skills
- adaptability and flexibility
- ability to meet deadlines
- information technology skills.

This list may appear daunting and quite demanding, but employers are looking for employees who can display the widest possible range of skills. Increasingly, because even low-level job roles are more demanding, employees need to have a wide range of skills and show the willingness to learn new skills. This is known as multi-skilling, which provides employees with a broad range of skills that can be transferred from one job role to another. A prime example would be an individual who has used the Microsoft Office package for an administrative job and has sufficient typing skills to take on secretarial work.

If an employee is multi-skilled and has a wide range of transferable skills, their employment prospects are improved. Employers look for flexible, well-trained and highly skilled individuals who can adapt to various changes in their job roles as well as accept and welcome the need to continually update their bank of skills and knowledge.

In the first instance it is the employee who should identify any areas of knowledge or skills that they feel they need to add to or improve. Certain areas ideal for personal development will be highlighted in appraisals or annual reviews. The personal development plans that arise from the appraisals will outline the key areas that the employee, supported by their supervisor or manager and ultimately the human resources department, feels are relevant to their job role.

In the meantime, other opportunities for personal development may arise, such as training courses, either within the organisation or arranged by local colleges or training agencies. The human resources department will routinely inform employees of training opportunities and employees should also look in the local press and libraries for notices announcing training programmes in the area. Many of these external training programmes will either be paid for or subsidised by the employer. If this is not the case, many of the courses have sliding scales of payment to make them affordable to almost any employee.

Over to you

On the move

Jess and Eve set up their IT training agency in the centre of London eight years ago. They have come under enormous pressure from competitors that have more staff and can offer a wider range of training courses. While they have continued to be successful, Eve and Jess have found it difficult to convince businesses to let them put on training programmes for their staff.

The 50 per cent increase in the rent for their offices was the final straw. It did not mean that they would not make a profit but it added to the pressure. For some years they had both wanted to relocate to Suffolk, where they had enjoyed holidays and had a number of friends. Between them they decided that they would move in five months and now had the problem of telling their employees.

Frank, Evelyn and Roger were full-time members of staff. They carried out all of the administration work, accounts, marketing and liaised with businesses, as well as trainers. They all lived in London and would probably be reluctant to move. Eve and Jess knew that they needed Frank and Evelyn because they were key members of staff. They could replace Roger.

All of the other employees were taken on when a training programme was up and running with a customer. They used a pool of about 20 different trainers dotted around the country. Moving to Suffolk therefore would not cause problems for the majority of the trainers.

Read the case study about Eve and Jess's business and then suggest how they should go forward with their plans. How should they handle telling their three full-time members of staff about their plans and their desire for two of them to move to Suffolk with them? What should they tell their trainers? What should they do about their current customers in London? What should they do to find out whether there is a need for a training company in Suffolk? What is the order in which they should do things?

2.5 Explain the purpose and benefits of treating others with honesty, respect and consideration
2.6 Explain why own behaviour in the workplace is important
2.7 Describe types of behaviour at work that show honesty, respect and consideration and those that do not

Most businesses attempt to strike a balance between making sure that all of the work which needs to be done is completed effectively and efficiently and trying to maintain good working relationships between the different members of staff.

Despite some very bad examples of employers who bully and harass their staff, the vast majority of businesses would prefer that their employees are happy. Happy and cooperative members of staff tend to be able to work together far more efficiently. They are not distracted by problems, so they can concentrate on producing good quality work.

The exact nature of business relationships will very much depend on the size, nature and structure of the type of business in which you work. You will have contact with a variety of people within the organisation, either on a routine and daily basis or occasionally when you need to work with them. Above all, you should be attempting to establish what could be called a productive working relationship with people. Productive working relationships can mean some or all of the following:

- that those involved are cooperative
- that others' feelings are considered
- that there is courtesy
- that people are respected and supported
- that people are loyal to each other
- that managers, team leaders and supervisors thank and praise people for doing a good job when appropriate
- that decisions made are reasonable

- that the reasons behind decisions are explained to those involved
- that people should listen to one another and try to understand the views of others.

There are many cases, of course, when circumstances create an unproductive working relationship atmosphere. These could include:

- the fact that people blame and distrust one another
- that a manager, supervisor or team leader is a bad leader and has favourites
- that some people will not listen to others
- that there is fighting between team members
- that some team members refuse to work as hard as the others.

Appropriate and inappropriate behaviours

APPROPRIATE BEHAVIOUR	INAPPROPRIATE BEHAVIOUR
Listen to others when they are speaking	Interrupt others
Take the blame for your mistakes	Blame others
Give your best at all time	Only work hard when you feel like it
Avoid gossiping	Listen to gossip and pass it on
Support other team members at all times	Criticise team members publicly
Show respect for others, whatever their position within the business	Behave differently to those in senior positions and show little respect for those you do not like personally
Be prepared to carry out additional work to help others	Never do more than you need to do and leave work dead on the finishing time

Give it a go

What would you do in the following situations?

1 You want a long weekend away to visit some friends. It is very busy at work and several people are off sick. You could rearrange your plans, or pretend you are ill and take the Friday off anyway.

2 One of your team members is very moody and is always criticising you. Should you ignore her, talk to your team leader or confront her?

3 You overhear a telephone conversation and one of the team is obviously having marital problems. Do you say nothing at all, tell some of the other team when he is not around or just confide in one person but swear them to secrecy?

There are many different qualities required of an individual to be an effective team member. Very few people will have all of the necessary personal qualities to be an ideal team member, but many will hope to acquire some of these qualities over time. Typical personal qualities could include some of the following:

- judgement – to be able to weigh things up and make a logical decision about what needs to be done

- initiative – the ability to make decisions on your own and work on your own

- integrity – to be trustworthy and dependable

- foresight – to be able to see what problems may be about to occur and alert the team to these possibilities

- energy – to show continued commitment to complete tasks, even if you are tired or bored

- drive – the ability to be enthusiastic and encourage others to work with you

- decisiveness – to be able to make a decision and to stick with it in order to get a task completed

- dependability – to show the rest of the team that you are reliable

- emotional stability – not to be moody, rude or argumentative

- fairness – to be able to see things from the point of view of others

- dedication – to show loyalty to the team and to the business

- cooperation – to be prepared to help others when requested

- understanding – to appreciate that it is not always possible for others to do things as you would do them.

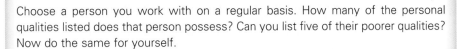

Give it a go

Choose a person you work with on a regular basis. How many of the personal qualities listed does that person possess? Can you list five of their poorer qualities? Now do the same for yourself.

When you work as a member of a team, various decisions will always have to be made and people will have different views about how to approach things. Most teams, although they are organised and controlled by a team leader, supervisor or manager, will tend to try to make decisions together. By imposing decisions or ways of doing things on the team, there is no guarantee that the team will accept or understand the decision that has been made. It is therefore important to discuss decisions before they are made and to try to reach an agreement on the way forward.

These negotiations and agreements about how to do things may occur formally at a meeting, or may develop through a series of informal conversations as work is being done. The important aspect is that everyone feels that their view has been listened to, even if the rest of the team have not necessarily agreed with them. Decisions and agreements need to bring in the views of as many of the team as possible. In doing this all of the team members, or at least the majority of them, will feel that they have made a contribution.

Normally it is advisable for each team member to be given the opportunity to contribute to the conversation about a decision and outline how they would go about doing something. Once all of the team have had a chance to put their point of view across, the way forward should be decided democratically, that is by majority decision.

It is not always possible, however, to set aside time for negotiations and democratic agreements and sometimes decisions have to be made quickly by the team leader, or by the team members who are directly involved in the work. On other occasions the team may have no choice whatsoever as the way in which a task must be approached has been determined by more senior management.

If you are interested only in yourself and what the job can provide you with, then you are probably not going to be a very good team member. Effective teams rely on cooperation and in order to be cooperative you need to have a number of qualities:

- you should be loyal to the team and supportive to the others
- you should be able to communicate easily and listen to what others say
- you should be happy to drop what you are doing and help another team member if they are in difficulties
- you should adopt a flexible approach to your work and realise that your day's plans may be changed at any minute
- you should be prepared to learn new skills which will help you and the team
- you should stick to your promises and if you have said that you will do something then you must make sure that it is done
- you should not expect other team members to always be cooperative, communicative or helpful
- you should think before you speak and be tactful
- above all, you should be as happy with the team's successes as you are with your own.

Not all people are the same; it would be a boring world if everyone was. Personality represents the way in which people think, feel, behave and relate to others. Some people are what is known as extroverts and are lively and sociable people. Others are introverts, who tend to be rather shy and find it difficult to communicate with others.

The problem with having a mixture of people with different personalities is that you will have to deal with them in different ways. You will find that most extroverts are quite friendly and confident. Yet while they are loud, lively and sociable, they can be quite excitable and highly strung. Introverts, meanwhile, can also be highly strung but are usually confident, calm, shy and somewhat trusting.

Give it a go

Although the results of this short questionnaire are never totally accurate, answer YES or NO to the following questions to see whether you are more or less extrovert or introvert.

1 For no apparent reason, do you sometimes feel happy and sometimes depressed?

2 Do you sometimes have mood swings without apparent reason?

3 Do you tend to be moody?

4 Does your mind often wander?

5 Do you start thinking about other things, even when you are involved in a conversation?

6 Sometimes do you have plenty of energy and at other times feel very tired?

7 Do you prefer doing things rather than planning to do things?

8 Are you at your best when you are involved in something that needs to be done immediately?

9 Are you usually the one who introduces themselves first to new people?

10 Do you tend to be fairly certain of what you are doing?

11 Would you consider yourself to be lively?

12 Would you be unhappy if you were not working as a member of a team?

SCORING:

For questions 1–6, give yourself 1 point if you said YES.

A score of 6 shows that you are rather emotionally unstable.

A score of 0 shows that you are emotionally stable.

For questions 7–12, give yourself 1 point for each time you said YES and 0 points for each NO.

A score of 6 indicates that you are an extreme extrovert.

A score of 0 indicates that you are an extreme introvert.

What is Evidence ?

Evidence can be reports, accounts, discussions and questioning.

■ 3. Be able to plan and be responsible for own work, supported by others

3.1 Agree realistic targets and achievable timescales for own work

Refer to 1.3 and 1.4 and then attempt the following activity.

Give it a go

Whether you are in work or studying this course at a centre, you will have a list of job tasks that need to be completed to a specified quality and a given deadline. A first step is to create a work log. Remember that this should be an ongoing document. Effectively it is a to-do list that needs to be updated and amended as required. Ideally, you should:

● have a time and date when the task was allocated to you

● have space to note the nature of the task or its title

● include a column to identify where you might find the resources necessary to carry out the task

● include an agreed deadline for completion

● include any special instructions regarding the way the task needs to be presented and to whom.

3.2 Plan work tasks to make best use of own time and available resources

Refer to 1.5 and then attempt the following activity.

Give it a go

In a busy work environment it is often difficult to judge just how much time you may need to carry out a task. You cannot predict when you will receive instructions to drop the work that you are currently doing in order to pick up something else, or perhaps help someone with their own task. Managing your time with plenty of competing calls on your daily work schedule means that planning ahead is very important. If you recall, there are ways in which you can identify the nature of tasks. Some are urgent, some are non-urgent, some are important, while others are not so important. You also need to appreciate that what may appear to be non-urgent and unimportant to you is urgent and important for someone else, as it may be holding up their work. It is all about prioritising. Return to your to-do list and alongside each of the work tasks give each one a code:

● urgent/important (UI)

● urgent/unimportant (UU)

● non-urgent/important (NI)

● non-urgent/unimportant (NU).

This should help you to prioritise the tasks on your to-do list.

Figure 201.5

3.3 Confirm effective working methods with others

Refer to 1.6 and 1.7 and then attempt the following activity.

Give it a go

It is not always the case that you will be required to carry out work alone – you may need the support of others. They may be providing you with information, they may have had to have carried out a task beforehand or they may be assisting you to do the task. The way in which you work will very much depend on your normal working practices. Some tasks are more suited for individual work, while others are very much team jobs. Using your work plan, look at your list and note down all of the tasks for which you will be relying on the work of others to complete, at least in some small part. Make sure that you organise these working arrangements with them and that they are aware of your priorities, which you should compare with theirs. Together you will be able to arrive at the right time and place to carry out the cooperative work.

3.4 Identify and report problems occurring in own work, using the support of other people when necessary

Refer to 1.8 and 1.9 and then attempt the following activity.

Give it a go

In a normal working environment, even if the bulk of the work is carried out individually, there are always others who can assist if you encounter a particular problem. It is perfectly acceptable to approach other people if you have identified a problem and you can think of no solution. Supporting other people in the working environment is incredibly important. Cooperation can make even the toughest of tasks and the heaviest schedules much easier. If you are in part-time or full-time work, note down recent examples of situations when you encountered a particular problem. Who did you go to for help in solving them? Is there one individual who seems to know all of the procedures and ways around problems? Are your work colleagues prepared to help even if they are busy themselves? How do other people deal with similar problems? Does anyone come to you for a solution?

If you are studying at a centre, you will have come across problems in understanding parts of either this unit or other units, or you may have struggled to generate evidence. Probably your tutor was your first port of call, but did you ask any of your colleagues? How did they tackle the problem? Was it a problem to them? Did they help you solve your problem? Have you helped other people solve their problems?

3.5 Keep other people informed of progress

Refer to 1.6 and then attempt the following activity.

Give it a go

Before deadlines to complete particular tasks are reached, many people in the workplace like to know the progress of the task and whether it is likely to be completed on time. Progress checking is commonplace. It is useful because it can alert you to potential problems in meeting the deadline, as well as warning the task setter that they may have to accept that it could take longer than anticipated. Progress checks are often made in team meetings. They can be formal statements of where the team is at with a particular task. Or they may just be informal feedback at a meeting. You will also discover that people will routinely ask you during the course of the day whether a particular task has been completed. You need to be able to give them a fairly accurate idea of whether or not you are on track with the task.

If you are in part-time or full-time work, progress checking will be fairly familiar to you. Giving progress reports will be part of your normal way of working. Note down how progress is reported to other interested people and whether this is a formal or informal process.

If you are studying at a centre, your tutor will have informed you about deadlines to complete various parts of each unit. This will probably have taken place in a tutorial, where you will have agreed with the tutor a series of deadlines. Your tutor will have checked to see your progress and expected you to be able to tell them where you are with each task that has been allocated. You could use notes from a tutorial meeting which includes a progress check as part of your evidence.

What is Evidence ?

Evidence can be observation, witness testimony, inspection of products and other evidence, including appraisals, performance reviews, letters, emails, memos, messages, minutes of meetings, to-do lists, work diaries and action plans.

3.6 Complete work tasks to agreed deadlines or renegotiate timescales and plans in good time

Refer to 1.5 and then attempt the following activity.

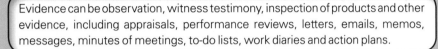

Give it a go

Following on from progress checking and reporting, you should have a clear idea as to whether tasks will be completed by the agreed deadline. You should also, therefore, know whether you need to negotiate a new deadline. It is important to get into the habit of being aware of any difficulties that you may encounter at the earliest possible point. When you give a progress report and you are behind with the task, it is better to tell the individual sooner rather than later and to renegotiate timescales.

In the workplace situation this is routine, as workloads are unpredictable. Think of some examples where you had to report that you were behind with a task and that you had to renegotiate a deadline. How did you go about doing that? Was there agreement? How did the individual you reported to take the news? Did they show understanding about your problems?

In collecting evidence for this unit and others there are constant deadlines and often some evidence is more difficult to generate than others. Opportunities simply do not arise and you may have to wait for a particular event, such as work experience, in order to gather this evidence. This may put some pressure on evidence gathering and may mean that timescales will have to be renegotiated. Again, you can use your tutorial time and notes from it as evidence of your negotiation regarding timescales.

What is Evidence ?

Evidence can be observation, witness testimony, inspection of products and other evidence, including appraisals, performance reviews, letters, emails, memos, messages, to-do lists, work diaries and action plans.

3.7 Take responsibility for own work and accept responsibility for any mistakes made

Refer to 1.10 and then attempt the following activity.

Give it a go

In the working environment everyone will have their own roles and responsibilities. Attached to these is a series of tasks that needs to be completed. You will be expected to take responsibility for your own workload and to accept the fact that on occasion you will make mistakes. These can be simple errors or they may be major ones that cause problems for others. If you are in full- or part-time work, a good place to start in identifying your responsibilities is to have a look at your job description. What are the expectations of you? How do you fulfil these expectations? Also think about mistakes, however minor, which you may have made. How did you handle the situation? What were the consequences of the mistakes? How did you put them right?

If you are studying at a centre then it is ultimately your responsibility to provide a high-quality range of evidence that covers each of the learning outcomes and assessment criteria. You will have been told by your tutor at the outset that it is ultimately your responsibility to put together your portfolio of work. Are there any guidelines or instructions related to this? How does your tutor ensure that you continue to take responsibility? Have you submitted evidence that has turned out to be insufficient, perhaps as a result of errors or mistakes? How did you handle this situation and what did you have to do to remedy the mistakes?

What is Evidence ?

Evidence can be observation, witness testimony, inspection of products and other evidence, including appraisals, performance reviews, letters, emails, memos, messages.

3.8 Follow agreed work guidelines, procedures and, where needed, codes of practice

Refer to 1.1 and then attempt the following activity.

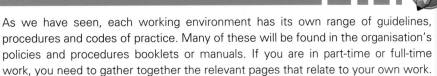

Give it a go

As we have seen, each working environment has its own range of guidelines, procedures and codes of practice. Many of these will be found in the organisation's policies and procedures booklets or manuals. If you are in part-time or full-time work, you need to gather together the relevant pages that relate to your own work. Note on these copies how they apply to you.

If you are studying in a centre, then the centre has their own guidelines, procedures and codes of practice. Collect copies of these documents and note how they apply to you, the work that you do, the tasks you undertake and the evidence that you gather.

What is Evidence ?

Evidence can be observation, witness testimony, inspection of products and other evidence, including appraisals, performance reviews and annotated organisational policies and procedures.

◼ 4. Behave in a way that supports effective working

4.1 Set high standards for own work and show commitment to achieving these standards

Refer to 2.1 and 2.2 and then attempt the following activity.

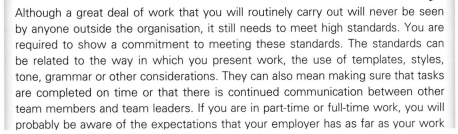

Give it a go

Although a great deal of work that you will routinely carry out will never be seen by anyone outside the organisation, it still needs to meet high standards. You are required to show a commitment to meeting these standards. The standards can be related to the way in which you present work, the use of templates, styles, tone, grammar or other considerations. They can also mean making sure that tasks are completed on time or that there is continued communication between other team members and team leaders. If you are in part-time or full-time work, you will probably be aware of the expectations that your employer has as far as your work is concerned. What are they? How do they relate to you? How do you ensure that you meet them or exceed them?

If you are studying at a centre, then the centre has a requirement for you to meet their high standards. There is an expectation that you will be able to show evidence that covers each learning outcome and assessment criterion. This is so that when it is checked it meets all of the standards required. Having produced evidence covering other learning outcomes and assessment criteria and assuming that they are acceptable, this is part way to showing this commitment. But how do you maintain that standard and understand what is required in each case?

What is Evidence ?

Evidence can be observation, witness testimony, inspection of products and other evidence, including appraisals and performance reviews.

4.2 Agree to take on new challenge(s) if they arise

Refer to 2.3 and then attempt the following activity.

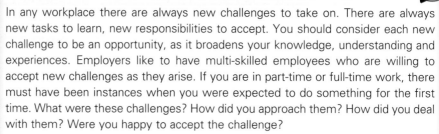

Give it a go

In any workplace there are always new challenges to take on. There are always new tasks to learn, new responsibilities to accept. You should consider each new challenge to be an opportunity, as it broadens your knowledge, understanding and experiences. Employers like to have multi-skilled employees who are willing to accept new challenges as they arise. If you are in part-time or full-time work, there must have been instances when you were expected to do something for the first time. What were these challenges? How did you approach them? How did you deal with them? Were you happy to accept the challenge?

For those with little work experience, each new part of a unit represents a new challenge. It may mean having to demonstrate your ability to do something for the first time. This is also a major part of the learning experience. How do you approach each of these new challenges? Do you find it difficult to cope with them? Do you see them as being a vital part of improving your overall learning and experiences?

What is Evidence ?

Evidence can be observation, witness testimony, inspection of products and other evidence, including appraisals, performance reviews, letters, emails, memos, messages, minutes of meetings, to-do lists, work diaries and action plans.

4.3 Adapt to new ways of working

Refer to 2.4 and then attempt the following activity.

Give it a go

There can be many reasons why work patterns, policies and procedures change. Sometimes the organisation is looking to improve procedures; in other cases there may be a legal reason for the change. There are other instances, such as reorganisation, relocation, expansion, all of which can radically change the way you work. Each time your employer chooses to change direction, your workload and the procedures could change. Note down any situations where this has happened and where you have had to relearn the way in which you carry out a task. How difficult was this for you? How long did it take you to adapt? Do you know what was behind the reason for the change?

For those studying at a centre, the whole way that the NVQ is assessed is entirely different from anything that you may have studied and been examined on before. It relies on creating a portfolio that is assessed. There are guidelines and requirements. How did you adapt to this new way of working? Have you found it more or less difficult than before?

What is Evidence ?

Evidence can be observation, witness testimony, inspection of products and other evidence, including appraisals and performance reviews.

4.4 Treat other people with honesty, respect and consideration

Refer to 2.5 and then attempt the following activity.

Give it a go

In whatever work environment you find yourself, it is important to treat others with honesty, respect and consideration. Working relationships are important. Each person relies on another, not only to make the job easier but also to make the atmosphere as enjoyable as possible. If you are in part-time or full-time work, what are your relationships like with other people? Is it strictly professional? Do you socialise? Do you trust each other? Do you respect one another's judgement? Do you consider your work colleagues and how do they respond to you?

If you are studying at a centre, you will be part of a group of different characters. How do you work as a group? Do you show and are shown honesty, respect and consideration?

4.5 Help and support other people in work tasks

Refer to 2.6 and 2.7 and then attempt the following activity.

Give it a go

This is all about team work and situations when you have been involved in team-based tasks and activities. It will have given you the opportunity to help and support one another. In your part-time or full-time work, how does this happen? Are there members of your group or team who are better at helping and supporting people than others? How do you help and support them? What do they expect from you and what do you expect from them? Does this make for a better and more efficient team?

For those studying at a centre, there is often an opportunity to carry out tasks that can provide you with evidence that is based on team-work activities. The individual parts of a task may have been allocated to individuals. This does not mean that they were left to do the work alone – they may have needed help and support from the rest of the group if they were struggling. It also would have speeded up the process and made it more efficient. How do these team-based exercises work? Do you offer one another help and support? Is this noted by your tutor or assessor when they observe you? What feedback have they given you? How have you responded to it?

What is Evidence ?

Evidence can be observation, witness testimony, inspection of products and other evidence, including letters, emails, memos, messages and minutes of meetings.

Pull it together

There is a wide range of evidence that can be gathered to cover each of the learning outcomes and assessment criteria. Your tutor and/or assessor will be able to help you to identify which assessment methods are the most appropriate for you. These will differ according to your personal circumstances.

The range of assessment methods can include:

- observation of performance in the working environment
- examination of work products
- questioning
- discussions
- witness testimony

- examining your own statements
- recognising any prior learning.

Specific evidence can include:

- annotated organisational policies and procedures
- work diary
- to-do lists
- work plans
- emails to colleagues seeking clarification or reporting problems
- appraisal or work reviews
- work requests or instructions
- minutes of team meetings
- feedback from colleagues
- personal development plans.

Improve Own Performance in a Business Environment

■ Purpose of the unit

This unit is about identifying ways of improving performance at work by encouraging feedback from others and maintaining a learning plan to record new learning and career opportunities.

■ Assessment requirements

There are only three learning outcomes for this unit. The focus is on using feedback to improve own performance, agree development needs using a learning plan and review progress against the learning plan, and agree further learning updates if required. The three parts of the unit are:

1 Understand how to improve own performance – the purpose and benefits of improving performance, encouraging and accepting feedback, how learning and development can improve your work, benefit the organisation and help you identify career options, describing possible career progression routes and development opportunities.

2 Be able to improve own performance using feedback – encouraging and accepting feedback from others, using that feedback to agree ways to improve your performance in completing workplace tasks.

3 Be able to agree own development needs using a learning plan – investigate and agree where further learning and development could improve your performance, confirm learning plan changes and follow a learning plan, review progress and agree further learning updates.

■ 1. Understand how to improve own performance

1.1 Explain the purpose and benefits of continuously improving performance at work

Everyone should strive to improve their performance. Organisations also strive to improve the performance of the whole of their workforce. As an individual, the purpose of continuously improving your performance at work is to make yourself a more valuable employee who is more efficient and reliable. As a consequence of your improved performance, the organisation will also be more efficient and effective.

You can achieve improvements in your performance by considering everything which you do to be a process of continuous development. Every time you carry out a new task you will be learning new skills and developing your flexible approach to work. As you work you will also be updating your existing skills, allowing you to progress and become more confident.

A good manager will always set aside time to look through the work which you are involved in and give you some advice as to your approach to that work. This may be formal or informal and may also take place as a scheduled event, or simply when the manager is checking your progress.

Having an experienced member of staff review your work can be very useful as they will be able to tell you about any mistakes you are making and point you in the right direction in terms of making your job easier and more efficient. These reviews can look at your general work during an appraisal or ongoing work as and when the opportunity arises.

Self-assessment does not mean that you have to be critical of yourself. Neither does it mean that you should praise yourself as to the efficiency or quality of your work. It means trying to step away from yourself and look at what you are doing. Have you met the targets which have been set? Are you able to stick to deadlines? Are you being cooperative, reliable, accurate and following procedures?

Even if you only take time at the end of the working week to reflect on how your week has gone, this is a step in the right direction to making a self-assessment of how you have worked.

Give it a go

Design your own self-assessment form. You could use this for either your course or your job. Your form should include suitable sections for you to fill in, including:

NAME

SHORT-TERM CAREER GOAL (within a year)

LONG-TERM CAREER GOAL (within 3–5 years)

CURRENT STRENGTHS (including areas of work you would like to develop)

CURRENT WEAKNESSES (including areas of work which you also need to develop)

SPECIFIC STRENGTHS AND WEAKNESSES (such as the quality of your work, your knowledge and skills, your personal skills, the quantity of work you produce, your interpersonal skills and your communication skills)

TRAINING REQUIREMENTS (any programmes of study which would help you reach your career goals)

1.2 Explain the purpose and benefits of encouraging and accepting feedback from others

Feedback is responses which you receive from other people in reaction to your work or your performance. Much feedback is informal – it may simply be a thank you for the work which you have done. You should be prepared, however, to receive both positive and negative feedback, as sometimes the work which you have done will not be of sufficient quality, or the person will not think that you can be relied on in the future.

Figure 202.1

The key purpose of encouraging and accepting feedback from others is to provide you with opportunities to improve areas of your work. It takes time for anyone to iron out any problems that they have, or weaknesses in their work. By encouraging feedback, more experienced employees can help you come up with solutions to many of the common weaknesses. This is an informal and ongoing process and sometimes the feedback will be positive, which will identify areas in which you excel. On other occasions it may be negative, but it will often be supported by suggestions on how to improve.

Many businesses have formal feedback, usually in the form of an appraisal system. Appraisals are reviews of progress and look at your abilities. Appraisals are opportunities for you and your supervisor to set targets and plans to improve your performance. These appraisals will allow you to talk about your job, what you plan to do in the future and whether you would benefit from additional training. Appraisals are confidential and aim to be positive. You should use these formal feedback sessions as they may be one of the few chances you have to talk about your work, uninterrupted, with your immediate superior.

Here you may again find either positive or negative feedback. It is rare to receive totally positive feedback, as you will believe that there is little you can do to improve your performance. Most appraisals have some negative feedback involved. They are criticisms of how you work.

It is always a good idea to think about any feedback session before it takes place. As we have seen, action planning is useful as it helps you identify areas where you are working well, as well as areas in which you are not performing well. Action planning suggests ways of dealing with these situations. You should not be too defensive about criticism, but if the criticisms are unfair then you should ask what you should have done or what you could do in order to improve. Overall, any appraisal should provide you with the means not to make the same mistakes in the future as you may have made in the past.

Setting targets in order for you to improve your performance is useful for the following reasons:

- they give you a clear idea of what you must do
- they identify the key areas which you want to develop
- they will give you satisfaction when you have achieved them
- they will improve your confidence about your abilities
- they will give you a vision of the future.

It is important to make sure that any targets are reasonable and realistic. In this respect, when setting targets you must:

- set specific targets about what you intend
- set realistic targets which are achievable
- don't be too ambitious
- focus on the positive – what you would like to do
- be as precise as possible by setting dates for reviews
- write down the targets so you can remember them
- don't set too many targets, otherwise none may be achieved
- try to set targets which you can achieve yourself, rather than having to rely on others to help you achieve them
- make them your own targets and try not to have targets imposed upon you.

Give it a go

Not many people would call Julia a particularly good manager. On the one hand, her department's work is always completed on time and she never overspends her budget. On the other hand, she has the department with the greatest turnover of staff in the whole organisation. People either love her blunt style or they cannot bear it. In the past week she has given out the following feedback to a variety of staff:

● 'Get a grip, Maureen, have that ready by the end of the day or you'll be staying here until it's done.'

● 'I don't want you to tell me what Mr Pearson said when he called; I want you to give it to me as a note.'

● 'Why can't you think ahead and make sure there is always photocopying paper in reserve? It is not down to me to order everything.'

In each of the examples of Julia's feedback there is something valuable to be learned. Suggest how she could have phrased each of the three comments so that the feedback would be of more value to the individual involved. Suggest what is valuable, regardless of the terminology, of each of the pieces of feedback.

1.3 Explain how learning and development can improve own work, benefit organisations, and identify career options

Training is normally a part of the appraisal system, but there may be regular training opportunities which are advertised within your business. If you feel that these training programmes would be of value to you, your team and the business, there is no reason why you should not enquire as to whether you could get involved. Generally, in terms of training, you should think about the following:

● What additional skills or training do you need?

● How will these new skills or abilities improve your performance?

● Is the training available?

● What will you have to give up in order to do the training?

● Is your employer prepared to support you during the training?

● What will you be able to offer the business after the training has taken place?

Organisations such as the Chartered Institute of Personnel and Development are very supportive of learning and development programmes. The benefits of learning and development are not only for the individual but also for the organisation itself. One good example is that training and development, whether it is formal education or learning on the job, means individuals are ready to take over key job roles.

Many businesses and organisations lose staff on a regular basis; they either move on to another business or organisation or they may retire. Each time a member of staff who has worked for the organisation for some time leaves, key expertise is also lost. Encouraging learning and development for all staff enables a business to identify successors for key posts. It helps them to plan their career paths and make sure that the business continues to run in an efficient way, even if an expert member of staff has left.

There are plenty of ways in which learning and development can go on as a regular part of the working week. In some cases businesses or organisations will encourage staff to attend external training courses, giving them time off in order to do this. They will also encourage staff to continue their education, perhaps in the evenings. However, many businesses and organisations have developed comprehensive training programmes that are carried out in-house. This begins with the induction of new members of staff, where all the basics are taught. The training continues with refresher courses for teaching of new policies and procedures, and those who have been identified through appraisals and reviews are selected for further training as team leaders or managers.

It is not always possible to identify a clear set of career options when you first join a new business or organisation. Career options will depend on not only your abilities and willingness to learn and develop but also the way in which the organisation works. Some organisations retain their staff for a very long period of time, which restricts career options for those who have not been there as long. Other businesses and organisations are not growing fast enough, so opportunities are limited. This may mean that some employees will have to look for career options elsewhere, or perhaps switch the type of work that they are doing for something that offers a better opportunity.

The main point of learning and developing is not only that the individual can improve their standards of work but also that the organisation benefits because it becomes more efficient and effective.

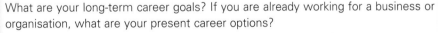

Over to you

What are your long-term career goals? If you are already working for a business or organisation, what are your present career options?

If you are not yet in work, what are your intended career goals? What career options exist in the local area?

The first step is often to develop a career action plan. To help you carry out these tasks, think about the following:

● self-assessment – what are your key skills and abilities?

● explore viable career options – with your current set of skills, what career options are open to you?

● occupation – will you be able to fulfil your long-term career goals by remaining in the same occupation?

1.4 Describe possible career progression routes
1.5 Describe possible development opportunities

Administration itself has a clear career path, even though this may mean having to change employers in order to reach the next stage. The broad career progression is:

- trainee administrative assistant or administrative assistant – providing basic administrative support, working under supervision and probably as a member of a team

- trainee administrative officer or administrative officer – someone who provides administrative support and also generates and implements procedures

- administrative team supervisor or office supervisor – someone who allocates tasks to team members and generally organises and monitors day-to-day administrative support

- personal assistant – an individual who provides day-to-day administrative support for managers or senior individuals in the business or organisation

- administrative section manager – someone who develops and implements procedures to meet the business's or organisation's needs. They plan, control and evaluate day-to-day administrative support

- company secretary or senior administrative manager – someone who ensures that the organisation or business complies with legal requirements.

Figure 202.2

Career development does not necessarily mean that you need to know exactly what you are going to be doing in five or ten years' time. What career development means is to slowly move forward, gaining skills, experience and qualifications, and taking note of areas of work that interest you and could form the basis of your career in the future. This is best done by regularly reviewing your performance. This can include part-time work, activities in school or college, and even reviews and reports from your teachers or tutors.

Figure 202.3

You can review your own performance or ask others to review your performance and appraise the way in which you can currently carry out work. You can also set yourself targets so that you can gradually improve your overall skills. There are a number of tables included in this section, which fall into the following categories:

- professional
- information handling
- interpersonal
- self-application.

Together these provide you with a series of checklists that you can use yourself or get others to complete to comment on your performance on your behalf.

Table 1 – professional

Skill	Current assessment	Improvement target
Appears smart and tidy		
Relaxed and confident in the company of others		
Enthusiastic and positive		
Gives the impression of being professional		
Gains and maintains attention and respect		
Learns and applies new information effectively		
Demonstrates knowledge of role		
Delivers work to an agreed level		
Able to adapt to change		
Willing to work to the satisfaction of others		
Keeps up to date in area of speciality or interest		

Table 2 – information handling

Skill	Current assessment	Improvement target
Understands meaning of written and verbal information		
Can see several points of view and weighs up alternatives		
Seeks out and uses facts where available		
Is unbiased and takes a rational approach		
Can use logical arguments and reasoning		
Can set priorities and targets		
Uses a system to keep track of work and deadlines		
Achieves tasks within required timescale		
Checks written work for errors before submitting		
Plans activities before starting them		
Can draw conclusions from a variety of information		

Table 3 – interpersonal

Skill	Current assessment	Improvement target
Can speak clearly		
Can summarise		
Can retain the attention of others		
Can use words or diagrams with correct spelling, punctuation and grammar		
Can use a variety of questions to get answers		
Can actively show interest when other people are talking		
Can take notes and identify key information		
Allows time for others to understand and contribute		
Can ensure that everyone has a chance to contribute		
Willing to share information with others		
Is respected by others		

Table 4 – self-application

Skill	Current assessment	Improvement target
Can come up with solutions to problems		
Can take actions without being told to do so by others		
Can make decisions		
Can tackle problems		
Can identify problems and recommend solutions		
Does more than the minimum required		
Monitors and checks work to make sure tasks are completed		

Skill	Current assessment	Improvement target
Can respond to new information		
Works well under time pressures		
Can work well with figures		
Happy to accept tight deadlines		

Give it a go

Without referring to anyone else, complete the four tables on your own. Then ask a friend or your assessor to complete the tables about you. How do they compare? What have they noticed about you that you missed? How can you best fill in the gaps in your skills?

Career development is all about recognising and seizing on opportunities that could increase your employability, general level of education, experience and skills. Opportunities arise at different times, both before you enter work and while you are in work. You should be looking for opportunities that will give you a chance to gain training, experience or qualifications whenever you can.

Typical types of career development include the following:

● induction – this is the initial period, just after you have started working for a business. The induction programme will tell you about the business, its procedures, policies and rules. It will explain to you how you are supposed to work and what the business expects of you

● training needs – a good employer will carry out what is known as training needs analysis, both on its new employees and on a yearly basis with its existing employees. The business will use your job specification, person specification and current abilities to help identify gaps between what you can do and what you are expected to do. The process should reveal any training that you require in order to get you up to scratch or to improve the way in which you carry out your job

● development plans – in many ways these are similar to training needs analysis, but they usually take a slightly less formal approach. The idea is to identify your longer-term career plans and to match any training or qualifications that may be of assistance to you. These are normally carried out on an annual basis and have agreed targets

● performance targets – these are minimum levels of work or output that you will be required to complete by your employer. Performance targets are difficult to set for some individual workers, so a departmental or section target may be set. These will require you to complete work by specified deadlines and very much depend on the type of work involved

- certificated training – this is training that you may be offered, which leads to recognised qualifications, such as an NVQ. These types of training are extremely useful for personal development as they allow you to demonstrate your ability to work at a particular level

Figure 202.4

- uncertificated training – these are normally in-house training programmes, designed specifically for the business, perhaps to update on policies and procedures. They are usually relevant only to the business in which you are working and may have no practical value if you switch jobs and move to another organisation

- personal development – there are a number of ways in which you can proceed with your personal development. Some may be formal and include, as we have seen, training needs analysis, various types of training and development plans. Personal development is your own ideal improvement plan, which would have to be agreed with your employer

- flexible working – this can simply be working odd hours, but more specifically it is your willingness to work in different areas of the business. This leads to what is known as multi-skilling, which is a measure of your ability to adapt to different types of work and your willingness to learn new skills so that you can be of greater use and value to your employer. You should seize chances to work in different areas of the business so you can get a better picture of what the business is all about and how particular tasks, carried out by different parts of the business, fit together

- progression opportunities – these are the opportunities that will present themselves for you to be promoted and to gain a higher paid and more valued post at work. By gradually taking on training and opportunities to work in different areas of the business you will have developed yourself to such an extent that your employer recognises you should be rewarded for your efforts. As your skills and experience improve, progression opportunities will present themselves. With each step you will gain access to higher-level work and begin the process of improvement once again so that you can seize the next opportunity for progression.

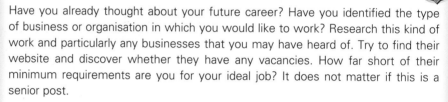

Over to you

Have you already thought about your future career? Have you identified the type of business or organisation in which you would like to work? Research this kind of work and particularly any businesses that you may have heard of. Try to find their website and discover whether they have any vacancies. How far short of their minimum requirements are you for your ideal job? It does not matter if this is a senior post.

Now try to work out the steps in your own development you would have to take in order to successfully apply for your ideal job.

What is Evidence ?

Evidence can be gathered using reports, accounts, discussions and questioning.

■ 2. Be able to improve own performance using feedback

2.1 Encourage and accept feedback from other people

Refer to 1.2 and attempt the following activity.

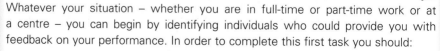

Give it a go

Whatever your situation – whether you are in full-time or part-time work or at a centre – you can begin by identifying individuals who could provide you with feedback on your performance. In order to complete this first task you should:

- note down who these individuals are, whether they are colleagues, supervisors, managers, tutors or assessors

- consider what they routinely see you performing in terms of work
- think about what areas of work you feel uncomfortable with at present
- decide which individuals could offer you valuable feedback to help improve your performance and confidence.

Create a suitable form, which you can give to the various individuals. Note that the forms may need to be different, as these individuals will observe you doing different things and may have a different opinion about your performance.

What is Evidence ?

Evidence can be collected via observation, witness testimony, reports, accounts and inspection of work products.

2.2 Use feedback to agree ways to improve own performance in the workplace

Refer to 1.2 and attempt the following activity.

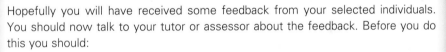

Give it a go

Hopefully you will have received some feedback from your selected individuals. You should now talk to your tutor or assessor about the feedback. Before you do this you should:

- comment on the feedback that you have received
- identify any areas of weakness and state how you think they could be addressed
- identify any strong areas.

You need to agree with your tutor or assessor as to how you could improve your performance by using the feedback that you have received.

What is Evidence ?

Evidence can be collected via observation, witness testimony, reports, accounts and inspection of work products. Specific sources could include letters, emails and memos.

2.3 Complete work tasks, using feedback given, to improve performance

Refer to 1.3 and attempt the following activity.

Give it a go

One of the difficulties in receiving feedback is ensuring that a suitable individual witnesses you carrying out that work. One of the ways of getting around this problem is to identify opportunities in the near future when you will be undertaking different work tasks and it is convenient for your selected individuals to observe you doing this. You should try to organise this before you carry out the first two parts of this learning outcome. Remember that you will have the opportunity to receive feedback only if someone witnesses you carrying out work.

You need to demonstrate your ability to carry out work tasks, get the feedback and then use it to try to improve your performance. You may wish to design a simple work diary that identifies when you will be carrying out specific tasks in the near future. You can usually tell what parts of the week will be allocated to particular jobs. Show this work diary to your selected individuals and see whether you can agree times when they can observe you at work.

What is Evidence ?

Evidence can be collected via observation, witness testimony, reports, accounts and inspection of work products. Specific evidence is tasks that you have completed.

■ 3. Be able to agree own development needs using a learning plan

3.1 Investigate and agree where further learning and development may improve own work performance

Refer to 1.3 and attempt the following activity.

Give it a go

Tasks such as this will often need some form of professional input. Your tutor, assessor, manager or supervisor may have an idea as to further learning and development opportunities. Most businesses and organisations have a human resources department. Within that department there will be individuals who are aware of formal and informal learning and development opportunities. There is a wide range of ways in which you could make use of their expertise and take their advice.

Remember that not all learning and development needs to lead to a certificate. In fact, some of the best learning and development goes on in a very informal way within the workplace environment. You can easily learn and develop by simply watching or shadowing an experienced member of staff. You can learn their techniques and their ways of dealing with situations. You can use their years of experience in having carried out a similar role to your own – they will know all the best ways to make sure that the task is carried out to a high standard and within deadlines. Many businesses and organisations will also use their human resources department to design specific training programmes. A key part of the human resources department's job is to look at training needs. They will examine appraisals or performance reviews in order to identify areas where additional training is needed. They can then organise specific training to cover those areas or gaps in what you are expected to do compared with what you can do at present.

You therefore need to investigate and agree where you may need further learning and development in order to improve your performance. Make sure you make use of any resources available to you in your business, organisation or centre.

What is Evidence ?

Evidence can be collected via observation, witness testimony, reports, accounts and inspection of work products. Specific sources could include letters, emails and memos.

3.2 Confirm learning plan changes

Refer to 1.4 and attempt the following activity.

Give it a go

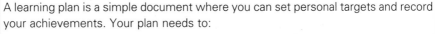

A learning plan is a simple document where you can set personal targets and record your achievements. Your plan needs to:

- cover what you have already done or achieved – this records all important learning that you have already carried out
- identify what you would like to learn, or achieve, in the future – this means identifying your goals
- identify your targets – what you will have to do on the way to getting where you want to be
- identify who can help – what support and guidance do you need?
- have a clear action plan – what do you intend to learn? What is the purpose of learning it? How will you know when you have done it?

The key part is also to keep your plan updated. You need to go through your learning plan on a regular basis and see whether you can add anything. Make sure that you review your plan regularly. Think about your goals (as these may change) and identify any new learning targets. It is advisable to create your own learning plan and keep a copy of this, which you could amend and date to show that you are updating it on a regular basis.

What is Evidence ?

Evidence can be collected via observation, witness testimony, reports, accounts and inspection of work products. Specific sources could include letters, emails and memos. Additional evidence could be provided by learning plans, appraisals and performance reviews.

3.3 Follow a learning plan

Refer to 1.4 and attempt the following activity.

Give it a go

The first stages of following a learning plan should be relatively straightforward, as you will be aiming to complete this course. However, you can use your learning plan in a number of ways from the outset:

● you can use it to identify work that you can carry out which can then be observed to provide evidence for one or more units

● you can identify areas of the units that you are going to struggle to find evidence for and work towards creating that evidence or the opportunity to produce that evidence

● you should also use the learning plan as your next logical step. What do you intend to do after you have finished studying these units? How might the studying of these units help you achieve other goals?

● you need to make sure that as you complete each learning outcome, assessment criterion or unit, you update your learning plan and check it to see whether there is evidence already generated that can be used elsewhere.

What is Evidence ?

Evidence can be collected via observation, witness testimony, reports, accounts and inspection of work products. The primary piece of evidence will be your learning plan.

3.4 Review progress against learning plan and agree further learning updates, if required

Refer to 1.5 and attempt the following activity.

Give it a go

A learning plan is a live document. It is specific to you and it should incorporate your long-term goals. Remember that it does not just have to fit in with the educational framework. So think beyond doing the next level of Business and Administration. Look to see if there are other areas that you can now develop. The learning plan is a written version of your career aspirations. It shows where you want to be in the future, where you are now and the steps that you have to take in order to get to your destination. You should review your progress on a regular basis. Consider this to be a lifelong learning plan. It may be difficult to think about where you might be in five or ten years' time, but by reviewing your progress and updating learning requirements it will give you a clue as to the direction in which you are moving.

Some people in full- or part-time employment will discover that a learning plan is in fact part of a learning agreement with their employer because it:

- identifies the learning outcomes or objectives that you wish to achieve
- identifies the strategies to meet the objectives or outcomes
- identifies the evidence you will need to produce to show that you have achieved.

By reviewing your learning plan you will be able to make the best use of the learning you do. It will focus your learning where it is most needed. It will help you identify the opportunities for learning and it will also prepare you for appraisals and performance reviews.

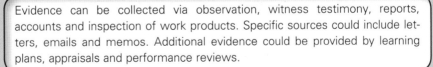

What is Evidence ?

Evidence can be collected via observation, witness testimony, reports, accounts and inspection of work products. Specific sources could include letters, emails and memos. Additional evidence could be provided by learning plans, appraisals and performance reviews.

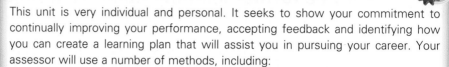

Pull it together

This unit is very individual and personal. It seeks to show your commitment to continually improving your performance, accepting feedback and identifying how you can create a learning plan that will assist you in pursuing your career. Your assessor will use a number of methods, including:

- observation of performance
- examination of work products
- questioning and discussion
- witness testimony
- learner statements
- prior learning.

Key examples of evidence that you will be able to use to cover the learning outcomes and assessment criteria are:

- appraisals
- work reviews and follow-up reviews
- feedback from colleagues
- learning or development plans.

Work in a Business Environment

■ Purpose of the unit

This unit is about being able to behave, and make contributions to work tasks and procedures, in a business environment in ways that support diversity, security and confidentiality at work, reduction of waste and improvement of efficiency.

■ Assessment requirements

There are eight parts to this unit. The first five parts introduce working relationships, dealing with security and confidentiality, waste disposal and recycling and sustainability. The eight parts are:

1 Understand how to respect other people at work – valuing diversity, being sensitive to others' needs, respecting other people, learning from others.

2 Understand how to maintain security and confidentiality at work and deal with concerns – the purpose and benefits of maintaining security and confidentiality, the organisational and legal requirements and the procedures in dealing with concerns about security and confidentiality.

3 Understand the purpose and procedures for keeping waste to a minimum in a business environment – the purpose of keeping waste to a minimum, how waste is generated, how it can be minimised, the use of technology to reduce waste, the purpose and benefits of recycling.

4 Understand procedures for disposal of hazardous materials – the benefits of procedures for recycling and disposal of hazardous materials.

5 Know how to support sustainability in an organisation – the purpose of improving efficiency and minimising waste, ways of improving work methods and use of technology to achieve this.

6 Be able to respect and support other people at work in an organisation – showing respect for people you work alongside, being sensitive to their needs, using feedback and guidance to improve your work, following organisational procedures and legal requirements in relation to discrimination legislation.

7 Be able to maintain security and confidentiality – following organisational procedures and legal requirements to keep property secure, keeping information secure and confidential and reporting concerns about security and confidentiality.

8 Be able to support sustainability and minimise waste in an organisation

– keeping waste to a minimum when working, using technology to minimise waste, following procedures for recycling and disposal of hazardous materials and maintenance of equipment.

■ 1. Understand how to respect other people at work

1.1 Describe what is meant by diversity and why it should be valued

Not only do businesses need a broad range of skills and talents, they also benefit from having a diverse workforce. Regardless of the background, values, customs and beliefs of individuals, all employees have similarities and this is the starting point for understanding them and appreciating diversity in the workplace.

Everyone has needs, interests and outlooks. Learning about these can contribute to a good working relationship. They will also have different interests outside of work. Whatever their background, at work the employees are there to accomplish mutual goals and to work effectively as a team. It is possible to pool common interests.

Diversity arises out of different backgrounds, different sets of values, customs that may be related to family history or different religious beliefs. Factors such as race, disability, age, gender and working patterns all make the workplace a diverse environment.

Figure 203.1

Some businesses and organisations have developed schemes to ensure that everyone is treated equally and that their differences are valued, as they make a major contribution to the workings of the organisation. They allow the organisation to look at things from different perspectives.

Businesses should try to promote equality of opportunity, to prevent unlawful discrimination and harassment and, on a daily basis, promote good relations between employees, regardless of their differences.

Give it a go

If you are in full- or part-time work, how diverse is the team? What steps does your employer take to ensure equality? How does the diversity of these individuals contribute to the working of your team?

If you are studying in a centre then you will also have a diverse group. What steps does your centre take to ensure equality? How does the diversity of these individuals contribute to the working of your group?

1.2 Describe how to treat other people in a way that is sensitive to their needs
1.3 Describe how to treat other people in a way that respects their abilities, background, values, customs and beliefs

Colleagues and supervisors will have different priorities. They will also have different workloads and commitments. Much work relies upon negotiating suitable times to work together and cooperating with others to fit around one another's busy schedules. In the case of requirements or demands by more senior members of staff, you may find that you do not have a choice as to when you carry out work on their behalf. They may decide the priorities; they may also decide how you will organise your workload. You need to be guided by them as they are the individuals who have the responsibility of ensuring that all work is done.

In order to ensure that you treat others with the respect they deserve, you should always:

● be courteous, polite and kind

● encourage others to express their opinions or ideas

● listen to what others are saying and do not interrupt them

● be prepared to use the ideas of others even if it means changing your own work and credit them for coming up with the idea if it is a successful one

● avoid insulting people

- avoid unnecessary criticism
- treat people the same, regardless of their age, race, religion, gender or origin
- include everyone in conversations, discussions and meetings and allow them to participate
- treat people as you would wish to be treated yourself.

It is important to remember that there are laws and regulations related to discrimination in the workplace. You will not need to know these in great detail, but it is valuable to understand their key purposes.

It is unlawful to discriminate against a person at work on the grounds of:

- sex
- race
- disability
- colour
- nationality
- ethnic or national origin
- religion or belief
- sexual orientation
- age.

Discrimination can be classed as being either direct or indirect. Direct discrimination happens when a person is treated less favourably at work because of their sex, race, religion, age, sexual orientation or disability – for example, a man is not selected for promotion because he is male.

Indirect discrimination happens when a particular employee cannot meet a requirement that is not supportable in terms of the work and they are disadvantaged as a result. For example, if an employer gives training only before 0800 in the morning, this would discriminate against people with young children.

Harassment is another form of discrimination. Harassment can include:

- verbal abuse
- suggestive remarks
- unwanted physical contact.

An employee can also be discriminated against if they are victimised because they have tried to take action about discrimination.

It is unlawful for an employer to discriminate against an employee on the grounds of their sexual orientation. This means that they cannot be discriminated against or harassed in the workplace because they are gay, lesbian, bisexual or heterosexual. All employees are protected whatever their sexual orientation.

It is unlawful for an employer to discriminate against employees on the grounds of their religion or belief. Religion generally means any religion, religious belief or similar philosophical belief. It does not include political beliefs. Employees are protected from discrimination whatever their employer's religion or belief, and whether they are already working for them or are applying for a job. If an employee has been discriminated against because of their religion or belief, they should get help from an experienced adviser as there is a strict three-month time limit for taking legal action on these grounds.

It is also worth remembering that unlawful discrimination takes place when an employee is paid less than an employee of the opposite sex for doing the same or similar work.

The Sex Discrimination Act (SDA) 1975 makes it unlawful for an employer to discriminate because of a person's sex or marital status when appointing someone to a post:

- in the arrangements made for deciding who should be offered the job
- in relation to any terms offered, such as pay, holidays or working conditions
- by rejecting an applicant or by deliberately avoiding consideration of an applicant.

The 'arrangements' for deciding who should be offered a job include:

- the job description
- the person specification, which is an assessment of the essential skills, experience and qualifications required to carry out the job
- the advertisement (this includes any advertisement of the post)
- the application form
- short listing
- the interview
- final selection.

The SDA does not just apply to recruitment and selection – it is relevant to all work situations. The law covers a broad range of workers, including contract workers. It applies regardless of length of service in employment or the number of hours worked. It allows for employees to take a case to an employment tribunal. If the case is successful, they will receive compensation for any financial loss they have suffered; an award for injury to feelings can also be made.

Under the Race Relations Act 1976 it is unlawful for a person, in relation to employment by him at an establishment in Great Britain, to discriminate against another:

- in the arrangements he makes for the purpose of determining who should be offered that employment; or

- in the terms on which he offers him that employment; or

- by refusing or deliberately omitting to offer him that employment.

Under this law, 'racial discrimination' means treating a person less favourably than others on racial grounds – which means race, colour, nationality or ethnic or national origins.

This law protects individuals against people's actions, not their opinions or beliefs. The Race Relations Act was amended in 2000, after the Stephen Lawrence inquiry, and now it extends to all public authorities, including the police. The act makes it unlawful to discriminate against an individual, either directly or indirectly, on racial grounds. This covers not only employment but also education, housing and the purchasing of goods, facilities and services. Discrimination can occur when an individual is treated less favourably because of their race, colour, culture or ethnic origin.

Direct discrimination takes place when an individual is treated less favourably because of their racial background, compared with someone else of a different race in similar circumstances. Indirect discrimination can take place when employment conditions would mean that a smaller proportion of people from a particular racial group would be accepted for a job vacancy.

Under the Equal Pay Act 1970, every employment contract is seen to include an 'equality clause' which guarantees both sexes the same money for doing the same or broadly similar work, or work rated as equivalent by a **job evaluation** study.

Don't forget

Job evaluation – an independent look at a particular job role to determine exactly what is involved in terms of duties and responsibilities.

The clause operates unless an employer can prove that pay variation between the sexes is reasonable and genuinely due to a material difference between their cases.

In 1983, the Equal Pay (Amendment) Regulations came into force. These give a person a right to claim equal pay for work of 'equal value' to that of a person of the other gender in the same employment, where there is no existing job evaluation scheme, and where there is no person of the opposite sex engaged in 'like work'.

In terms of recruitment and selection, it is therefore illegal for an organisation to offer a job at a lower rate of pay to one gender compared with a similar offer to someone of the other gender.

The Equal Pay Act made it unlawful for employers to discriminate between men and women in terms of their pay and conditions. Discrimination could be identified when men and women were doing the same or very similar work but were being paid or treated in different ways.

When the Equal Pay Act was introduced in 1970 the pay gap between men and women stood at 37 per cent. Five years later it had closed to 30 per cent. The Equal Pay Act extends to requiring equality in the contract of employment. It covers pay, conditions, bonuses, holidays and sick leave. The act has also been extended to require employers to give equal pay in redundancy, travel, pension contributions and pension benefits.

The key to the Equal Pay Act is comparable work. If an individual believes that they are being treated or paid less well than an individual of the other gender, they need to find a comparator. This needs to be a person who does a similar job and has similar status in the business. They can, of course, compare themselves to their predecessor who held their job before they joined the company. If it can be proved that another individual or the previous post holder had better working conditions and better pay, then there is a right to claim that the business has broken the Equal Pay Act.

The individual making the complaint has to use an Equal Pay questionnaire in the first instance and then refer the case to an employment tribunal if the employer does not accept their claim.

The Disability Discrimination Act 1995 (Amendment) Regulations came into force on 1 October 2004. The amendments were introduced as a result of the European Directive on Equal Treatment in Employment and Occupation. The directive prohibits direct and indirect harassment on the grounds of:

- religion or belief
- disability
- age
- sexual orientation.

This applies to the fields of employment, self-employment, occupation and vocational training. The main reason for the changes to the existing Act was a desire to expand the discrimination protection to:

- employees
- contract workers
- police officers
- job applicants.

The law prohibits harassment against disabled people and removes the old threshold which meant that employers with less than 15 employees were excluded from disability discrimination laws.

The Employment Equality (Sexual Orientation) Regulations 2003 came into force to prevent employers from treating their staff less favourably on the grounds of their sexual orientation. Employers are required to investigate and take appropriate action if individuals are discriminated against because of their sexual orientation. At the same time the Employment Equality (Religion or Belief) Regulations 2003 came into force, making it illegal to directly or indirectly discriminate on the grounds of an employee's religion or beliefs. This act includes specific dress codes related to religion or beliefs and for employees to consider prayer times and religious observance.

In October 2006 the Employment Equality (Age) Regulations came into force. These new regulations apply to both employment and training. For the first time they outlaw both direct and indirect age discrimination. They also tackle harassment or victimisation on the grounds of age. The regulations make an impact on retirement, but also affect the following:

● they remove the upper age limit for unfair dismissal and redundancy rights

● they allow pay and non-pay benefits to continue when they are related to an employee's length of service with an organisation

● they remove the age limits for statutory sick pay, maternity pay, adoption pay and paternity pay

● they remove the upper and lower age limits for redundancy schemes.

There is no fixed state retirement age in Great Britain. The government intends to raise the age at which state pensions are paid to 65 for both men and women by 2020.

Employers set mandatory retirement ages; this new legislation allows employees to continue working beyond this date, should they so wish.

Over to you

Are copies or summaries of these pieces of legislation available either at your workplace or at the centre? Where would you go to find information? Who would you turn to at your workplace or centre if you felt that behaviour towards you broke one of these laws? Have there been any examples of any kind of discrimination in your workplace or centre?

1.4 Describe ways in which it is possible to learn from others at work

Almost everything that we know how to do we have learned from someone else. Regardless of qualifications or education there is still a great deal to learn from the people we work with on a daily basis. All of this information has been communicated to us by someone else. While we all learn from our experiences, over the course of our lives we will continue to learn through straight education, personal learning and, importantly, from the advice and experience of others.

It is always wise to take any opportunity we have to learn new ideas, processes, tricks and techniques. There is an enormous amount of experience in the workplace and there is also experience in your group, as everyone has had different life experiences.

In business terms, learning and gaining information and support is known as networking. It can give you contact with many different people with different experiences. You can learn things from them and they can learn things from you. You should be looking for ways to learn in almost everything that you do.

Watching someone carry out a series of tasks, observing work in progress, listening to people's descriptions of their normal working day and any opportunity you may have to see other parts of a business or organisation at work can all be valuable.

It is often a good idea to try to link up with a senior or long-serving member of staff. They can show you how to follow the procedures and you can draw on their experience. This is a very valuable form of individual training and learning. The experienced employee has a thorough practical working knowledge. They can alert you to potential difficulties and give you tips on how to deal with problems.

Figure 203.2

Most businesses create procedures by talking to those who carry out the duties which the procedures will cover. These individuals are aware of the difficulties and steps which need to be taken in relation to particular types of tasks. By asking the experts how they would ideally do a particular job, the business can begin to create a handbook which outlines the procedures. These manuals can then be used as a reference for individuals carrying out these tasks in the future. The manuals can be updated as procedures change or are amended for various reasons.

Businesses do not usually circulate copies of a manual and expect people to read it from cover to cover and understand what is now required. New procedures are often supported by training events or individuals who were involved in the writing of the manual provide support for others who were not more directly involved. This is known as mentoring and the mentor can be considered to be an expert in these particular procedures and can help other employees through the difficult process of understanding the new procedures.

In order to see whether the new procedures are being used properly, and to track their effectiveness, a business may create a series of documents or forms. These forms will need to be completed by those using the new procedures. They confirm that particular steps outlined in the procedures have been followed and can also serve as a useful way of highlighting difficulties with the new procedures.

In larger organisations where new procedures are being put in place, it may not be possible for those using the new procedures to contact those who have designed the procedures. These larger organisations need to provide support and normally this can be achieved by individuals encountering difficulties sending memos or emails to named people responsible for dealing with the difficulties.

Over to you

Just to prove that even the most straightforward tasks have been learned by having them explained or demonstrated to you, think about who taught you how to do the following:

- tie a shoelace
- use a kitchen gadget
- open a bank account
- make a cup of tea
- use a computer.

What is Evidence ?

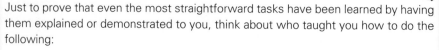

Evidence can be supplied by reports, accounts, discussions and questioning.

2. Understand how to maintain security and confidentiality at work and deal with concerns

2.1 Describe the purpose and benefits of maintaining security and confidentiality at work
2.2 Describe requirements for security and confidentiality in an organisation
2.3 Describe legal requirements for security and confidentiality, as required
2.4 Describe procedures for dealing with concerns about security and confidentiality in an organisation

The key purpose of security is to protect the buildings, employees, equipment and information. Part of this is obviously to prevent theft or deliberate damage to the business's or organisation's property.

In many cases you may be asked to deal with information as part of a task which involves you having to respect confidentiality. Information may not only be confidential, it may also be sensitive and therefore security needs to be paramount. To begin with, confidential or secure information may not be suitable to leave lying around your desk. Neither may it be appropriate for you to ask others their opinion of it, or what to do with it. Here are some examples of confidential information:

- personal details about other employees (their addresses, bank account details and telephone numbers)
- appraisal information or confidential notes, letters or memos about employees
- payroll details (salaries and pay scales)
- business information (such as product details, suppliers, costs and prices)
- plans (ideas and plans to be undertaken by the business in the future)
- lists of customers (which could be of interest to competitors).

You will not always find that confidential or sensitive information is labelled as such and you should use your judgement before letting anyone else see it. The following list suggests some basic steps to take:

- be careful about photocopying – you might leave a document in the copier or someone could be looking over your shoulder
- make sure you lock the documents away and do not leave them lying unattended on your desk

- make sure you seal envelopes if the documents have to be distributed to other people

- make sure you use the shredder to destroy unwanted documents or copies

- check with your team leader or supervisor to make sure that particular documents are confidential

- if you have a confidential document on your computer, switch off the screen or close the document before leaving the computer

- ensure you choose a password which is easy to remember without you having to write it down – something personal to you that will be difficult to guess

- be careful about the information you disclose over the telephone.

Figure 203.3

There are also concerns about a business's or organisation's knowledge. Inventions, ideas and written material that have been created by the business or organisation are known as intellectual property. Certain inventions and ideas can be protected by a patent. This is a way of registering and protecting an invention or idea. Confidential information or copyright material, which has been created by the business or organisation, has a commercial value. A good example would be a list of customers, which, if it were to be passed on to a competitor, might cause the business or organisation to lose sales. Work and material created during work hours are normally owned by the employer and the employer needs to take steps in order to protect that information.

Most businesses and organisations will have procedures related to security and confidentiality. All employees should take reasonable steps to ensure that security and confidentiality are maintained. If an employee feels there is a problem, it is usual for them to report the situation to their immediate team leader, supervisor or manager. Some larger organisations have security personnel whose sole responsibility it is to deal with these matters.

Over to you

Think of some examples of confidential information you may have access to. What would be the implications if they were seen by the wrong people?

You may occasionally be asked by outsiders to provide either sensitive or confidential information regarding the business. If you are unsure as to whether or not you should say anything, you should promise to get back to the customer or individual and then check with your team leader or supervisor. You should never disclose information such as:

● personal information about other employees

● information about other customers

● information about the business's plans

● information about the business's financial situation.

You should also never repeat what you have been told to anyone except the person you are supposed to tell.

Sometimes different parts of businesses are very competitive with each other and a manager's plans may be considered to be confidential as the manager may not wish any other manager to know what they are aiming to do in the future.

Give it a go

Read the following telephone conversation and then answer the questions.

'Good morning, Devon Holiday Cottages.'

'Hello, this is Clive, is that Sarah?'

'Yes, it is.'

'I don't know if you remember me, Sarah, but I work for Framlingham Stationery and I visited you with the sales rep last month.'

'Yes, I do, Clive. Hello, what can I do for you?'

'I was wondering if you could sort me out a cottage for August to fit six people?'

'Yes, I don't think that will be a problem. Do you want me to send you a brochure?'

'Yes, that would be useful, but I wanted to talk to you about prices. I talked to Simon, the sales rep, on the way back from your office and he told me that you had sorted him out a 20 per cent discount for a holiday next July.'

'Did he really?'

'Yes and I wondered if you could do me the same deal.'

to protect the environment when it disposes of equipment. Some examples of best practice include:

- removing whole toner cartridges intact so that the toner does not enter the water system

- careful handling of computer monitors so the glass or screen is not broken; a professional organisation would have to remove any pollutants, such as lead

- not burning electrical cables but rather shredding or reusing them

- recycling the printed circuit boards in mobile phones if possible.

Over to you

Consider the equipment that you use on a daily basis. How often is it replaced? Is it replaced only when it has broken down and cannot be repaired, or is it replaced on a regular basis? What happens to the old equipment?

What is Evidence ?

Evidence can be supplied by reports, accounts, discussions and questioning.

5. Know how to support sustainability in an organisation

5.1 Outline the purpose of improving efficiency and minimising waste
5.2 Describe ways of improving own working methods and use of technology to achieve efficiency and reduce waste

Working conditions within an organisation can differ, depending on the employee's department, where they are situated and their importance. The technology used and the surroundings or the number of people with whom the employee works can also differ. Individuals' qualifications and skills differ, as do the ways in which these are used in a specific job.

Government laws may have an impact on working conditions. Your basic working conditions are governed by health and safety rules. It has long been accepted that employees work much better if the employer takes note of the following:

- that the workplace is well lit

- that the workplace is kept at a constant temperature, regardless of the weather
- that the workplace is well decorated
- that efforts are made to encourage health and fitness and to reduce sickness
- that the hours worked can be flexible to take account of employees' personal commitments (for example, child care)
- that employees receive regular training and the opportunity to gain qualifications
- that employees' skills are rewarded – this could either be with money or with improved chances of promotion
- that experienced employees are encouraged to stay with the business by receiving more money and other benefits
- that pay and conditions should be attractive and compete with those of other businesses offering the same types of jobs.

The working conditions that you experience, as an administrator, will be very different to those experienced by someone working in a factory. You may work in a carpeted office, with window blinds and comfortable seats. Someone in a factory may have to work in a dirty, noisy environment, be standing up all day and do hard, physical work.

Figure 203.6

Over to you

Consider either your business or your centre. Think about the environment in terms of the points we have mentioned in this section of the unit by doing the following:

1 Identify the type of environment in which you work or study.

2 Try to list the specific advantages and disadvantages of this layout.

3 Make some suggestions about any improvements to the office layout.

4 Word process your suggestions and attach them to a covering memo to your tutor or supervisor.

There are a number of ways in which small changes in working practices and the use of technology can improve efficiency and reduce waste. We have already seen that reusing paper and setting the printer to produce draft copies are good ideas. But there are other simple measures, including:

- using paperclips instead of staples – 72 tons of metal would be saved every year
- replacing disposable pens with refillable ones
- reusing padded bags and polystyrene beads
- reusing cardboard boxes
- repairing equipment rather than replacing it
- ensuring all mailing lists are up to date to avoid sending out unnecessary post
- encouraging employees to either cycle or walk to work or to use public transport (car sharing is also a good idea).

Over to you

Are there any recycling or environmental schemes being run at your workplace or centre? Are employees encouraged to think about minimising waste and about recycling? Can you think of any ways this could be improved?

What is Evidence ?

Evidence can be supplied by reports, accounts, discussions and questioning.

■ 6. Be able to respect and support other people at work in an organisation

6.1 Complete work tasks alongside other people in a way that shows respect for backgrounds, abilities, values, customs and beliefs

Refer to 1.1 and 1.3 and then attempt the following activity.

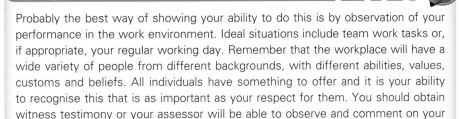

Give it a go

Probably the best way of showing your ability to do this is by observation of your performance in the work environment. Ideal situations include team work tasks or, if appropriate, your regular working day. Remember that the workplace will have a wide variety of people from different backgrounds, with different abilities, values, customs and beliefs. All individuals have something to offer and it is your ability to recognise this that is as important as your respect for them. You should obtain witness testimony or your assessor will be able to observe and comment on your respect and support as a major part of the evidence.

6.2 Complete work tasks with other people in a way that is sensitive to their needs

Refer to 1.2 and then attempt the following activity.

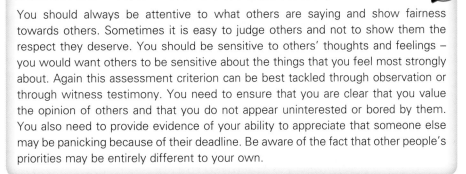

Give it a go

You should always be attentive to what others are saying and show fairness towards others. Sometimes it is easy to judge others and not to show them the respect they deserve. You should be sensitive to others' thoughts and feelings – you would want others to be sensitive about the things that you feel most strongly about. Again this assessment criterion can be best tackled through observation or through witness testimony. You need to ensure that you are clear that you value the opinion of others and that you do not appear uninterested or bored by them. You also need to provide evidence of your ability to appreciate that someone else may be panicking because of their deadline. Be aware of the fact that other people's priorities may be entirely different to your own.

6.3 Use feedback and guidance from other people to improve own way of working

Refer to 1.4 and then attempt the following activity.

Give it a go

There are a number of ways in which you can receive feedback and guidance from other people. You may wish to create your own form. Some good examples are to consider a number of different areas at the same time and ask people to comment on them. This is rather like an appraisal form. Consider the following areas:

- timekeeping
- availability
- organisational skills
- approachability
- communication skills
- contribution to the team.

Ask individuals to grade you from 1 to 6, 1 being excellent and 6 being improvement. You could also add in a space for general comments. This should alert you to areas where you may need guidance to improve your way of working.

6.4 Follow organisational procedures and legal requirements in relation to discrimination legislation, as required

Refer to 1.3 and then attempt the following activity.

Give it a go

This will need to begin with an investigation as to whether your workplace or centre has an equal opportunities policy. The vast majority of organisations will have a policy and a series of procedures in line with legal requirements. Obtain a copy of this and mark on it how each of the parts of the policy could apply to you.

What is Evidence ?

Evidence can be supplied by reports, accounts, discussions and questioning. Further evidence can be generated using minutes of meetings, memos, emails, appraisals and performance reviews and annotated organisational policies and procedures.

■ 7. Be able to maintain security and confidentiality

7.1 Keep property secure, following organisational procedures and legal requirements, as required
7.2 Keep information secure and confidential, following organisational procedures and legal requirements
7.3 Follow organisational procedures to report concerns about security/confidentiality, as required

Refer to 2.1–2.4 and then attempt the following activity.

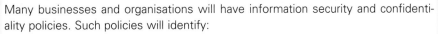

Give it a go

Many businesses and organisations will have information security and confidentiality policies. Such policies will identify:

● why the policy is necessary

● legal requirements

● why records are kept

● security management

● who should share data and information

● communications – including security of networks, home working, use of laptops, telephone security, email, internet, postal and verbal communications

● responsibilities of management and staff

● potential risks

● equipment security, including protecting equipment, hard drives, routing cables and power supplies

● access to data – who can access what type of data and from where

● incidents – data backup and virus control.

Does your workplace or centre have such a policy? If so, try to obtain a copy of it and note down those areas of the policy which would apply to your own situation.

What is Evidence ?

Evidence can be supplied by reports, accounts, discussions and questioning. Further evidence can be generated using minutes of meetings, memos, emails, appraisals and performance reviews and annotated organisational policies and procedures.

8. Be able to support sustainability and minimise waste in an organisation

8.1 Complete work tasks, keeping waste to a minimum
8.2 Use technology in work task(s) in ways that minimise waste
8.3 Follow procedures for recycling and disposal of hazardous materials, as required
8.4 Follow procedures for the maintenance of equipment in own work

Refer to 3.1–3.6, 4.1–4.2 and 5.1–5.2 and then attempt the following activity.

Give it a go

Many businesses and organisations have begun to introduce sustainability policies. These aim to address all of the key issues, such as waste minimisation, recycling and the general impact of the business or organisation on the environment. They will begin by stating the basic principles, which will include:

- complying with legal requirements and codes of practice
- considering sustainability in all business decisions
- explaining to staff about the policy and how to implement and improve it
- making outside organisations and individuals aware of the policy
- reviewing, updating and improving it on a regular basis.

The organisation will then go on to identify a number of practical steps, which can include:

- encouraging staff to use public transport, walk or cycle to work and to meetings
- avoiding travel where other alternatives are available
- trying to reduce emissions
- minimising use of paper and office consumables
- reusing or recycling office waste

- buying energy-efficient equipment
- buying electricity from a renewable energy source
- buying fair-trade products if possible
- encouraging employees to carry out voluntary work.

Does your workplace or centre have a sustainability policy? If it does, you should try to obtain a copy of it and again note where the policy impacts on your own areas of work. If the organisation does not have a sustainability policy, you should suggest why it should have one and recommend areas that should be addressed.

What is Evidence ?

Evidence can be supplied by reports, accounts, discussions and questioning. Further evidence can be generated using minutes of meetings, memos, emails, appraisals and performance reviews and annotated organisational policies and procedures if available.

Pull it together

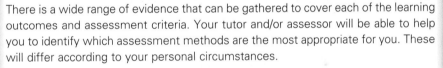

There is a wide range of evidence that can be gathered to cover each of the learning outcomes and assessment criteria. Your tutor and/or assessor will be able to help you to identify which assessment methods are the most appropriate for you. These will differ according to your personal circumstances.

The range of assessment methods can include:

- observation of performance in the working environment
- examination of work products
- questioning
- discussions
- witness testimony
- examining your own statements
- recognising any prior learning.

Specific evidence can include:

- annotated organisational policies and procedures
- minutes of team meetings
- feedback from colleagues
- reviews and appraisals
- task lists
- work requests
- personal development plans.

Unit 206 Communicate in a Business Environment

■ Purpose of the unit

This unit is about being able to communicate clearly and accurately, in writing and verbally, with other people in a business environment.

■ Assessment requirements

To meet the assessment criteria for this unit, learners must use both written and verbal communication. This means that there are eight parts to this unit:

1 Understanding the purpose of planning communication – why it is important to know the needs of the audience, different communication options and when to use them.

2 Understand how to communicate in writing – sources of information, basic principles for electronic forms of written communication, using the right language, organising, structuring and presenting, checking accuracy, grammar, punctuation and spelling, using plain English, proofreading and checking, identifying important and urgent work, organisational procedures for saving and filing written communication.

3 Understand how to communicate verbally – clear presentation, contributing to discussions, active listening and summarising.

4 Understand the purpose of feedback – how to get feedback and why it is important in developing communication skills.

5 Be able to plan communication – purpose of communication and the audience, and selecting the right method.

6 Be able to communicate in writing – finding information, clear and accurate organisation, structure and presentation, use of language, accurate grammar, spelling, punctuation and plain English, proofreading and checking, identifying important and urgent work, meeting deadlines and keeping copies.

7 Be able to communicate verbally – clear and accurate communication, making contributions, active listening, asking relevant questions, checking meaning has been understood.

8 Be able to identify and agree ways of developing communication skills – getting feedback and using it to improve own communication skills.

1. Understand the purpose of planning communication

1.1 Explain reasons for knowing the purpose of communication

Each communication, whether it is written, verbal or a diagram, is in fact a message. Each communication has a purpose. It may be to give an instruction, provide information or request information. The way in which each communication is made depends on the situation. Sometimes communications have to be presented in a particular way. In other cases a less formal approach can be used.

Effective communications in business organisations is essential. It is important not only when dealing with people and organisations outside the business but also within the business itself. Managers and employees often have to work under enormous pressure and they also have to work accurately and make the right decisions. In order to do this there has to be effective communication.

Every day information flows in and out and around an organisation. All of this has to be checked, read, understood and communicated to individuals and to departments, or to other organisations. Sometimes written communications are chosen; on other occasions verbal communication is used. The choice and the exact type of communication used depend on the circumstances – some types of communication suit the situation better than others.

Give it a go

There are lots of different options, even when the communication is between one person in an organisation and another. What types of written communication do you think a manager might use in these situations? What is the purpose of the communication? What is the outcome that you hope the communication will achieve? Should the communication be formal or informal?

● telling someone that they have a pay rise

● telling all employees about the Christmas party

● telling employees about changes to car park arrangements

● showing the results of research to other managers in the business

● inviting another manager from a different part of the business to join them for lunch after a meeting.

As we will see, organisations use different types of communication, depending on whether it is an internal or external communication. Internal communication is with those who work inside the organisation. In smaller businesses a great deal of information is passed on in a straightforward way, through discussions, conversations and meetings. In larger businesses this can become more complicated. Not only are different departments in different parts of a building, but they may even be in different parts of the country, or the world. This means that different sorts of communication have to be used.

The situation can become even more complicated when dealing with external communications. Organisations may have to communicate with individual customers or groups of customers. Some of the customers may be non-English speaking, or English may be their second language. Customers from different cultures may expect communications to be in ways familiar to them. Other customers may have specific needs; they may have a hearing impairment or they may be young children. Above all, the purpose of planning communication is to be:

- clear about what you are trying to get across in the message
- clear about what you hope the message will achieve.

It is important to be able to identify whether it needs to be a formal or an informal communication. It is also advisable to make sure that your communication:

- is as brief as possible
- uses appropriate language
- avoids **jargon**.

Don't forget

Jargon – a technical term, or a special word or abbreviation, that has a specialised meaning, which may not be understood by others.

Over to you

Clara has been working as a personal assistant to the managing director for just two months. She has a busy job and she often has to take phone calls and pass on the messages to her boss. Over the last week she has been making a lot of mistakes. Her boss was at lunch on Wednesday and a customer came to see him. Clara took the customer's name but spelled it wrong. Later on her boss gave her the telephone number of another customer to call. Clara wrote down the number in the wrong order and she was too embarrassed to ask her boss to give her the number again. Today Clara's boss had a meeting nearly 200 miles away. He normally drives, but he decided to take the train. He asked Clara to check what time the trains left from the nearest station, but again she copied the departure time down incorrectly. Clara's boss has just called her to tell her that he has had to wait an extra hour for the train, as he missed it by 10 minutes. He will now be late for the meeting.

> **QUESTION**
>
> Look at the list of Clara's mistakes and for each one you should suggest how those mistakes are likely to affect both the business as a whole and her boss. What do you think Clara's boss should do about all of these mistakes?

1.2 Explain reasons for knowing the audience to whom the communication is being presented

There are times when it is more appropriate to use verbal communication rather than written communication. There are also situations when an informal communication is better than a formal one. It is not a simple question of whether the audience to whom the communication is being presented is part of the same organisation or individuals from outside the organisation.

Some types of communication are better in specific situations. If you need to write something formal to a customer, then a business letter is the right choice, rather than a note or an email, which are less formal. Knowing the audience helps you eliminate communication methods that are not appropriate and to focus on communications that are ideal for the particular job.

1.3 Describe different methods of communication

Communication in business is constant and varied. It enables information and ideas to be passed from one person to another. These can include orders and instructions, feedback or the product of tasks and activities.

A business will use a wide variety of methods of communication. They broadly fall into two categories: verbal or written. The following two tables look at the basic differences between written and verbal communication.

Verbal communication

Advantages	Disadvantages
Communication is quick	The listener may not be able to hear clearly
Communication is cheap	The speaker has to be clear about what they are saying
The voice can be used to highlight important points	The messages cannot be too long or too complicated
The listener can give immediate feedback	It is easy for the listener to be distracted if they are working in a noisy environment
The listener can confirm that they have understood	If the speaker and listener disagree, there could be an argument or disagreement
Body language and facial expressions help make explanations easier	There is no record that the conversation took place

Written communication

Advantages	Disadvantages
Ideal for **formal** communication	Preparing the communication can be time consuming
A record is created	It must have no errors and be accurate
The record allows others to read the communication and refer to it	Poor layout and design look messy
Copies can be made for others to read	Spelling mistakes give a bad impression
Long and complicated messages can be fully explained	Ideally it should not be handwritten, as it needs to be easy to read
Diagrams and instructions can help understanding	The communication may take longer to arrive than would be ideal

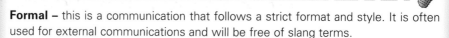

Don't forget

Formal – this is a communication that follows a strict format and style. It is often used for external communications and will be free of slang terms.

Even the simplest memo or letter must follow a particular format and set of conventions. These are rules which require the person who is creating the business document to follow particular steps in terms of the way in which the document will look. Each different type of business communication, or document, has a different set of formats and conventions. By following these

Figure 206.1

formats and conventions, the person or people who receive or see the communication will have a much better chance of understanding the information contained in it.

Because each type of business document has a different format and a set of its own conventions, it is important to tackle each of these one at a time. We will first show you the standard formats and conventions and then you will have an opportunity to prepare a business document yourself using those formats and conventions.

Written communication

Business letters

Normally a business letter is sent to an individual outside the organisation itself. Letters may be written for a number of purposes, including:

● contacting potential customers – people who are either buying or may buy the organisation's products or services

● communicating with suppliers – which are other businesses that may provide items such as products, photocopy paper or office equipment to the organisation

● in answer to a customer complaint

● to tell lots of existing customers about a new product the business may be about to make available

● contacting a potential employee who has applied for a job with the organisation.

Give it a go

We've given you five reasons why a business might write a business letter. Can you think of any others? Write down your other reasons for an organisation writing a business letter. Remember that a business letter goes out of the organisation.

Business letters need to be neat, accurate and well presented as businesses see their letters as a reflection of their professionalism in all things that they do. They will tend to use headed paper, which means that many of the details in the following list are printed onto the paper and appear on every letter that leaves the organisation. This also means that the person preparing the letter does not have to type these details every time a letter is sent out. The headed paper will usually contain the following information:

● name and address of the business

● telephone and fax number of the business

● email address of the business

- website address of the business

- registered address of the business (this could be a different address to the normal postal address of the business)

- the business's registration number (this is a number given to the business by Companies House where most businesses have to register that they have been created)

- names of the business's owners or directors

- names of other businesses associated with the business, such as professional organisations.

Figure 206.2

A business letter will be ordered in a certain way to make sure it contains all the necessary information. As well as the name and address of the business on the headed paper, it will contain:

- the name and address of the recipient (the person the letter is being sent to)

- the date the letter is being prepared or sent

- sometimes a reference – which can be the initials of the writer or a set of numbers. This will help the writer of the letter know where to file it and also keep all the paperwork together if there are lots of letters relating to the same subject

- the word(s) URGENT or CONFIDENTIAL which also helps the recipient to recognise how important the letter is

- a salutation – this is the start of the letter and could be Dear Mr Smith or Dear Sir. If the name of the recipient is known, it is usual to use it and start with their name. If the name of the recipient is not known, it is more appropriate to use Dear Sir or Dear Madam

- a subject heading – which will help the recipient see immediately what the letter is about

- the paragraphs contained in the letter come next

- the complimentary close – this is the way the letter ends. If Dear Sir or Madam has been used in the salutation, the letter is ended with Yours faithfully. If the name has been used, for example Dear Mr Smith, then Yours sincerely is used in the complimentary close

- the printed name of the person sending the letter (and their job title) will come after the complimentary close, leaving enough room for their signature

- if the letter includes any additional items, this is indicated at the end of the letter by the word 'Enc.' or 'Encs' for more than one enclosure.

Different businesses will have different ways for how their business letters are displayed. For example, some may prefer to 'indent' at the beginning of each paragraph (this means spacing in so that the first line is a few spaces away from the left-hand margin). When writing a business letter, it should be remembered that it needs to have a beginning, a middle and an end:

- the beginning – should contain the reason for writing and may refer to a previous letter, or telephone call or document

- the middle – provides the recipient with details of the information you wish to give them. This may involve giving instructions, or asking for information. The middle could consist of several paragraphs and numbered or bulleted points could be used to break down detailed information

- the end – should be used to review what has already been stated. It could also include any action you have promised to take or anything you wish the recipient to do. The final sentence usually takes the form of a simple, closing statement, such as 'Please let me know if you require any further information'.

Odd or confusing addresses should be double checked before the letter is sent out, particularly if there is an incomplete postcode. Important points to remember are:

- check the spelling of the recipient's name

- check the spelling in the address line matches the salutation in the letter

- check that each part of the address begins on a new line

- check that you have included the postcode.

Standard conventions	Description
Headings	Subject heading – so the reader can see what the letter is about as soon as they open it
Standard formats	Include your own and the reader's addresses
	Include a salutation (Dear Mr, Ms, Mrs, Miss, Dr, etc.) or Dear Sir or Madam
	Use blocked layout (unless the organisation does it differently)
	Use the appropriate complimentary close – Yours faithfully or Yours sincerely
	Remember to sign the letter
	If an enclosure is to go into the envelope with the letter, indicate this with Enc. or Encs
Methods of addressing addressee	Use full name if known in the address but the salutation will be simply their title (Mrs, Mr) and surname
Methods of closing	Yours faithfully is used when you start with Dear Sir or Madam
	Yours sincerely is used when you have started the letter with their name

Advantages and disadvantages of business letters

Advantages	Disadvantages
Can be personalised	Can be rather formal
Can be a standard format	May not convince the reader to respond
Can deal with a single problem or issue	Can take too much time if a separate letter has to be written each time
Has a professional look if correctly formatted	May be delayed in the post
Can be used as a simple covering letter when sending other information	Can give a bad impression if content is not accurate and format is not well presented

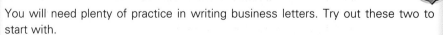

Over to you

You will need plenty of practice in writing business letters. Try out these two to start with.

You work in the human resources department of a business and you have received a letter from someone who has applied for a job with you and has been invited to come in for interview. They cannot make the time set for the interview as they have to go to hospital for a small operation, but have told you they could make the same day and time the following week. Your business is very keen that the interview should take place. Write a letter to Mrs Susan Dodd, 75 Chancery Lane, West Bromwich, WB41 5DT, dated today, informing her that you would still like to interview her, but can only make next Friday at 11.30 in your office. You can imagine you are using your company headed paper.

Imagine that your first job of the day, at a busy supplier of garden furniture, sheds and fences, is to listen to the voicemail and jot down the names and addresses of people who have requested brochures. You have noted down the following names and addresses and the brochures which they have requested:

Mr Richard Sutherland, 7 Old School Villas, Stradbroke, near Eye, Suffolk, IP49 3BN – he wants the garden sheds brochure and the wheelbarrows brochure

Ms Frances Hathaway, 42 Station Road, Huntingfield, Suffolk, IP14 2PS – she wants the gates and fence panels brochure

Dr L James Franklin, The Manse, The Street, Metfield, near Harleston, Suffolk, IP12 4BP – he wants the compost bins brochure and the wheelbarrows brochure

The Reverend Kenneth Smith, The Maltus Vicarage, Mulbarton, near Norwich, Norfolk, NR31 2EE – he wants the fence panels and the sheds brochure

Design a standard letter that could be sent to any customer requesting a brochure. This means you will need to leave the name and address, the salutation and the details of the brochures enclosed blank.

Now complete the standard letter, with the correct details, for each of the four customers who have requested the brochures.

Email

Email, or electronic mail, enables people to send text messages, pictures and files to other people via the Internet. In order to send and receive email, both the sender and the receiver need to have email software, such as Microsoft's Windows Live Mail. Most email software packages allow you to write, send, receive, store and manage emails. The sender and the receiver need to have an email address. Many email addresses are available free through websites such as Yahoo.

Electronic mail allows the sender to send the same email to several people at the same time, providing they have the correct email addresses. Email is a fast and convenient way of getting in contact with people as the messages can be sent and received almost instantly or at least in a few minutes, unlike normal posted mail which can take several days to arrive at its destination. Email allows businesses to send messages and receive messages from other businesses, or individuals, anywhere in the world.

Email allows businesses and individuals to communicate without having to use a telephone, or having to write, print and post a formal business letter. Because emails can be sent at any time of the day or night, and on any day of the week, messages can be sent and received without worrying about whether the post will be collected or delivered.

Emails are ideal not only for sending simple messages but also for sending complex messages and they can allow you to attach various other documents to the email. Emails can be printed and stored.

It is vital to get an email address absolutely right. Unlike some forms of post, which allow you to confirm whether the person has received your letter, there is no double-check for emails. If you type in the wrong email address, the email message may disappear for ever, although some email systems inform you that the email message could not be delivered because the address was wrong. The problem is that if you type the incorrect email address, but this is in fact the email address of another person, it will be delivered to them. It is therefore very important to make sure that the email address is completely accurate and it is often a good idea to decide to reply to an email, rather than type in the email address yourself. By replying to an email you are returning a message to the email address from which you received a message in the first place.

Standard conventions	Description
Headings	Use subject header to state what the email is about
Standard formats	If formal, follow the normal business letter format
	If informal, there is no need to follow any particular format
Methods of addressing addressee	Use 'Dear Mr, Mrs, Ms' etc. if formal
	You can use 'hello' or 'hi' if you know the person and the email is informal
Methods of closing	Use the appropriate complimentary close if the email is formal
	Use 'Regards' or 'Best wishes' if the email is informal

Advantages and disadvantages of email

Advantages	Disadvantages
Can be sent instantly	There is no way of knowing whether the email has been opened by the recipient
Saves on telephone costs, stationery and postal charges	There is no way of knowing whether the email has been opened by the person it was addressed to
Can be sent or received anywhere	The sender and the recipient both need to have Internet access and email accounts
Email system stores all sent and received messages for later reference	Computer faults may lead to the loss of all email records if they have not been printed out
Email addresses can be stored and accessed without having to retype each time	
Hard copies can be printed out if needed for records	

Memorandum (memo)

An inter-office memorandum is used by businesses to communicate between different departments within the same organisation. They are often called memos and are usually shorter than a business letter. They usually deal with only one particular subject, but when more than one point is being made it is normal to number each one. Memos are not signed in the same way as a business letter, although the sender will often initial it at the end. A memo can be compared with a business letter in the following ways:

- both should always be dated

- both often have a reference, which helps to identify where the document should be filed and can be quoted in future communications

- URGENT, CONFIDENTIAL, PRIVATE or PRIVATE AND CONFIDENTIAL can be used on both business letters and memos

- enclosures are indicated on business letters, but memos are often not placed in an envelope. Any additional paperwork accompanying the memo is identified as an attachment and the letters 'ATT' are placed at the bottom of the document.

As with a business letter, a memo should be structured. It should provide any background information required at the beginning of the memo (this may be the reason why the memo is being written), followed by a series of paragraphs and ending with a short review of what has been proposed or requested. A memo, despite being more informal than a business letter, should always be checked for accuracy and should include only appropriate information.

Standard conventions	Description
Headings	Often pre-printed and relevant information can be inserted
Standard formats	Usually more informal a way of communicating, and can often be handwritten
Methods of addressing addressee	There is no salutation, as in a business letter, but often the recipient's name is included at the beginning of the memo
Methods of closing	There is no complimentary close and a signature is not always required, but the sender will sometimes initial at the end of the memo

Advantages and disadvantages of memos

Advantages	Disadvantages
Pre-printed headings remove the need to write out the same thing several times	Because they are paper based they often have to be filed
Can be handwritten or typed	They are more formal than just handwritten notes and often require the recipient to act on them
The pre-printed headings can be saved on computer as a template	
Memos are a much less formal method of communication	
They can be used as reminders	
They can be used as a notice to a large number of members of the business	
They can be sent to a number of different individuals	

Over to you

Imagine that you have been asked by your employer to write a memo to all your colleagues who use the car park at the back of the business's buildings. In two weeks' time the car park is going to be closed for four days because of some work that needs to be carried out on the fencing that surrounds the area. You and your colleagues will have to park in the public car park opposite and the owners of your business have agreed that they will pay the parking fees, provided all those involved produce appropriate receipts. Write one memo, addressed to ALL STAFF, and tell them of the arrangements, which take effect from Monday–Thursday inclusive the week after next.

Forms

Businesses use a variety of forms for a variety of reasons, including some of the following:

- application forms – for those wishing to apply for a job in the business

- employee record forms – for those working in the business. These may include forms that log details of medical conditions, overtime worked, expenses claimed or travel undertaken on behalf of the business

- visitor record forms – to identify who has visited the business, who they called to see, at what time and when they left the building

- customer record forms – which would be completed in order to ensure that the business can contact the appropriate customers when, for example, they decide to try a new product or when they consider that the customer may wish to purchase something from them.

Give it a go

Can you think of any more reasons why a form would have to be completed for a business's records? If so, write down those you can think of and give a brief reason why each would be needed.

Over to you

Thinking back to the memo you sent regarding the use of the public car park for four days, you are now to design a form which allows all those involved for this time to claim their car parking fees from the business. Think about the questions you need to ask each of those involved and remember that not all those people necessarily parked for each of the four days. Get someone to check your form to make sure you haven't made any mistakes or missed out something vital. If possible, your form should be word processed.

Agendas

Meetings are held in all businesses and they can be formal or informal in nature, depending on the type of business and the type of meeting. All meetings, however, tend to produce varying forms of documentation and tend to be held for the following reasons:

● to share information

Figure 206.3

- to discuss new ideas or proposals

- to maintain interest

- to ask for assistance

- to report back on an activity

- to report on progress

- to discuss problems.

The document used to inform individuals about the forthcoming meeting and the nature of what is to be discussed at that meeting is called an agenda. The following basic information is given at the top of an agenda:

- date of the meeting

- time of the meeting

- venue (place) of the meeting.

There are a number of other common items that appear on the agenda, these are:

- apologies for absence – this will always be item 1 on the agenda and will be the apologies received from members not able to attend the meeting. Apologies are sent to the meeting via the chairperson

- minutes of the last meeting – this will be item 2 on the agenda and will be the checking for accuracy of the minutes (the written record) of the previous meeting held (if any). Once this checking of the minutes of the last meeting has been done, the chairperson will sign them as being a true and accurate record of what took place at the previous meeting

- matters arising – this, the third item on the agenda, relates to the matters arising from the minutes of the last meeting.

Following these three common agenda items, the chairperson will list those issues that are to be discussed specifically at the meeting. There could be any number of these items and it could be that certain individual employees are given the task of presenting information to the meeting on any number of agenda items.

- AOB – this is short for 'Any Other Business' and is an agenda item which gives the members of the meeting the opportunity to introduce any matters they wish to discuss which have not been included on the agenda

- date of next meeting – the final item on the agenda allows the members of the meeting to decide the date on which they will meet again.

Safety Representatives Meeting

A meeting of Safety Representatives will be held in the business suite on Friday 25 January 201- at 1100.

Agenda

1 Apologies for absence
2 Minutes of the last meeting
3 Matters arising from the minutes
4 Report on research into safety issues on the factory production line
5 Report on financial cost implications of the proposed extension to the production line
6 Any other business
7 Date of next meeting

Minutes of meeting

The minutes of the meeting are an accurate, written record of the meeting and they are provided for all those who attended, as well as those who offered their apologies and could not attend. The minutes are distributed after the meeting and will appear in the same order as the items on the agenda. Minutes include the following information:

● an account of those present at the meeting

● an account of the discussions which took place during the meeting

● any specific jobs given to individuals during the meeting

● any reports received from individuals during the meeting

● any specific actions that have to be taken before the next meeting

● any specific decisions made or votes taken during the meeting.

Minutes do not have to be a word-for-word account of what was said, but should be brief and to the point, and they must be accurate.

Give it a go

Get together with your fellow students and decide on what you would like to discuss at a meeting of your group. Make it something that needs a bit of research – your tutor may come up with some issues that might need to be discussed as a group. Now create an agenda for the meeting and print enough copies for all those you wish to invite. Include all the common agenda items, as well as the specific items you are proposing to discuss. In this, your first meeting, you may not have any comments to make when it comes to items 2 and 3, but when you have future meetings you will feed back to the meeting the results of this first meeting.

Figure 206.4

Whatever type of notice you are involved in preparing, the following guidelines should help:

● remember that not many notice boards are very large, so don't use paper which will take up all the space and might hide other notices

● make the notice bold enough to grab attention

● don't use too much text, but state clearly and concisely what it is you want noticed

● make sure the reader knows what they have to do – if they have to contact someone, make sure that person's name and contact address or number are clear

● put a date on the notice so that the reader can tell when it was placed on the notice board and also so that the reader will know if the notice is still current or is out of date.

Good design of a notice is important. You want the notice to have impact and attract attention. You could include any of the following:

● bullet points (● ◊ □ ▫ or ●)

● different fonts to **make** *words* more or less obvious

● different font size to make important words stand out

● the use of CAPITAL letters or **bold** or <u>underline</u> and *italics* to make text stand out

● the use of sub-headings to break up the text

● pictures or graphics to add emphasis.

Verbal communication

The common business language across the globe is English. Verbal communication can be a live message, such as a conversation, or a recorded one, such as on a voicemail. Verbal communications can include:

- discussions with colleagues or customers
- conversations between employees or with customers
- formal or informal meetings
- receiving instructions
- asking questions
- attending an interview
- giving or listening to presentations
- telephone, **teleconferencing** or **videoconferencing**.

Don't forget

Teleconferencing – using modern digital switchboards it is possible for a number of people to have a live telephone conversation or discussion at the same time.

Videoconferencing – using the Internet or a secure telephone line, individuals in different parts of the country or the world can take part in a live meeting with sound and vision.

Body language – this is gestures, eye movements and facial expressions, all of which can reinforce verbal communication.

Many verbal communications that take place in a working environment are face to face and informal. This allows individuals to read one another's **body language**. Employees will be expected to carry out verbal communication in many different ways, often dependent on the type of person they are speaking to. Later in this unit we will look at the ways in which information can be presented verbally and how to get ideas across clearly.

1.4 Describe when to use different methods of communication

Above all, communication needs to be effective. It is vital for all business activities. People need to be able to make accurate, well-informed decisions and this can be achieved only if they have access to information and relevant information has been communicated to them.

The communication process involves starting with a message and deciding who needs to know that information. The message needs to be prepared in such a way that the person it is intended for will be able to make sense of it. It needs to be in the right format and language for them. This is known as encoding. Encoding simply means choosing the right way to communicate the message, whether it is in writing or is relayed verbally.

Sending the message is known as transmission. This can be as simple as sending an email, or leaving a message on a voicemail. The main point is to choose the most foolproof way of getting the message across. This may mean following up to make sure the message has been received, or supporting it with additional information.

Once the message has been received the receiver will listen to it or read it. Ideally, they should feed back to the sender. This confirms not only that they have received the message but also that they have understood it.

There are other things to take into account, as these can affect the type of communication method:

● Does the communication have to be formal or can it be informal?

● Is the communication an internal or external one?

● Is the information confidential or non-confidential?

● Is the message urgent or non-urgent?

Give it a go

Here are some examples of communication. In each case can you identify their features using the list above? Can you suggest the ideal method of communication for each one? Identify which of the communications require follow-up or confirmation of receipt.

● Communicating to a colleague that their child's school has called and that their daughter is not well and needs to see a doctor.

● Communicating that a customer has cancelled a meeting scheduled for next week with a colleague.

● Communicating that the managing director is visiting your office next Tuesday at 1000 hours and wants to see all staff for a meeting at 1030.

● Communicating to a customer that there has been a delay with their order and it will be another two weeks before they receive it.

● Communicating to all employees that the business has been sold but that their jobs are not at risk.

What is Evidence ?

Evidence for these four assessment criteria will come from an assessor observing your performance in a work environment, an examination of your work products, question and answer sessions and discussions. Evidence can also be generated by providing witness testimony, examining your own statements and recognising any prior learning.

■ 2. Understand how to communicate in writing

2.1 Identify different sources of information that may be used when preparing written communication

There is a wide variety of sources of information. The range of this information will depend on the type of work that you are involved with and the nature of the business or organisation. Typically, you will use some or all of the following:

● documents – these can be letters, reports, memos, company information, product details, financial reports

● directories – from simple telephone directories to more specific industry directories, listing businesses and organisations involved in particular sectors

● telephone lists – these may be lists of customer or supplier contacts or they may be telephone details of employees or perhaps applicants for jobs

● company catalogues – these can either be from the business or organisation itself or from customers or suppliers and can be used to compare the range of products and services offered

● price lists – these usually accompany company catalogues or may be simple lists of products and services that are on offer from a variety of suppliers and again they can be compared.

It would be impossible for everyone to read every relevant piece of information. It is therefore vital that someone takes responsibility for analysing the data and the figures and for identifying what may be relevant and what is not relevant.

Also, many facts and figures are presented in ways which are not immediately useful, either to the business or to particular departments. Again, someone has to take responsibility for looking through the data, finding what is relevant and then presenting it in a useable format.

Figure 206.5

Whenever you are required to analyse, extract or adapt information, you need to think about what is, and what is not, relevant to the person or group of individuals you are preparing the information for. The more relevant the information, and the shorter the summary of that information, the more likely it is that the reader is able to understand the relevance of what they are being shown.

If you were asked to look through a long document and find specific information, you would be given guidelines as to what to summarise and what to leave out. You would also probably be told that particular information is needed for a particular purpose. It would be impossible and time consuming for people attending a meeting to read through long and complicated documents before the meeting. Equally, the meeting would be slowed down by those individuals having to refer to that document several times. The skill is to identify information which is or is not appropriate to include in a business document, which summarises or presents in a different way the information contained in a larger document.

Give it a go

Imagine you are working as an administrative assistant for a shop and it is the end of January. One of your responsibilities is to keep a record of overtime worked in the shop. The shop manager wants to know how much overtime has been worked over the Christmas and January sales period. Your information is based on a time sheet of overtime which you send monthly to the personnel department at the business's head office. You will need to find the relevant overtime figures for the period 15 December–7 January inclusive. The shop manager is interested only in the total number of overtime hours worked, not those worked by individuals.

December overtime worked (hours)				
December	1–7	8–14	15–21	22–28	29–31
Sharon	0	2	3	5	4
Clive	2	2	2	2	2
Robin	3	4	4	4	4
Petra	2	2	0	2	4
Alex	5	0	0	5	2
January overtime worked (hours)				
January	1–7	8–14	15–21	22–28	29–31
Sharon	5	2	2	2	2
Clive	9	4	3	2	1
Robin	11	2	3	2	1
Petra	2	5	2	2	0
Alex	5	0	0	2	2
Clare	5	4	4	4	1

You should present your total overtime figures in the form of a memo to the shop manager, Katie Walsh.

Sometimes you will be asked to use more than one document or source to extract information and compile it into a new format. You will need to be careful, as the information which is in one document may not be exactly the same as the information which is in the other document. In this case you need to make sure that you are using the right information – it is probably safer to check back with the person who has asked you to look at the documents about which set of figures or facts they would like you to use.

When you are using two different sets of documents you will probably be creating information that has not been created before. This may mean that you will need to make calculations. You may also need to collect some information from one document and add it to information from another document, creating a third document which is a summary of the other two.

Give it a go

Refer back to the last activity. The shop manager has now asked you to calculate the total cost of the overtime over the same Christmas and January sales period. Katie has given you a confidential summary of the hourly pay rates and grades of the staff. You must now calculate how much the overtime cost the business over the same period of time. You will need to add up the total hours worked by each member of staff and multiply that by their hourly pay rate. Then find the total for all staff.

	Pay rate (per hour)	Grade
Sharon	£7.54	Assistant manager
Clive	£6.42	Senior sales staff I
Robin	£5.94	Sales II
Petra	£5.68	Sales I
Alex	£6.42	Senior sales staff I
Clare	£4.98	

Again you should give Katie your answer in the form of a memo.

Sometimes the instructions which you receive to carry out a particular task may not be very clear – it is always best to ask before you begin working if you are unsure about what you are supposed to do. Whoever has asked you to carry out a task for them will be more pleased that you have asked and made sure that you are doing the right thing, rather than receiving something which is not what they wanted.

Give it a go

Following on from the last activity, you have just received a memo from Katie.

MEMORANDUM

TO: **FROM:** Katie Walsh

REF: KW/Overtime   **DATE:** 2 February 200-

Total overtime figures

I am afraid that the figures which you have supplied me are incorrect. You have forgotten that overtime payments are 50% more than the hourly pay rate. You have also forgotten that Petra has now been promoted to Sales II.

Please amend the figures immediately – I require this information by 3.00 pm at the very latest.

2.2 Describe the communication principles for using electronic forms of written communication in a business environment

Emails enable you to send text, pictures and files using email software, such as Windows Live Mail. You are able to write, send, receive, store and manage emails. Both the sender and the receiver need to have email addresses. Emails can also be sent to several different people at the same time. It is a convenient way of sending messages to individuals, as they can be sent and received almost immediately.

Email allows contact with people without having to use the telephone, or having to write, print and post formal documents. Emails are ideal for sending simple messages, but they can also be useful in sending complex ones with other documents as attachments. The receiver can print or store emails and attachments if they wish.

Emails have many advantages, including:

● they can be sent instantly

● they save on costs, such as postage and printing

● they can be sent and received anywhere there is an Internet connection

● they can be stored for later reference

● email addresses can be stored

● hard copies can be printed out if necessary

● time differences around the world are not a problem.

However, there are some disadvantages, including:

● it is not always clear whether the receiver has got the email, or whether it has been opened

● internet access and an email account are necessary for both sender and receiver

● computer failures could lead to the loss of all email records

● the fact that care has to be exercised in opening attachments on emails, or clicking links in emails. Attachments must be virus scanned and unless you trust the link being given in the email, you should not click on it.

2.3 Describe the reasons for using language that suits the purpose of written communication

Vocabulary is your use of words, the way in which your choice of words has to change in different circumstances. You cannot always expect people to understand what you are saying if you use jargon terms or complicated words that they are not familiar with – you would not be expected to understand what others were saying if they bombarded you with words that were difficult to grasp. Use of vocabulary is not about intelligence, showing off by using complicated words, or even trying to impress someone. The most important thing about your use of vocabulary is that whoever you are talking to or writing to understands what you mean. After all, talking and writing are about communication and to make it a two-way communication, both sides need to understand what the other is saying.

We have looked at the various ways in which information can be passed on to others and the ways in which complicated information can be 'translated' into different formats to suit particular readers. Style is often a personal way of passing on that information to others, but in some cases, businesses will have preferred ways of doing this. Style can actually mean several different things:

- it may mean that the business has a preferred way of formatting documents, such as letters, and may well have preferred ways of opening or closing letters

- style may also mean that the business has preferred spellings, such as using 'z' instead of 's' in words such as organisation (organization)

- style can also be set out in the use of particular forms, which the business expects everyone to use

- style may be conversational (write like you speak) or technical (which assumes the reader will understand technical jargon) or formal (which will require you to be polite, tactful and clear about what you say or write).

Style, in most cases, means that you have to know how to speak or write in particular circumstances. The business may have codes or rules about this and expect you to follow them at all times. Normally, style differs in the following situations:

- you will have a particular style when dealing with colleagues at work who are on the same level as you are (and probably know you quite well)

- you will adopt a different style if dealing with someone who is senior to you

- you will adopt a different style if dealing with customers or suppliers

- you will use another style for writing, depending on the type of business document or format

- you will have yet another style if you are preparing a document which will be read by others whom you do not normally work with.

Give it a go

Have a look at the following types of communication style. One could be used in an email, another in a formal business letter to a customer and the other in a telephone message for your manager. Can you identify which one is suitable in each case?

1 'I regret, therefore, that under current company policies we cannot refund your payment at this time.'

2 'Toni, get me the figures for last month when you've got a chance, cheers, Mike.'

3 'When you were at lunch, Mr Sinclair called. He is keen to talk to you about an order, but wouldn't confirm his order until you have spoken to him. Can you call him back please between 3 and 4 this afternoon? His number is 07924443333.'

Tone means putting something across in the right kind of way to get the right kind of reaction from the person you are communicating with. This means that you will adopt a different tone in different cases to match the needs of the person you are communicating with, otherwise they may not understand or appreciate what it is you are saying or writing. Tone can depend on the type of individual you are addressing in speech or in writing. Tone will be different in the following sets of circumstances:

Type of person	Tone to be used
Person working with you, not senior to you	Friendly, familiar tone, not too formal, can use jargon if you both understand it
Person working with you, senior to you	Friendly, but not too familiar. You may need to be formal, you can use jargon
Customer	Friendly, polite and respectful. The customer may always be right, but sometimes they are not. You must be clear, forceful, but not rude
Supplier	Friendly, polite, quite formal. Depends on how well you know the supplier. They will expect you to be rather formal but need you to be clear

2.4 Describe ways of organising, structuring and presenting written information so it meets the needs of an audience

It is not always the case that your adaptation of information will be required in the same format as the original documents you used. Facts and figures which are hidden in paragraphs of text may need to be converted into tables, charts or diagrams. Equally, charts and diagrams may have to be converted into text, with explanations as to what the figures actually mean.

When you are given instructions to analyse, extract and adapt information, you will also be told how the information you are working on needs to be presented. For the most part, adapted information needs to be put in a format which is easy to understand and can be used for quick reference.

You have received yet another memo from Katie, who needs to present the information which you have given her at a shop managers' meeting. She doesn't want to stand and read out the figures – she wants to pass around a chart to the other managers. Here are your revised figures:

	Overtime rate per hour	Hours of overtime worked	Total overtime earnings
Sharon	11.28	15	169.20
Clive	9.63	15	144.45
Robin	8.91	23	204.93
Petra	8.91	8	71.28
Alex	10.13	12	121.56
Clare	7.97	5	39.85

Insert the figures on a spreadsheet and produce a chart of your choice for Katie to use. Katie wants each employee's name and the total overtime earnings for each person shown on the chart.

In most cases you will either be requested to present information in a particular way, or it will be left to you to decide which is the most appropriate format. This means that once you have analysed and extracted information from a variety of sources, you will then have to choose the most appropriate document or format in which to present that information. As we already know, some types of business documents and formats are more or less relevant and applicable in different circumstances.

Sometimes it will be obvious which type of document or format you should choose. In other cases you may well have to think about how you are going to present the information, as this will affect how you adapt that information.

Sometimes it is useful to break down the document with headings, so that you make individual sections smaller. You can do this by giving each paragraph its own heading. At times you may want to use numbered paragraphs, which can also have a heading.

If you are making a series of points, then rather than presenting them as a single paragraph it may be valuable to break them up by using either bulleted points or numbered points. This automatically highlights those points as being particularly important within the document.

2.5 Describe ways of checking for the accuracy of written information

It is important that business information is accurate. Incorrect figures, dates or facts can cause enormous problems. The address on an envelope could cause an unnecessary delay, or a mistyped email address could mean that a vital message does not get through. Even jotting down telephone numbers needs accuracy. It is always best to double-check – sometimes it is too late to confirm the number once the caller has hung up.

It is sometimes impossible to see mistakes in your own work, so it is a good idea to get someone else to check it with you. Some basic accuracy tips include:

- reading back information, facts and figures to a caller to ensure that you have written down the correct information

- getting someone to check documents before you despatch them

- proofread everything thoroughly

- don't just rely on the spell-check facility on the computer, as this does not recognise names of towns, people or the use of certain words, such as 'whether' and 'weather'.

2.6 Explain the purpose of accurate use of grammar, punctuation and spelling

Poor or inaccurate spelling in a business document can be very annoying for the person receiving the document. This would be the last thing a business would want – to upset its customers or suppliers because of a simple thing like spelling a word wrong. Nevertheless, these errors do occur and unfortunately the only way that an individual can practise to improve their spelling and the use of the English language is to keep on thinking about it.

If you are not very good at spelling, then you need to make sure that you:

- pay attention to the spell-check facility on your computer – if the machine identifies a spelling error it will underline the word in red. If it identifies a grammatical error it will identify the words or phrase in green

- get used to using a dictionary – it is all very well saying how can I use a dictionary if I don't know how to spell the word, but if you get into the habit of having a dictionary on your desk and double-checking each time you are not sure, you will find you will eventually be able to spell several of the words you are unsure of

- get used to asking someone else – most people prefer to see a correctly spelled word because the individual writing it has asked for help rather than constantly having to tell them to go away and do the typing again. If you are unsure how to spell a word and can't find it in the dictionary, ask for assistance from a colleague.

Lots of people have problems with the plural of words. A plural of a word means 'more than one', so the plural of dog is dogs. A plural is usually formed simply by adding an 's', as in the example of dogs. However, some words can be both singular (one) and plural, such as 'sheep'. Other words need more than just 's' to transform them into a plural. For example, words ending in 'y', such as 'library' or 'facility', require the 'y' to be removed and 'ies' added to the end to make the plural – 'libraries' and 'facilities'. Words ending in 'ss', for example 'mass', usually require an 'es' to be added to give the plural, i.e. 'masses'.

Some nouns ending in 'f' or 'fe' need to drop the 'f' to make a plural and replace it with a 'ves', for example 'calf' in plural is 'calves' and 'knife' in plural is 'knives'.

Give it a go

See if you can write the plurals of the following words:

Donkey	Record
Family	Jacket
Ability	Paper
Gateau	Embarrass
Architecture	Knife
Leaf	Life

If you know you have a problem with spelling, then every time you come across a word you needed help with, write it down correctly. This may sound a bit like getting ready for a spelling test at school, but it is the only way you will get to grips with the problem. The more times you practise spelling it, the better you will become.

Over to you

The following words are those that people often have problems in spelling correctly. Use these words to start off your list of words you can spell correctly.

Acceptable	Hygienic
Accommodation	Initial
Assessment	Initiative
Behaviour	Liaise
Budgeted	Necessary
Colleague	Receive
Committee	Receipt
Convenient	Recommended
Criteria	Separate
Definite	Transferred
Environment	Undoubtedly

Another confusing area of spelling to some people are the words 'their, there and they're'. These three words sound the same but have different meanings. They are likely to occur when writing any form of business communication or document and it is easy to confuse them and use the wrong word, but this can make nonsense of a sentence. You should try to remember the following:

● their – this form of the word means 'belonging to them' and could be used to describe 'their' work, or 'their' children, or 'their' home. Their is the plural of words such as his, her or its

● they're – this form of the word means 'they are' and is like 'I'm' or 'We're' in that a letter is missed out

● there – this form of the word is used to show a place or to indicate something, for example 'There is' or 'Go over there' or 'I'll meet you there'.

Over to you

Correct the deliberate mistakes in the following sentences:

1 The girl went their because she was the only one.
2 There happy to be doing that kind of work.
3 The children has always enjoyed there time at the beach.
4 We told her we would be happy to meet her their.
5 We met them after they had collected they're belongings.

Punctuation refers to full stops (.), commas (,), question marks (?), dashes (–), semi-colons (;), colons (:), apostrophes (') and capital letters. There are some golden rules to help you remember:

● a full stop should be used at the end of a sentence

● a capital letter should be used at the beginning of a sentence and when using the names of people and places (proper nouns)

● a question mark is used to replace a full stop at the end of a sentence when a question has been asked in the sentence

● a comma is a way of identifying a pause in the middle of a sentence and can sometimes be replaced with a dash (–). It is also used to separate a list of words or to separate linking words, such as 'therefore' and 'however' from the rest of the words in the sentence:

'We will all be happy when he is back, and safe again with us.'

'We will all be happy when he is back – and safe again with us.'

● a semi-colon is used almost as a replacement to a full stop, but it breaks up one complete sentence which needs a break in it, but which has to remain as one sentence rather than two short ones:

'We were thinking of going on holiday again in September; June seems such a long way off now.'

● colons are used when a list is included in a sentence:

'We will have to take lots of items with us: the beach ball, the umbrella and something to wear if it turns cold.'

The apostrophe is commonly used in written communication and often causes confusion. There are two different uses to the apostrophe:

● to show that a letter or letters have been missed out of a word, e.g. 'I'm' for 'I am' or 'won't' for 'will not'

● to show that something belongs to someone or something, e.g. the manager's car or the dog's tail. This is known as the possessive apostrophe.

There is only one exception to the use of the possessive apostrophe and that is the word 'it'. When you see the word 'it's' it always means 'it is' because you do not put a possessive apostrophe into its: 'It's a good car but its paintwork is in a poor state of repair.'

Over to you

Try to place the apostrophe in the correct place in the following:

1 Claires desk

2 The directors office

3 Jons dog

4 The girls coat

5 The girls couldnt find their pens and pencils.

6 Its a nice day isnt it?

If you were unsure in this last activity, turn around the words to read:

1 The desk **of** Claire

2 The office **of** the director

3 The dog **of** Jon

4 The coat **of** the girl

in order to show who owns the items. When there are several owners of something, the apostrophe goes after the 's', for example the companies' shareholders or the bees' hive.

Over to you

The following sentences contain no punctuation. Rewrite or retype them, inserting the correct punctuation marks throughout:

1   The naughty boy was told therefore to report to the headmistresss office the next morning bringing with him his latest school report his outstanding homework and his packed lunch

2   maurices car was always giving him problems so he decided he would sell it soon and buy himself something brighter quieter and more reliable

3   When we all go to greece this year we have made a decision that we will travel by boat it is so much more relaxing than the airport

4   She expects to depart the station at 4 oclock and to arrive at birmingham just before it gets dark

5   if there late then we will have to find somewhere to sit and wait for them to arrive that should not be to difficult

Give it a go

The ten sentences below are all incorrect in some way. Find the mistakes in each and write or type them out correctly:

1   Me and Rosie enjoyed our day at the seaside but we didn't see nobody we knew.

2   Brian is the one what said it in the first place and we all blamed him.

3   The secretary told us that one of the letters what were sent out was full of mistakes.

4   My teacher is good at learning me the different ways of spelling words.

5   Chris and Laura said they would of come to the party but they was away for the weekend.

6   Pamela and me will be able to attend the meeting but Susie Charlotte and Tim will be away on holiday.

7   There friends sent them fewer cards than there family did send.

8   The sun shined all day it was only when it begun getting dark that it turned coolest.

9   If you will make sure the letter gets posted by Monday I would have been very relieved.

10 At Easter all of them what like to go to church to celebrate the resurrection of Christ do so.

2.7 Explain what is meant by plain English, and why it is used

The use of plain English is important as it tries to eliminate jargon or confusing information. Plain English aims to make sure that everything is clear and concise. In Britain, businesses and organisations can apply for a Crystal Mark. This is a system that was set up by the Plain English Campaign. It is a seal of approval for the clarity of a document and is now internationally recognised. The Plain English Campaign produces a number of free guides that explain how to write in plain English and there is also a list of alternative and clearer words that can be used instead of jargon. Plain English aims to ensure that anyone reading a document can understand it without being bombarded with jargon, odd terms or phrases and unnecessary complexity.

2.8 Explain the need to proofread and check written work

We have discussed throughout this unit the importance of using the correct format for business communications and making sure that they are well presented. However, none of these considerations will make any difference to the impression given in a business document unless the use of the English language is good.

Although our reliance on computers includes the use of word processors, which have a spell-check facility built in for checking the spelling, it is very important that all documents are proofread to make sure there are no errors. A word processor cannot be relied upon to identify words that are spelled correctly but are the wrong word. All types of documents, from memos and business letters to reports, articles and job descriptions, need careful checking. Mistakes can creep in, particularly in the use of punctuation, grammar, spelling and the general use of English, which can end up making the sentence or paragraph both confusing and hard to understand. The careful checking of all finished work is therefore essential.

Give it a go

Proofread the following text and identify the spelling and use of English errors that appear.

A verb is a word what describes a action. It is sometimes known therefore as a doing' word. For e.g. 'The manager open the door'. A sentence is not compleat withough a verb. For example 'The new ofice layout a big success'. This does not make a compleat sentence without the missing varb – is. The doing or action words in a sentence is usually the verbs.

2.9 Explain how to identify work that is important and work that is urgent

On a daily basis you are likely to deal with a number of tasks and communications with different priorities. They can usually be broken down into four different groups:

● urgent and important – these need to be done immediately and need maximum priority

● urgent but not important – not quite as vital as urgent and important, but still need immediate attention

● important but not urgent – vital information that must not be forgotten, but does not need immediate attention

● neither urgent nor important – does not need immediate attention and is usually routine work, but it still needs to be done.

It is not always a simple case that communications will be marked as being either important or urgent. The other complication is that some work, which is both urgent and important, can also be complicated and may actually take a good deal of time to complete.

Work is likely to come in from a variety of places. Some may be work that arrives as correspondence, or documents. Other work may be required as a result of email or voicemail messages. More work may come as a result of meetings, discussions or decisions that have been made during the day. Balancing all of these competing tasks is difficult at times and requires organisation.

2.10 Describe organisational procedures for saving and filing written communications

A vital part of administrative support is the storage and retrieval of information. This means saving and filing written communications. Although most businesses rely on their computerised systems for saving and filing information, it is still the case that a large number of physical documents also need to be saved and filed.

Whether the information is being stored digitally or conventionally using filing cabinets or storage boxes, a key to it all is indexing. This involves using a logical and effective way of recording documents and storing them in an efficient system so that they can easily be retrieved when required.

All documents need to be arranged and stored. They can be placed in consecutive order, such as using a simple alphabetical index. Other businesses prefer to give codes to specific documents. In *Unit 219: Store and Retrieve Information* we look at many of the different ways in which information can be stored and retrieved. We also cover good practice and classification methods.

What is Evidence ?

Evidence for these ten assessment criteria will come from an assessor observing your performance in a work environment, an examination of your work products, question and answer sessions and discussions. Evidence can also be generated by providing witness testimony, examining your own statements and recognising any prior learning.

■ 3. Understand how to communicate verbally

3.1 Describe ways of verbally presenting information and ideas clearly

As we have seen, any form of verbal communication involves exchanging information between a sender and a receiver. The sender will have a particular reason for sending the message and will expect a certain response from the receiver. Above all, the receiver has to understand what is being said, otherwise there will be misunderstanding and confusion.

Broadly speaking, verbal communication can have one or more of the following purposes:

● to inform – simply to pass on information

● to confirm – to acknowledge understanding or to agree dates and decisions

● to promote – to try to persuade somebody to do something or buy something

● to make a request – to ask for information, place an order or ask someone to do something for you

● to instruct – to give orders or allocate tasks.

This means that it is important to establish the purpose of the verbal communication, then figure out the best way to achieve this, so that your communication gets across in the clearest possible manner. It is always worthwhile planning how you are going to do this. Your options will usually be:

● face to face – either in a one-to-one formal or informal situation or in a meeting. Particularly in the case of a formal face-to-face situation or a meeting, you should note down what it is that you wish to say to remind yourself to cover all of the key points or questions that you may have

● remote verbal – this can mean using the telephone or perhaps teleconferencing or videoconferencing. These are live conversations and need to be planned and prepared in a similar way to a face-to-face situation. But remember, you will not have the benefit of being able to use non-verbal communication on the telephone or using teleconferencing

- voice messages – many people are thrown if a telephone extension goes to voicemail. You should prepare for this eventuality, having noted down the key things that you wish to say. Do not make your telephone message too complicated – stick to the basic information that you need to get across and request that the individual contacts you, or promise that you will attempt to contact them again at a specific time.

Whatever the reason for the verbal communication, it is important to consider the following:

- What is the best way of getting the message across?
- When is the best time?
- As the communication is verbal, does a record need to be kept of what has been said?
- Are you expecting feedback and how can you request this?

In any organisation there may be different forms of verbal communication, including:

- conversations that take place in the office or at a person's desk
- brief chats in the corridors or at lunch breaks
- informal meetings, when one or two employees talk about something
- formal meetings, when groups of employees are called together to make decisions
- when one member of staff is giving instructions to another
- when talking to customers, either in person or on the telephone.

There are many points that need to be considered when carrying out any form of verbal communication. These include:

- whether or not the message is being made clear
- the pitch and tone of the voice being used
- whether the recipient is listening or paying attention to what is being said
- whether the recipient feels free to ask questions
- when not to speak or interrupt
- the body language used.

Body language can take several forms and includes the following:

- facial expressions
- gestures

● posture

● how close we are prepared to get to another person

● eye contact.

3.2 Explain ways of making contributions to discussions that help to move them forward

Preparation is often the key to being able to make a valuable contribution to discussions. It is good practice to read through agendas for meetings and always to be aware of the purpose of team meetings and discussions. Going into a meeting or discussion without knowing the purpose or subject of the meeting will greatly inhibit your ability to make any valuable contribution.

Good team meetings encourage all those attending to make a contribution, as good teams recognise that each individual has their own perspective on situations and ways to deal with them.

Every team has its own mix of individuals. Some members work quietly in the background and are happy for others to make the important decisions. Some teams are a combination of difficult characters, often competing to make decisions and to appear to be in charge. A team needs to be a good mix of individual members, each with their own set of skills, abilities and experience. They are there to support each other.

In team meetings, for example, it is important to look at all of the information available, tasks and objectives to be met and any other factors that may affect the way in which the team can operate in the near future. Normally, teams will consider the following:

● they will look at where they are at the moment

● they will consider deadlines and whether these will be achieved

● they will prioritise deadlines and goals

● each team member will have an opportunity to express their opinion

● once opinions have been expressed, the team will try to reach an agreement

● individual team members will be given, or will volunteer to do, certain jobs

● the team members will request any resources they need to carry out their work.

It is vital to remember that even in difficult meetings, which require difficult decisions, you should try to remain calm – as you will have to work with these team members once the meeting is over. Provided you have carried out your own tasks and have volunteered to do work when it is needed, there is no need to be defensive or aggressive. This is particularly true if other members of the team have not fulfilled their part of the workload.

Usually a set period of time is put aside for the team to have a meeting. This is a limited amount of time and things need to be discussed and decisions made. A meeting is worthless if no decisions are made and therefore the conversation needs to be driven along so that the team can agree a particular way forward. There are always members of teams who will wish to talk about a situation and never come to a conclusion. If this is allowed, it will disrupt the team's work in the next few days or weeks after the meeting.

3.3 Describe methods of active listening
3.4 Explain the purpose of summarising verbal communications

People speak at a rate of 100–175 words per minute. It is very easy to let your mind drift and think about other things when other people are talking. In order to cure this you will need to actively listen or listen with a purpose. If you find it difficult to concentrate, try repeating their words (in your head) to reinforce the message. Listening is an important verbal communication skill. We all listen to a number of people during a single day, but not many of us can remember what was said in these conversations. As a useful backup, it is always a good idea to try to take notes, particularly of important conversations or instructions. This will allow you to remember what has been said.

Throughout the course of any working day, most people could receive instructions from a number of people. Being able to listen effectively is even more important if the person giving instructions is not sure of a number of things, including:

● the exact details of what they need to tell the listener

● how interested or receptive the listener is

● how knowledgeable the listener is about the subject of the instructions.

In order for the listener to understand the instruction they have to:

● hear the instructions clearly

● interpret the instructions

● evaluate their response to the instructions

● act upon the instructions and make use of the information they have heard.

If we are to make good use of our listening skills it is important to:

● concentrate on what is being said

● avoid becoming distracted

● repeat the words or phrases used in the conversation

● look at the person speaking and respond

- be ready for the other person to stop speaking

- ask questions and comment on what has been said.

Give it a go

In pairs, get your partner to tell you about a recent holiday or an outing they have taken. Let them talk to you for 3 minutes about their visit but do not interrupt them or ask them questions. Now recount everything that you have remembered about their visit. Did you remember most of it or did they have to remind you about some things?

Now swap roles and repeat the process.

What is Evidence ?

Evidence for these four assessment criteria will come from an assessor observing your performance in a work environment, an examination of your work products, question and answer sessions and discussions. Evidence can also be generated by providing witness testimony, examining your own statements and recognising any prior learning.

■ 4. Understand the purpose of feedback in developing communication skills

4.1 Describe ways of getting feedback on communications
4.2 Explain the purpose of using feedback to develop communication skills

One of the main objectives of communication is to get feedback from other individuals. They can make comment on the communication and give their opinion. Feedback can come in different forms:

- it can come as an immediate response, or a considered one at a later date, either verbally or in writing

- it can result in new instructions being given, or more information provided.

Your audience or the individual(s) that you are communicating with will be able to provide you with valuable feedback. Sometimes they will give you verbal or non-verbal reactions to your communications. You should pay close attention to this feedback. It will not only give you confidence that they have understood your message, but will also give you valuable pointers as to how to improve your communication techniques.

If you discover that there has been some kind of misunderstanding with a communication, then even negative feedback will be valuable. This will help you to restate the message in a different way, taking the feedback into consideration. Feedback is meant to be a supportive process. It reinforces your communication techniques. But remember, it also aims to correct problems and change the way you do things. Always consider the following:

- feedback is usually given on the basis of mutual trust rather than blame
- feedback, in order to be valuable, needs to be specific and also needs to be clear and concise
- feedback needs to be timely and to refer to specific communications
- feedback needs to be agreed and accepted in order for it to be valuable
- feedback, in terms of its value to you, may be variable. Some may give you useful feedback which is positive, while others may simply be negative and offer no suggestion
- feedback should not overwhelm you and make you feel inadequate
- you should ask for feedback, even if you are certain that your communication was correct.

Above all, feedback allows you to see yourself as others see you. It allows you to adjust the way in which you communicate and move towards a gradual improvement across all of your communication techniques.

If the instructions given or the explanation of tasks are not clear, then the person receiving the instructions should always make sure that they fully understand what is involved. Sometimes this involves asking a series of questions in order to obtain more information or to clarify the set of instructions.

Someone needing to clarify instructions or the objectives will obviously need to have more than a 'yes' or 'no' reply to their questions. They may want full answers. The following things should be remembered:

- it should always be clear what is being asked
- the question should not repeat something that has already been asked or said
- the way a question is asked can make a big difference – take care not to sound sarcastic or funny
- the question should be asked at the appropriate time and not when someone else is speaking.

Over to you

Turn the following 'yes' or 'no' questions into questions that would require a longer answer.

Did you enjoy your holiday?

Did you go out at lunchtime?

Was the bus on time?

Did you see many people you knew at the cinema?

Have you eaten much today?

Once you have done this, ask one of your colleagues these questions. Then ask them how clear your questions were and whether or not you should have phrased them slightly differently to get the best answer.

Asking reasonable questions about what is expected is acceptable. Sometimes people are too busy to answer questions, but it is always better to get a question answered than try to continue a task with unclear instructions.

Any task will have an objective, either for the individual, the team of people involved or the business as a whole. In order to carry out the task properly and meet the objectives, the listener will have to be clear about:

● why the instructions have been given

● for whom the work is being done

● the outcome of the task involved

● when the task has to be completed.

Clarification means making clear or dealing with any confusion that might arise out of the objectives. The clearer the objectives, the better chance the person instructed to carry out the task will have of achieving them.

The clarification of objectives can come from those who have set the objectives in the first place. This means that that person will need to explain clearly what the objectives are. Based on this, the person given the instructions will then set in motion all of the steps needed to fulfil the objectives.

What is Evidence ?

Evidence for these two assessment criteria will come from an assessor observing your performance in a work environment, an examination of your work products, question and answer sessions and discussions. Evidence can also be generated by providing witness testimony, examining your own statements and recognising any prior learning.

■ 5. Be able to plan communication

5.1 Identify the purpose of communications and the audience(s)

Refer to 1.1 and 1.2 and then try the following activity.

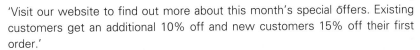

Give it a go

'Visit our website to find out more about this month's special offers. Existing customers get an additional 10% off and new customers 15% off their first order.'

What is the purpose of the communication and what are the likely audiences? How might this message be communicated?

5.2 Select methods of communication to be used
5.3 Confirm methods of communication, as required

Refer back to 1.3 and 1.4 and then try the following activity.

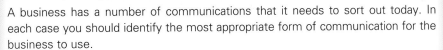

Give it a go

A business has a number of communications that it needs to sort out today. In each case you should identify the most appropriate form of communication for the business to use.

1 To invite a manager from another office within the business to attend a meeting and lunch afterwards.

2 To present the results of some research to all managers in the business.

3 To tell all employees about a change to car parking arrangements.

4 To inform a customer that their order will be delivered tomorrow.

5 To apologise to a customer who has left three messages on voicemail and has not yet been contacted.

What is Evidence ?

A wide range of evidence can be provided to demonstrate your competence. Examples of evidence can include:

● communications log

● information searches

● draft communications

- amended documents
- emails, memos, faxes and letters
- copies of messages or notes that you have passed on to others
- forms that you have completed yourself
- notes that summarise key points
- presentations
- minutes of meetings indicating your contribution
- feedback on your performance
- action or development plans.

■ 6. Be able to communicate in writing

6.1 Find and select information needed for written communications

Refer back to 2.1 and then try the following activity.

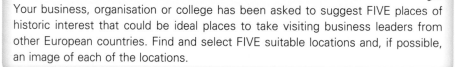

Give it a go

Your business, organisation or college has been asked to suggest FIVE places of historic interest that could be ideal places to take visiting business leaders from other European countries. Find and select FIVE suitable locations and, if possible, an image of each of the locations.

6.2 Organise, structure and present information so that it is clear, accurate and meets the needs of the audience
6.3 Use language that suits the purpose of written communication and the audience

Refer to 2.3 and 2.4 and then try the following activity.

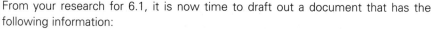

Give it a go

From your research for 6.1, it is now time to draft out a document that has the following information:

- the name and location of each of the five sites chosen
- one short paragraph for each of the five sites, describing the historic importance of each

- an indication as to whether any or all of the sites would be suitable for a welcome reception for visiting business people
- at least ONE image of each of the FIVE sites.

You can choose the most appropriate form of written communication to present your information.

6.4 Use accurate grammar, spelling and punctuation, and plain English to make sure that meaning is clear

Refer to 2.6 and 2.7.

You want the information from the previous activity to have as wide a readership as possible, so the language needs to be clear. Bear in mind that people from other European countries may read your information. A good way of checking that it is clear is to use the Fog Index, which measures the readability of English writing (see below). Check your work by carrying out the following activity.

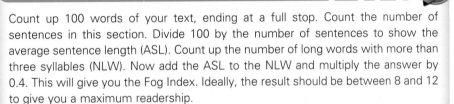

Give it a go

Count up 100 words of your text, ending at a full stop. Count the number of sentences in this section. Divide 100 by the number of sentences to show the average sentence length (ASL). Count up the number of long words with more than three syllables (NLW). Now add the ASL to the NLW and multiply the answer by 0.4. This will give you the Fog Index. Ideally, the result should be between 8 and 12 to give you a maximum readership.

6.5 Proofread and check written communications and make amendments, as required

Refer to 2.5 and 2.8 and then try the following activity.

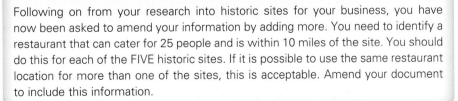

Give it a go

Following on from your research into historic sites for your business, you have now been asked to amend your information by adding more. You need to identify a restaurant that can cater for 25 people and is within 10 miles of the site. You should do this for each of the FIVE historic sites. If it is possible to use the same restaurant location for more than one of the sites, this is acceptable. Amend your document to include this information.

6.6 Confirm what is important and what is urgent
6.7 Produce written communications to meet agreed deadlines
6.8 Keep a file copy of written communications sent

Refer to 2.9 and 2.10 and then attempt the following activity.

Give it a go

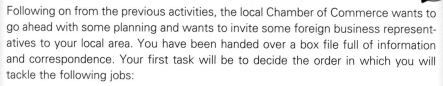

Following on from the previous activities, the local Chamber of Commerce wants to go ahead with some planning and wants to invite some foreign business represent-atives to your local area. You have been handed over a box file full of information and correspondence. Your first task will be to decide the order in which you will tackle the following jobs:

- confirm by email to 25 European businesses that you have received their details and that they are booked in to attend meetings from 22 to 25 September

- contact a centrally located 3-star or better hotel and block book 25 rooms

- confirm with the first historic location on your list that you wish to use it for a welcome reception on 22 September

- book evening meal at your chosen restaurant for 40 people

- design and get printed 100 invitations for the welcome reception

- send travel details, location of hotel and rough itinerary to all 25 European business representatives

- contact at least five large employers from the local area and request they provide speakers for the events

- arrange an itinerary that takes in historic sites, transport hubs and examples of local businesses.

Assume that you have two months before 22 September. Note down when each of these tasks will have to be completed and how you will check whether the deadlines have been met. Make sure you keep a file copy of all the research you carried out in the previous activities. Word process a copy of your prioritisation list and ensure you also have kept a file copy of this document.

What is Evidence ?

A wide range of evidence can be provided to demonstrate your competence. Examples of evidence can include:

- communications log
- information searches
- draft communications

- amended documents
- emails, memos, faxes and letters
- copies of messages or notes that you have passed on to others
- forms that you have completed yourself
- notes that summarise key points
- presentations
- minutes of meetings indicating your contribution
- feedback on your performance
- action or development plans.

7. Be able to communicate verbally

7.1 Verbally present information and ideas to others clearly and accurately

Refer to 3.1 and then carry out the following activity.

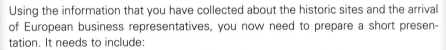

Give it a go

Using the information that you have collected about the historic sites and the arrival of European business representatives, you now need to prepare a short presentation. It needs to include:

- a summary of your suggested locations
- an explanation as to how you have ordered the urgent and non-urgent preparation work for the arrivals
- suggestions as to what additional tasks may need to be carried out, giving deadlines as appropriate.

Your presentation should be made to your assessor as a representative of the local Chamber of Commerce and it can be videoed if required.

7.2 Make contributions to discussion(s) that move the discussion forward

Refer to 3.2 and then carry out the following activity.

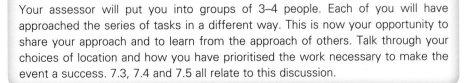

Give it a go

Your assessor will put you into groups of 3–4 people. Each of you will have approached the series of tasks in a different way. This is now your opportunity to share your approach and to learn from the approach of others. Talk through your choices of location and how you have prioritised the work necessary to make the event a success. 7.3, 7.4 and 7.5 all relate to this discussion.

7.3 Actively listen to information given by other people, and make relevant responses

Refer to 3.3 and then carry out the following activity.

Give it a go

When you have completed your contribution and series of suggestions during the discussion, you need to ensure that you listen to the information given by the other members of the group. You need to prove that you have actively listened to them and this can be done in the following ways:

- encourage or prompt them to explain anything that you feel is unclear
- make notes of their key points and solutions to problems
- ensure that each member of the group has had an opportunity to contribute to the discussion.

7.4 Ask relevant questions to clarify own understanding, as required
7.5 Summarise verbal communication(s) and agree that the correct meaning has been understood

Refer to 3.4 and then carry out the following activity.

Give it a go

Ensure that all members of the group discussion understand and agree a common way forward in organising, prioritising and setting deadlines for all of the tasks that would be necessary for the event. At the end of the discussion the group should summarise the discussion in their own words. You should then compare your summaries with those of the others to ensure that the correct meaning and decisions have been understood by all.

What is Evidence ?

A wide range of evidence can be provided to demonstrate your competence. Examples of evidence can include:

- communications log
- information searches
- draft communications
- amended documents
- emails, memos, faxes and letters

- copies of messages or notes that you have passed on to others
- forms that you have completed yourself
- notes that summarise key points
- presentations
- minutes of meetings indicating your contribution
- feedback on your performance
- action or development plans.

■ 8. Be able to identify and agree ways of developing communication skills

8.1 Get feedback to confirm whether the communication has achieved its purpose

Refer to 4.1 and then carry out the following activity.

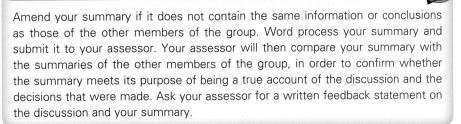

Give it a go

Amend your summary if it does not contain the same information or conclusions as those of the other members of the group. Word process your summary and submit it to your assessor. Your assessor will then compare your summary with the summaries of the other members of the group, in order to confirm whether the summary meets its purpose of being a true account of the discussion and the decisions that were made. Ask your assessor for a written feedback statement on the discussion and your summary.

8.2 Use feedback to identify and agree ways of improving own communication skills

Refer to 4.2 and then carry out the following activity.

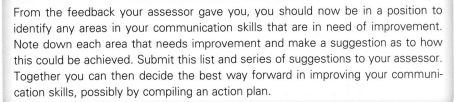

Give it a go

From the feedback your assessor gave you, you should now be in a position to identify any areas in your communication skills that are in need of improvement. Note down each area that needs improvement and make a suggestion as to how this could be achieved. Submit this list and series of suggestions to your assessor. Together you can then decide the best way forward in improving your communication skills, possibly by compiling an action plan.

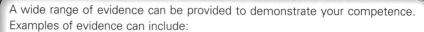

What is Evidence ?

A wide range of evidence can be provided to demonstrate your competence. Examples of evidence can include:

- communications log
- information searches
- draft communications
- amended documents
- emails, memos, faxes and letters
- copies of messages or notes that you have passed on to others
- forms that you have completed yourself
- notes that summarise key points
- presentations
- minutes of meetings indicating your contribution
- feedback on your performance
- action or development plans.

Pull it together

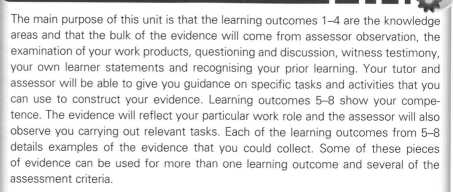

The main purpose of this unit is that the learning outcomes 1–4 are the knowledge areas and that the bulk of the evidence will come from assessor observation, the examination of your work products, questioning and discussion, witness testimony, your own learner statements and recognising your prior learning. Your tutor and assessor will be able to give you guidance on specific tasks and activities that you can use to construct your evidence. Learning outcomes 5–8 show your competence. The evidence will reflect your particular work role and the assessor will also observe you carrying out relevant tasks. Each of the learning outcomes from 5–8 details examples of the evidence that you could collect. Some of these pieces of evidence can be used for more than one learning outcome and several of the assessment criteria.

The following activity has been designed in order for you to create additional evidence if there are areas in which you are finding it difficult to demonstrate competence.

You have recently become the personal assistant of the managing director of Elizabeth Francis Advertising Associates. You used to work as an administrative assistant for Liz, the boss. You know how she likes to do things and you see this as a great opportunity. You need to show her that you are capable of doing all the work that she has given you. Liz is not in the office very often, as she spends a lot of time with her clients and talking to designers, photographers and artists. Liz is not exactly demanding, but the last personal assistant survived only three months before she was sacked. In fact, Liz has had four personal assistants in the past two years. Eight other people work for the agency, but there are lots of others who do contract work and they need clear instructions and guidance at all times.

The following activities represent a typical working day and Liz is out of the office for the next three days. When you sit down at your desk you find that there are a number of different things in your in-tray, which Liz has left you to deal with.

Liz's speech

From time to time Liz is asked to talk about advertising and marketing. She actually enjoys it and also sees it as a chance to talk to potential customers. She wants to get an advertising message across in her speech and you will need to read her instructions in the memorandum and refer to her notes to help you put together a five-minute speech for her.

MEMORANDUM

TO: PA   **DATE:**

FROM: Liz   **REF:**

Speech to Chamber of Commerce

On Friday of next week I've been asked to speak at the monthly Chamber of Commerce meeting on the subject of advertising. I want to be able to say how important advertising is and what its role is in business. I have attached some handwritten notes for you, but I need you to put these together for a five-minute (no more than that, I think) speech. The main point of the exercise is to tell them about advertising; I don't mind if you mention some of the things it can't do, but be upbeat and positive. Don't forget these are business people and they want solid information that does not waste their time.

Liz's notes

Advertising is often seen as a waste of money.

It pushes up the prices and they have to be passed on to the customer.

It is, however, a great opportunity for business – why?

Because:

You use advertising to make sales – this allows businesses to get extra income at times when sales are low or disappointing.

You can use advertising to push up sales when the business might be tempted to drop prices to get extra customers. After all, when sales pick up you will only be tempted to increase prices again.

You can use advertising to help you reduce the amount of goods that you have in the warehouse. We know how expensive it is to have lots of stock sitting around doing nothing; it ties up the business's money. Advertising will help to increase demand and lower stock levels.

Hope this is of some help to you.

Liz's memorandum

On a scrap of paper Liz has left you a note to remind you that the architects are coming in next week. At the last staff meeting she promised to circulate a form, asking all members of staff what they felt about open plan offices. Liz wants to knock down some of the partition walls and make a more attractive workspace for everyone. This would mean that senior members of staff would not have their own offices any more; they would have their own areas that could be partitioned off and have meetings with their clients in their own part of the office space.

Liz has asked you to write a memorandum for all staff and to design a simple form that they could fill in as a record of their comments on the plan. You remember a conversation that you had with Liz and she said: 'I have spoken to everyone about this, but they won't be pleased if I just make a decision without consulting them. At the end of the day, we need to improve the offices and I'll only change my mind if there are some really good reasons for not going open plan.'

Her note goes on to say that you must not write in the memo that the decision has actually been made, but rather say that the open plan idea is a good one and that Liz is very keen to go ahead with it.

You will need to write a memorandum that covers these points and you will need to attach to it a basic form that would allow members of staff to make comment about the proposals to go open plan.

Preparing a notice and an agenda

The meeting about the open plan office proposal is due to take place next Thursday in the board room at 10am. Liz wants you to make it part of a general staff meeting, which can cover several points that she thinks need discussion. As usual, several members of staff have sent in requests of items to be included on the agenda. Liz has suggested that the following agenda items should be included:

● the open plan office proposal (including feedback from the staff)

● the new contract with Clinch Communications

● the proposed staff weekend in Paris to celebrate winning the Goodlad Publishing account.

You will need to produce an agenda and a notice of this meeting, as requested, including two further suggestions, one by Linda asking for a discussion about the lack of photocopy paper, which is causing problems for her design department, and the other from Kevin, who wants to thank all staff who were involved in winning the Brondale Electronics advertising contract.

An information sheet

Following the circulation of the memo about the open plan office proposal you have had a number of comments back from various members of staff. Liz will want you to summarise the comments and try to show in your summary the strength of feelings and opinions if possible. The following comments need to be noted:

● 'I think it is a great idea and I would find it far easier to supervise the staff' – Linda

- 'I really think it would mean a lot of extra noise and disruption to my work. If we did go open plan I would want to have screens around me' – Kevin

- 'The advantages in terms of work flow and communication would be great. I think that the open plan system would really work for us in client fulfilment' – Hassan

- 'I really think that we need some way of reducing the amount of noise that will be generated in one big space' – Felicity

- 'The lack of privacy would be a real problem, especially when I am trying to talk to clients. I don't think that it will be very professional if I have to ask people to keep the noise down' – Frank

- 'There will be far more opportunities to be flexible about the way we do things; I think it is a good idea' – Justine

- 'I will be able to see everything that is going on, that's both good and bad' – Hari

Using these comments, summarise the main points that have been made by the staff. You have also noticed a scribbled note – Liz wants you to prepare a confidential memo for her, noting which members of staff are actually in favour of the open plan proposal.

Work with Other People in a Business Environment

■ Purpose of the unit

This unit is about working within a team, sharing responsibility with others to make sure that a team can achieve agreed goals and objectives.

■ Assessment requirements

There are ten parts to this unit. The first six parts introduce organisations, goals and objectives, communication and teams. The ten parts are:

1 Understand how your role fits with organisational values and practices – the sector in which your organisation operates, its missions and purpose and a comparison of your organisation with other types of organisation in your sector, an outline of your responsibilities, how your role fits into the organisation's structure and contributes to its operations, the organisation's policies, procedures, systems and values relevant to your role.

2 Understand how to work as part of a team to achieve goals and objectives – the purpose of working with others, how team work can achieve positive results, the purpose and benefits of agreeing work goals and plans, supporting team members, the purpose of agreeing quality measures.

3 Understand how to communicate as part of a team – the purpose of communicating with team members, the different methods of communication and when to use them.

4 Understand the contribution of individuals within a team – the purpose of recognising strengths of others, valuing diversity, respecting other team members.

5 Understand how to deal with problems and disagreements – types of problems and disagreements, methods of dealing with them.

6 Understand the purpose of feedback when working as a team – the purpose of giving and receiving constructive feedback, using feedback to improve own work and that of the team.

7 Be able to work in a way that fits with organisational values and practices – following organisational policies, systems and procedures, applying organisational values, working with outside organisations, seeking guidance about policies, systems, procedures and values.

8 Be able to work in a team to achieve goals and objectives – effective communication with team members, contributing to the agreement of work objectives and quality measures, ensuring goals and objectives

are achieved, providing support to team members, showing respect for individuals in a team, ensuring own work meets agreed quality standards and is on time.

9 Be able to deal with or refer problems in a team – identifying problems and disagreements, resolving those problems and disagreements or referring them.

10 Be able to use feedback on objectives in a team – contribute to providing constructive feedback on achievement of objectives, receive and use constructive feedback.

1. Understand how your role fits with organisational values and practices

1.1 Describe the sector in which your organisation operates

There is a wide range of organisations and they differ a great deal, but they all have some common features, including:

- they all use resources (such as human beings, money and materials)
- they all provide something (maybe a product or a service)
- they often compete with other business organisations.

Each business, or business organisation, will undertake a variety of tasks or functions to make sure that it operates well within the area in which it is involved. Some of these functions include:

- managing employees – usually through a human resources department
- selling products or services – providing the customers with the required product or service
- distributing the product or service – to make sure that the customer can get what the business provides
- purchasing products or services – by ordering stock to help the business make its own products or services
- marketing a product or service – by carrying out research to find out what customers need and making sure they know what the business is offering for sale
- keeping financial records – to monitor the success of the business.

Organisations have to make sure that when they make a choice, it is the right one. They do not always have the same purpose as other businesses, but all organisations have considerations and choices to make. These often involve the most effective way to use their resources in order to meet the business's objectives, or to make a profit.

Sectors in which business organisations operate

Generally speaking, business organisations fit into two different sectors:

- private sector organisations – including sole traders, partnerships, private limited companies, public limited companies and charities
- public sector organisations – including public corporations and local authorities.

Private sector organisations

Private sector organisations are independent of the government and include:

- sole traders – organisations that are usually owned and run or operated by one person, for example the owner of a newsagents

Figure 205.1

- partnerships – organisations owned by groups of people, for example a group of solicitors

Figure 205.2

- limited companies (private and public) – organisations owned by share-holders, will have either Ltd (Limited) or Plc (Public Limited Company) in their name

Figure 205.3

- charities – organisations which do not function necessarily in order to make a profit but to make money for the cause they are representing, for example Oxfam

Give it a go

Using a copy of the Yellow Pages for your local area, first of all identify at least ten sole traders. How have you identified these organisations as being owned by a sole trader? What did you look for to make your decision as to whether or not these organisations were sole traders?

Answer the same questions for at least ten partnerships, five limited companies and five public limited companies, and five charities that operate in your area.

Public sector organisations

The public sector consists of organisations that are either owned or controlled by the government. The most common forms of public sector organisation are:

- government departments, or the civil service – these are departments which are responsible for running government activities in a specific area, such as the Department for Business, Enterprise and Regulatory Reform (BERR), which assists businesses of all types

- local government – such as county, metropolitan, district or borough councils that provide services, assist businesses and promote the area in which they are involved

- public corporations or enterprises – these are also known as nationalised industries and provide services in a particular part of the economy. The Bank of England is a public corporation.

Industry sectors

Another way of classifying different types of business is to identify their industrial sector. There are three main sectors:

- primary sector – these are businesses where raw materials are generated. Good examples are agriculture, fishing, mining, quarrying and forestry. They provide all the basic raw materials that are used by manufacturing to make products, or for power generators to make electricity

- secondary sector – these are businesses that manufacture products. They transform raw materials into finished products. A good example would be a paper factory that transforms pulped wood into different types of paper, which can then be used to make magazines, books and newspapers

- tertiary sector – these businesses are often referred to as the service sector. They are involved in retail, transport, banking, healthcare and distribution.

Some businesses have operations in two or even three of the industrial sectors. An oil company may be involved in drilling for oil in the primary sector; it then processes the oil to make petrol in the secondary sector and sells it through a chain of petrol stations in the tertiary sector. Sometimes the primary and secondary sectors are referred to as the industrial sector.

1.2 Describe your organisation's missions and purpose

All business organisations, whether they are small, medium or large in size, will have purpose – a set of aims or objectives which they wish to achieve. The purpose of most organisations is to be successful and they will aim to achieve this objective in all of their day-to-day activities. However, there are some things that can affect whether or not a business is able to meet its objectives, including the following which may be out of the control of the organisation itself:

● the laws may change – such legal changes might affect the way an organisation produces its products, for example, or the way in which it advertises them to the customer

● internal problems – financial difficulties, for instance, can affect the way an organisation works towards meeting its objectives

● change in ownership – for example, a sole trader becoming a partnership can affect the original business's objectives and require the new partnership to draw up a new set of aims or objectives under their new circumstances.

A good starting point for any business that is just starting out is to write down its main aims, purposes and objectives in what is known as a business plan. Having written a business plan, however, the business owners would have to be aware that they need to be flexible. The environment in which the business is operating can be constantly changing and the objectives will change along with it.

Objectives are the medium- to long-term targets which help the business to achieve its 'mission statement'. Examples of business objectives that could be included in a business plan are different for each organisation, but could include any of the following, depending on the organisation involved:

● to be successful

● to make a profit

● to break even – this means that the business would want to make enough money to pay its bills, but not necessarily to make a profit

● to sell products

● to sell services

● to survive.

Obviously, it is in everyone's interests to identify the organisation's exact business objectives. In addition, business objectives can differ from time to time.

There are a number of different methods of ensuring that employees know about the business's objectives. Employees must have a true picture of what the organisation needs. Organisations will use some of the following to make sure they keep their employees up to date with changing objectives:

- staff meetings
- newsletters
- company newspapers
- bulletin boards
- notice boards
- email messages
- press statements or press releases
- organisational videos
- letters or memos sent directly to all employees.

Mission statements (corporate objectives)

An organisation's mission statement is different from a business plan because it looks more at what the organisation as a whole stands for. In other words, it is an agreement between the managers and the employees of the organisation regarding a number of goals. Everyone involved in the business will have an opinion about the way goals should be achieved, or at least share some ideas about how they will be achieved.

A business's fundamental policy will be contained within a mission statement. It will describe the organisation's business vision, including its values and purpose. Mission statements tend to be a statement of where a business wishes to be rather than a description of where they are at the present time. A business may choose to include within its mission statement a vision of how it wishes its employees to respond, react and fulfil the needs of its customers.

Businesses will try to ensure that whatever is contained within their mission statement will be achieved. Often they put in place employee development programmes and training, so they can meet the objectives stated in their mission statement.

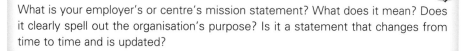

Over to you

What is your employer's or centre's mission statement? What does it mean? Does it clearly spell out the organisation's purpose? Is it a statement that changes from time to time and is updated?

1.3 Compare your organisation to other types of organisation in your sector

There are many different ways in which you can compare organisations, including:

● the type of legal structure

● the size

● the purpose

● the number of employees

● the different departments

● the way they are organised

● the type of customer or other businesses and organisations they routinely deal with

● the industrial sector in which they operate.

Perhaps one of the first areas to investigate is the mission or purpose of the organisation before going on to examine areas such as location, number, size and purpose of different departments, outlets, offices or other key features.

It is sometimes very difficult to compare organisations because they differ so much. There are many reasons why this happens. It may be to do with the way in which the organisation has grown, how old the organisation is, how it goes about doing its work and its **organisational culture**.

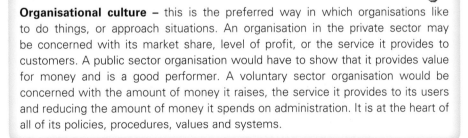

Don't forget

Organisational culture – this is the preferred way in which organisations like to do things, or approach situations. An organisation in the private sector may be concerned with its market share, level of profit, or the service it provides to customers. A public sector organisation would have to show that it provides value for money and is a good performer. A voluntary sector organisation would be concerned with the amount of money it raises, the service it provides to its users and reducing the amount of money it spends on administration. It is at the heart of all of its policies, procedures, values and systems.

1.4 Outline your responsibilities
1.5 Describe how your role fits into your organisation's structure
1.6 Describe how your role contributes to the organisation's operations

Knowing what your role is in an organisation begins with your initial interview, where you are told to some extent what will be expected of you. When you receive your contract of employment, a job description may well be included. This will outline your role in the organisation, either as a team member or as an individual who is working to support others in the organisation.

The job description tells only part of the story and you should be prepared to be flexible and adaptable, as you may be asked to carry out other duties which are not on the job description. Whether this is the case or not, the term 'clarity of roles' means knowing in a variety of circumstances exactly what is expected and how your work relates to a larger activity as a whole.

In your regular work and in work which you are not that familiar with, organisational procedures can help you understand the processes involved in getting particular tasks completed. Organisational procedures will suggest the ideal ways in which the business wants particular things completed. These will be a series of steps, supported by checks, to make sure that everything has been covered and completed to the business's, and probably the customers' satisfaction.

These organisational procedures will set out the requirements of a particular task. They will be a series of instructions which should alert you to the fact that particular documents have to be referred to, other documents and forms completed and other individuals involved, either to check what has been done or to pass on that information to them at a particular stage of the activity.

Organisational procedures which suggest the requirements of an activity can help you, as an employee, make sure that everything has been done and will also assure the business that all the necessary steps have been taken in line with its policies and procedures.

Give it a go

Think of one particular activity you carry out routinely in either your job or while studying at college. Can you think of at least three benefits to yourself and three for the business as a whole of having procedures in place to follow in the completion of this activity?

Job descriptions

A job description explains what the job involves and is useful for a business to match the right person for the job. If your job is in a human resources department of a business, it is likely that it will involve writing job descriptions for any vacancies that occur. A job description would include the following:

- the job title – the title of manager or supervisor would be included if the job includes the new employee having responsibility for and authority over other employees
- where the new employee would fit in within the business; in other words, their position within the structure of the business
- the tasks and activities that the new employee will be required to carry out
- the roles and responsibilities that are required of the new employee.

The amount of detail included on a job description will depend on the type of job that is being described. There will probably be more details given for a job with management responsibility than for a job for a junior person with few responsibilities. The following illustration shows the typical headings on a job description.

JOB DESCRIPTION

Job title:

Department/Function/Section

Wage/Salary range

Main purpose of the job

Duties and responsibilities

Responsible to:

Responsible for:

Give it a go

Look through the job advertisements in your local paper. Choose an advertisement for a job you think you would like to do at some time. From the advertisement, see if you can write a brief job description for the job involved. Choose an advertisement that has a lot of detail, although you may be able to think of some hidden duties that are not included in the newspaper.

If you can't find any suitable job advertisements, choose from one of the following occupations and write your job description around that job role:

- office junior
- assistant to office manager
- receptionist
- accounts clerk
- mail room assistant.

You may find that talking to family, friends and colleagues will help you to complete the duties and responsibilities section.

As well as a job description, sometimes a business will draw up a person specification. This is more of a description of the kind of qualities the person should have to satisfactorily carry out the job. A person specification is the business's checklist of the ideal person for the job and will include a description of:

- the experience required
- the necessary skills
- the physical characteristics the person needs to have – including things such as their height, weight, hearing or eyesight, which could affect their ability to do the job
- the qualifications required – a computer expert, for example, would need the qualifications to prove they could do the job
- the personality and temperament required – this is important if the job involves working closely with other employees, customers or new employees, or leading a team
- the level of motivation required – this is their ability, for example, to work alone and not be supervised and the pride they take in doing the job.

Give it a go

Go back to the job description activity and now, for the same job role, draw up a person specification. What qualities or attributes would the person need to do that particular job?

Over to you

Using a clerical assistant job as an example, prepare a list of criteria which you would consider to be essential, desirable or just required. These criteria may include some or all of those we have given you already, as well as some of the following:

- current achievements (qualifications, driving licence, etc.)
- aptitudes (social skills, listening skills, communication skills, legible handwriting)
- interests (relevant sports or leisure activities)
- personal circumstances (whether they are willing to work overtime or at weekends, etc.)
- physical attributes (appearance and ability to speak clearly, for instance).

1.7 Outline the policies, procedures, systems and values of your organisation that are relevant to your role
1.8 Outline who you would consult if unsure about organisational policies, procedures, systems and values

Policies are broad guidelines that determine the way in which an organisation operates. Its procedures are the preferred ways in which it wants specific tasks or activities to be performed. The systems are the supporting mechanisms that allow the procedures to be followed. The values of an organisation are often part of its organisational culture and may include providing excellent customer service and feedback, value for money, open and honest dealing and public accountability.

All organisations work in different ways and have different systems and procedures which they expect their staff to carry out in the course of their day-to-day duties.

The operation of administration procedures is important since the organisation's activities must be coordinated and planned. If inadequate administration procedures are in operation, the organisation may suffer from a lack of efficiency and effectiveness since it does not have access to all relevant information. Administration procedures inevitably involve some form of filing, whether it be a paper-based filing system or one housed within a computer system.

Businesses and organisations will have a series of other procedures. These will include:

- health and safety – this will need to follow the requirements of health and safety legislation and will provide guidance to employees on ensuring that the workplace remains a healthy and risk-free environment

- security and confidentiality – these will include procedures to ensure that the building, the business's or organisation's property and confidential information remain safe

- grievance and disciplinary procedures – these will also follow legislation, but will state how an employee can bring a complaint to the notice of the employer and the procedures to be followed to investigate that grievance. The disciplinary procedure will state unacceptable behaviour and the sanctions that can be brought against the employee. It will also state the stages involved in the disciplinary procedure.

The systems which an organisation has in place should aim to establish a means by which the operations it carries out can be assessed. Most administrative systems are a series of sub-systems, which can be split into additional sub-systems. It is, therefore, important that the organisation monitors all parts of the system. The systems should be designed in such a way that they can be changed to meet the requirements of the organisation.

Administrative procedures obviously play a vital role. They are the means by which the organisation is able to operate as a whole. Any organisation can have good ideas and well-motivated employees, but without procedures to ensure that functions are carried out, these may be unsuccessful. Information received into the organisation has to be processed in some way before it can either be stored (in which case it could be retrieved later) or disseminated (sent to different people) around the various departments. Alternatively, the information may need to be sent out from the organisation in a different format.

The following table shows us what information may come into a business, what the business may need to do to that information and the type of information that may leave the business.

Type of information that may enter a business	How information may be processed by the business	Type of information that may leave a business
Fax	Filed on a computer	A reply or response in writing
Telephone message	Sent around the different departments	A reply or response via the telephone
Email message		
Business letter	Filed in a filing cabinet	A bill to a customer
Money from a customer	Discussed at a meeting	A payment to a supplier
Bill from a supplier	Followed up by a member of staff	
Order or enquiry from a customer	Analysed by managers	
	A report produced	

An organisation will need to process the information that comes into the business. This can be done in a number of ways, depending on the type of business and the type of information. These are the generally accepted descriptions of administration procedures:

- ways of doing things that are set down as rules and regulations by the senior managers
- activities carried out by managers to meet the objectives of the organisation
- activities carried out to ensure the control of the day-to-day running of the business.

The running of an organisation requires an organised approach if it is to be efficient and effective. Administrative tasks will be carried out at all levels of the organisation. In a larger organisation, administration will be carried out by the administration department, but in smaller businesses the administration may be carried out by a single individual who will be responsible for all forms of administration. Whoever is responsible for carrying out these tasks, the basic purpose for these procedures remains the same:

- to provide support systems for all resources used by the organisation
- to keep records relating to the activities of the organisation
- to monitor the performance of the business's activities.

The business will have administrative procedures in place that aim to make sure:

- information is stored in the right place (either on a computer or in a paper-based filing system)
- information can be found easily once it has been stored (either on a computer or in a paper-based filing system)
- information can be copied or printed (using a photocopier or a printer) and passed on to all those employees who need to see it
- information can be received easily by the business (via the fax machine or through email messages and the postal system)
- those wishing to send information to the business can do so easily and without problems
- information needing to be sent out of the business can be done so easily (via fax machine or through email messages and the postal system)
- those who are meant to receive the information being sent out of the business do so easily and without problems
- the physical resources (materials, components and items such as stationery, envelopes, etc.) the business's employees need to carry out their tasks are available when needed. This is known as stock.

The activities of an organisation may be classified as routine or non-routine. Routine activities mean those carried out on a regular basis. Some individuals will be responsible for administration functions which will not differ regardless of any other activities carried out by the organisation. Examples of such functions may include:

- opening the mail each morning
- filing business documents in a filing cabinet.

Although many businesses and organisations will have written records of their procedures, it is always important to check that you understand these policies, procedures, systems and values. Some of this will have been covered during induction and some businesses will also run training programmes to refresh people's knowledge or to inform them of changes. If in doubt, you should always consult your immediate team leader, supervisor or manager.

Give it a go

Write down another five routine activities which would be carried out on a regular basis by employees of an organisation.

Other employees will be required to carry out a series of non-routine activities. They will have to be more adaptable as daily demands will differ greatly. These individuals will not be able to predict the demands upon them with any great accuracy. On a single day they may have a series of meetings or tasks to perform without prior notice or instruction.

Routine functions of an office can be easily organised throughout the organisation if the correct procedures are in place to handle them. An office organised in this way will base its procedures on experience and will know with considerable accuracy the demands that will be placed upon it. In situations when an individual or department must carry out a non-routine function, they must be able to rely upon a separate series of procedures to support them. It may be the case that a support system has to be created for that specific purpose if the non-routine task needs to be carried out so frequently that it becomes routine.

The purpose of procedures

An administrative procedure would need to be in place to track the activities of the business. All organisations will have their own procedures, but generally they will all have a way of keeping track of some of the following aspects of their activities:

- the cost of the purchases that the business has made
- the names of those the business has made purchases from
- sales levels of the business's products or services
- the customers who have bought the business's products or services
- any enquiries made by customers

- payments made by customers

- payments outstanding from customers

- payments the business has made to suppliers

- payments outstanding to suppliers

- information about the employees (human resources) of the business (employee records)

- details of training undertaken or required by employees

- information about the levels of stock (physical resources) held by the business

- records of meetings held within the business.

Give it a go

Think about your job, or the activities you have to carry out while studying this course. Do you have your own procedures in place that help you make sure you work efficiently and effectively? Do your procedures help you work towards meeting your own objectives? Write down at least five procedures that you use routinely in order to complete the different tasks required of you.

Larger organisations tend to have more procedures than smaller ones. Some procedures are very formal because they are dictated by law, such as health and safety procedures, but others are dictated by the business's objectives, or what they have discovered to be the best way to do things. Some procedures are required to ensure the business's confidential information is not leaked out, or because there is a need for security of information or the business's buildings. The following could be examples:

- all visitors to the business have to check into reception on arrival at the business's buildings

- employees wishing to do photocopying have to complete a form in order to obtain their paper

- employees wishing to obtain a file from the filing room (centralised filing) have to complete a form and have it signed by a senior manager

- all mail being delivered to the organisation, or sent out of the organisation, has to be dealt with by a mail room (centralised mailing) and then distributed to each department by the mail room employees.

Give it a go

Why do you think it would be a business's procedure to have all mail handled through a centralised mail room? Write down what you consider to be the advantages and disadvantages of using this type of procedure.

Benefits of procedures

A business would not want procedures just for the sake of having them. They have to be an advantage to the business, particularly if setting up the procedures and then running those procedures costs the business money. There are a number of reasons why a business could benefit from having procedures in place.

Procedures allow a business to carry out all of its activities in an organised way. The decisions about the organisation's objectives will be made and then the procedures will help the business's managers and employees to achieve those objectives.

If a business's employees are organised in the way in which their activities or tasks are carried out, then the impression or image they give their customers and the general public is good. A good image is important for businesses. They will want their procedures to give this image and will try to make sure, for example:

- all paperwork that leaves the business gives a good impression because it is neat, accurate and well presented

- all information requested is sent out quickly to the right person, at the right time

- all messages received are dealt with promptly and efficiently

- all customers, or people likely to become customers, receive the same high level of service from employees

- employees are aware of the need to keep confidential or sensitive information safe

- the business's buildings and employees are kept healthy and safe

- they are following government laws in the way in which they carry out their activities.

Organised businesses will also have the following benefits:

- the business's customers are more likely to return and buy again (repeat business)

- the business's customers are more likely to recommend the business to others, which could bring them new customers.

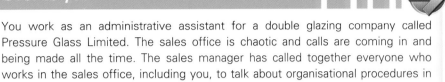

Over to you

You work as an administrative assistant for a double glazing company called Pressure Glass Limited. The sales office is chaotic and calls are coming in and being made all the time. The sales manager has called together everyone who works in the sales office, including you, to talk about organisational procedures in dealing with customers. She wants the business to have a definite way of dealing with customers who ring the business. At the meeting the following ideas were suggested and your sales manager thinks they are all good. She wants you to put them in some kind of sensible order. These will be the new organisational procedures.

We need to say Pressure Glass Limited, how can we help you?

Don't forget we need to tell them about our latest products.

We need to ask them what they want and who they want to speak to.

We really should pick up the phone before six rings.

We should put them straight through to the right person if they are around.

If we promise to send something out, it must go out the same day.

We should tell them we can organise for someone to visit them in 48 hours at the maximum.

We mustn't forget to tell them we're the best in the area.

We have got to make sure all letters are checked before they go out – we don't want them to have any mistakes.

If someone is not available, tell them we'll promise to make sure they call them back.

We should make sure any letters or brochures go out first class.

What is Evidence ?

This can be candidate reports, accounts, professional discussion and questioning.

- deciding what the team's main objectives are
- deciding which of the team's goals need to be achieved to reach the objectives
- deciding on the strategies (how to do it) needed to achieve the objectives
- deciding who will do what in the team to achieve the objectives.

Team planning usually takes place at meetings set aside to decide what the team has to do and how it will achieve these goals. In the meeting the following would be looked at:

- they would evaluate where they are at the moment (look at their progress)
- they would then consider any deadlines which are coming up to achieve particular goals
- they would decide how to prioritise the goals or deadlines
- the team would hope to reach an agreement on all of the above issues so that everyone has had a chance to say what they feel
- the team would then allocate individual responsibilities to team members arising out of the priorities and deadlines
- finally, the team would allocate resources to the team members to help them achieve and deal with the responsibilities that they have been given.

2.4 Describe situations in which team members might support each other
2.5 Describe ways of providing support to other people in a team

When you work as a member of a team there will be times when you need support and there may be situations when others need your support. This can often mean offering to help either to clarify a situation or to assist a colleague to complete work. Talking through situations and offering advice is always a good idea. It may mean reorganising your work, as different parts of the team's work may prove to be more complicated and time consuming than anticipated. Thus team members need to be flexible. They also need to be aware of any problems that other team members are having, which in turn means being open with each other and generally supporting each other for the good of the team.

The exchange, or swapping, of information between team members is vital in order to make sure that any tasks, series of tasks or major objectives are achieved. Continual communication between the team members means that everyone is kept up to date with the progress of the project and that any problems which occur can be dealt with by the team as a whole. It also means that information collected by one of the team is available to all of the others, as they may need these facts and figures to carry out their part of the task.

Exchanging information can happen as a regular process (such as having regular meetings to exchange information) or it can be passed on as and when the information becomes available. Above all, there needs to be a foolproof way of making sure that information collected or received by one of the team does not simply become missed or overlooked and not exchanged with the others. If this happens, the whole idea of working as a team begins to break down.

The process of exchanging information can be either formal or informal, as we can see in the following table.

FORMAL	INFORMAL
Meetings	Conversations
Reports	Email messages
Memoranda	Business notes
Circulated documents (with sign-off sheets to show they have been seen)	
Presentations	
Updates or newsletters to all team members	

Give it a go

Think about the following situations when information would need to be exchanged among team members. Which method of information exchange would be the most effective?

1 The deadline has been brought forward by two days to complete the task.

2 New figures are available in one week's time.

3 A key team member will be off sick for at least a week.

4 A team member has just received a message for another member to make a telephone call.

5 Part of the team have finished their part of the task and want the rest of the team to see what they have done and discuss it.

Team work relies on cooperation, as each of the team relies on the others in order to do their work. Cooperation means being helpful, available and open to suggestions. This means that in order for the team to have cooperative members, the following has to occur:

● the members should be more concerned about the needs of the rest of the team rather than themselves

● the members of the team should try to work in a friendly and sociable atmosphere

members and have worked with them before, this latest task may have shown you different aspects of their personalities. Key things to consider are:

● How did you decide to approach the task in the way you did?

● What could you have done to have made the task easier?

● Did you take account of everyone else's opinion when you planned the task?

● Were you and other members of the team happy with the workload allocated to you?

● Were you and the other team members happy with the outcome of the task?

● How could your team's performance and your own be improved if you were asked to do this task again?

Feedback is a valuable tool. Feedback consists of comments and suggestions received from others in a constructive manner, in order to help improve performance. Feedback is not meant to be critical; it is meant to support individuals and give them insight into their contributions to team work. Simple, positive feedback can include:

● thanking people for doing something well

● thanking them for helping solve a problem for you

● praising their commitment

● celebrating successes and combined effort.

Good feedback is all about trying to assess where a person might need help and then helping them find solutions. You should encourage feedback from others and listen to what people have to say. Even negative feedback can give you something of real value, so ensure that you listen to it. You should always ask questions to clarify what went wrong. Think about how you can use the feedback.

Good feedback can help improve working relationships, as it encourages openness and the sharing of ideas.

What is Evidence ?

This can be candidate reports, accounts, professional discussion and questioning.

■ 7. Be able to work in a way that fits with organisational values and practices

7.1 Follow organisational policies, systems and procedures relevant to your role
7.2 Apply relevant organisational values across all aspects of your work

Refer to 1.7 and 1.8 and then attempt the following activity.

Give it a go

Where did you learn about the organisational policies, systems and procedures relevant to your job role? Can you identify the organisational values that you are expected to apply to your work? You may have encountered these in a number of ways:

- at induction, where you were introduced to the organisation and its way of operating
- through your supervisor or team leader
- as a result of carrying out work and following instructions
- from a staff manual or handbook
- from templates provided or broken-down descriptions of procedures
- from regular training
- from special training.

Identify all of the situations where you have learned about policies, systems, procedures and values. You will need to show evidence that you have followed and applied them.

What is Evidence ?

This can be candidate reports, accounts, professional discussion and questioning. It can also be supplied by observation of workplace activities and witness testimony.

7.3 Work with outside organisations and individuals in a way that protects the image of your organisation, when relevant
7.4 Seek guidance when unsure about organisational policies, systems, procedures and values

Refer to 1.7 and 1.8 and then attempt the following activity.

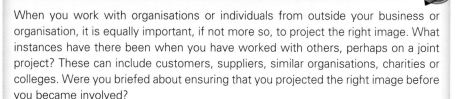

Give it a go

When you work with organisations or individuals from outside your business or organisation, it is equally important, if not more so, to project the right image. What instances have there been when you have worked with others, perhaps on a joint project? These can include customers, suppliers, similar organisations, charities or colleges. Were you briefed about ensuring that you projected the right image before you became involved?

Where would you go to find guidance about policies, systems, procedures and values if you were unsure about them? Are there individuals you can turn to? Or are these all written down and available to be studied if required? Have you had to seek guidance in the past and was the guidance you received clear?

What is Evidence ?

This can be candidate reports, accounts, professional discussion and questioning. It can also be supplied by observation of workplace activities and witness testimony. Good examples of sources include minutes of meetings, memos, letters and emails.

8. Be able to work in a team to achieve goals and objectives

8.1 Communicate effectively with other people in a team

Refer to 3.1 and 3.2 and then attempt the following activity.

Give it a go

You may well be able to provide specific evidence that you communicate effectively with other people when you are working in a team. The following activity is designed to take you through the six requirements for learning outcome 8 of this unit. For each of the six parts you will need to make a comment about your performance. This can be supported by observation and by witness testimony.

The Pharaoh

Your assignment is to submit a bid to the Egyptian Pharaoh, who wants you to build him one or more pyramids. Your bid will take the form of a 5-minute presentation.

Three or four of you will work as the team to produce the bid and another one of the group will act as an observer. That person will note down how you have agreed certain things during the activity and tell you later which roles they think each of the team members have adopted. You will need the following to carry out the activity:

● paper

● card for building your model of the pyramid or pyramids

● scissors, glue, rulers, pens, flip chart and a calculator.

Your team task

Your team is a business which builds pyramids. You have been approached by the Pharaoh. He is likely to live another 10 years. The Pharaoh wants you to build him an impressive monument. He is not sure whether he wants one big pyramid or two smaller ones. It is your decision as to what to build. He is also not sure where he wants the pyramid(s) to be built. Again, he wants you to give him your recommendations.

The Pharaoh has put aside 10.5 million gold pieces. If you spend more than that he will have you executed.

He also wants to see the completed pyramid(s), so you have 10 years to build. If you do not have the pyramid(s) finished within the 10 years, he will die and leave instructions that you are to join him in the pyramid(s) once they are completed.

For the presentation you will need to use a scale model, or models and flip chart paper. On the flip chart paper you will need to show your calculations and other information you feel is important. Your presentation needs to include:

● the proposed site

● the size of the pyramid or pyramids

8.5 Show respect for individuals in a team

Refer to 4.3 and then attempt the following activity.

Give it a go

The observer plays an important role in the activity, as they are the individual who notes down what you have agreed and the roles played by each member. The observer should also comment on the way in which each of the team members behaved towards the others. Did they show respect to each other even if they were under pressure?

8.6 Make sure own work meets agreed quality standards and is on time

Refer to 2.6 and then attempt the following activity.

Give it a go

Comment on your own contribution to the task. Were you happy with the outcome in terms of work product, specifically the model and flip chart? What about the presentation? How did this go? Did you complete the task on time within the 1-hour deadline?

What is Evidence ?

This can be candidate reports, accounts, professional discussion and questioning. It can also be supplied by observation of workplace activities and witness testimony.

■ 9. Be able to deal with or refer problems in a team

9.1 Identify problem(s) or disagreement(s) in a team
9.2 Resolve problem(s) or disagreement(s) within limits of own authority and experience
9.3 Refer problems, as required

Refer to 5.1 and 5.2 and then attempt the following activity.

Give it a go

Working in a busy office environment will always mean there are problems and disagreements. Some of these can be solved relatively easily, but others will be new to you and the problems will have to be referred to others. If you have experience of dealing with problems, you should note down the nature of those problems and how they were resolved. Were you able to resolve them yourself? Or did they need to be referred to someone in a more senior position?

If you do not have any specific experience of dealing with problems, you can refer to the activity that you carried out for learning outcome 8 of this unit. You should:

- identify any problems or disagreements within the team
- explain how these problems or disagreements were resolved
- explain why you may have had to refer the problems to your tutor, observer or assessor.

What is Evidence ?

This can be candidate reports, accounts, professional discussion and questioning. It can also be supplied by observation of workplace activities and witness testimony. Good examples of sources include minutes of meetings, memos, letters and emails.

■ 10. Be able to use feedback on objectives in a team

10.1 Contribute to providing constructive feedback on the achievement of objectives in a team

Refer to 6.1 and 6.2 and then attempt the following activity.

Give it a go

If you have experience of working as a member of a team, this should be a relatively easy criterion to meet. You may already have evidence that you have provided constructive feedback on the achievement of objectives in a team situation. If not, you will need to do this at the next opportunity. Consider the following areas:

- How did the team perform overall?
- Were deadlines met?

- Were there any problems within the team?
- Did all team members contribute?

Remember that you need to provide constructive feedback, so these are suggestions as to how slight changes could be made in the future in order to improve overall performance.

If you do not have experience of providing feedback or the opportunity in a workplace situation, you could use the activity that featured in learning outcome 8 of this unit.

What is Evidence ?

This can be candidate reports, accounts, professional discussion and questioning. It can also be supplied by observation of workplace activities and witness testimony. Good examples of sources include minutes of meetings, memos, letters and emails.

10.2 Receive constructive feedback on own work
10.3 Use feedback on achievement of objectives to identify improvements in own work

Refer to 6.1 and 6.2 and then attempt the following activity.

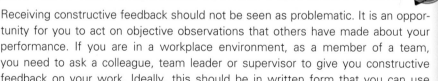

Give it a go

Receiving constructive feedback should not be seen as problematic. It is an opportunity for you to act on objective observations that others have made about your performance. If you are in a workplace environment, as a member of a team, you need to ask a colleague, team leader or supervisor to give you constructive feedback on your work. Ideally, this should be in written form that you can use as direct evidence. Use this feedback and identify areas that are in need of improvement. How will you achieve these improvements? What might be involved? Is it a question of having more experience, freedom or training?

If you are not in a position to receive feedback from a workplace, you should use the observer's remarks from the activity that you carried out in learning outcome 8. What comments did the observer make about your work? How do you respond to them? Has it helped you to identify areas in need of improvement?

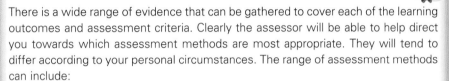

What is Evidence ?

This can be candidate reports, accounts, professional discussion and questioning. It can also be supplied by observation of workplace activities and witness testimony. Good examples of sources include minutes of meetings, memos, letters and emails. Other good evidence are appraisals and performance reviews.

Pull it together

There is a wide range of evidence that can be gathered to cover each of the learning outcomes and assessment criteria. Clearly the assessor will be able to help direct you towards which assessment methods are most appropriate. They will tend to differ according to your personal circumstances. The range of assessment methods can include:

- observation of performance in a working environment
- examination of work products
- questioning
- discussions
- witness testimony
- examining your own statements
- recognising any prior learning.

Specific evidence can include:

- annotated organisational policies and procedures
- appraisal or work reviews
- minutes of team meetings
- feedback from colleagues
- feedback to colleagues from yourself
- internal communication with colleagues
- communication that seeks guidance
- development plans
- information about involvement in team work
- referring problems
- discussing problems
- task or project plans.

Produce Documents in a Business Environment

■ Purpose of the unit

This unit is about preparing high-quality and attractive documents to agreed layouts, formats and styles to meet agreed deadlines.

■ Assessment requirements

This unit requires you to produce documents, use resources and technology and follow procedures when you produce documents. There are five parts to the unit:

1 Understand the purpose of producing high-quality and attractive documents in a business environment – different types of documents and styles, different formats and the purpose of producing high-quality and attractive documents.

2 Know the resources and technology available and how to use them when producing documents in a business environment – types of resources available and ways of using them, different technology available for inputting, formatting and editing text.

3 Understand the purpose of following procedures when producing documents in a business environment – agreeing content, style and deadlines, organising content, integrating and laying out text and non-text, checking finished documents, purpose of storing documents safely and ways to do this, confidentiality and data protection, the purpose and benefits of meeting deadlines.

4 Be able to prepare for tasks – confirming the purpose, content, style and deadlines for documents.

5 Be able to produce documents to agreed specifications – preparing resources, organising content, using technology, formatting and producing documents to agreed styles, integrating non-text objects, checking for accuracy, editing and correcting, clarifying document requirements, safe and secure storage, presenting documents to required format within agreed deadlines.

1. Understand the purpose of producing high-quality and attractive documents in a business environment

1.1 Outline different types of documents that may be produced and the different styles that could be used

Businesses communicate with their customers, with their suppliers and with one another. We will be looking at the following types of written communication in this unit, but you could also refer to *Unit 206: Communicate in a Business Environment*, where there is more information about business communications, formats and styles:

- letters – which tend to be used by businesses to be sent to customers rather than for internal use

- memoranda – these are in effect shortened versions of a letter, which can also be sent as emails and are always internal documents

- reports – these are detailed investigations into a particular subject and are almost exclusively internal documents

- emails – both internal and external, allowing the user to send text and pictures and attach files

- agendas – which are a list of subjects that will be discussed at a meeting. Again these are for internal use and are circulated only to those who will be attending the meeting

- minutes of meeting – these are a summary of a previous meeting and detail what was discussed, decisions made and who is responsible for carrying out further research or tasks. This is an internal document

- completing forms and designing forms – guidelines to complete forms and how to design simple forms

- business notes – usually a handwritten form of business communication

- articles – such as newsletters and press releases where persuasive communication is required

- leaflets and advertisements – for passing on messages and information, as well as trying to generate sales and interest

- summaries – condensing long and complicated documents for ease of understanding.

Business letters

Business letters should follow a specified format as laid down by the business or organisation. They need to use headed paper and should be neat, accurate and well presented. The order of a business letter is standardised and must always include the name and address of the person to whom the letter is being sent. It will need to be dated and at the start the person should be addressed in the correct manner, preceded by 'Dear'. It may be necessary to include a subject heading.

The bulk of the letter is paragraphs of text, which should be logically organised. It is important to match the close with the salutation. At the foot of the letter it should be signed, with the name of the person and their job title beneath. If the letter is to include anything with it, this should be indicated.

Memoranda

Memoranda are internal written communications that are usually shorter than business letters. Many businesses also require people to sign or initial memos. The standard format is to have to, from, date and ref and many businesses will use templates that employees can complete.

Report writing

Report writing is a far more complex procedure. Reports aim to identify problems and find solutions. Some will be progress reports, or they will focus on particular areas of activity. There are plenty of different ways in which reports can be written, but they should always have a title page followed by what is known as terms of reference. This lays out what the report has been asked to achieve. This is followed by a section headed procedure, which explains how the information was gathered. The main body of the report is the findings, which are simply what has been discovered. Most reports will then finish with a conclusion, which is a summary of the findings. In some cases reports will also have recommendations, which are made on the basis of the findings and conclusions.

Reports often have a series of appendices that includes all the charts, diagrams and tables that are relevant to the report.

Emails

Emails are an extremely common form of both internal and external communication. They are very flexible, allowing people to send text and pictures and attach files or images. Multiple emails can be sent out without having to write individual versions of the email, or to print out and post the communication. There are no strict conventions regarding emails, as it will very much depend on the recipient. It is generally accepted that emails should not be typed in capital letters, as this infers shouting and is considered rude. Simple, informal emails can be sent internally, while slightly more formal versions should be used for external recipients. It is important to always ensure that the email address is correct and that something relevant is put into the subject box, as effectively this is the same as the ref in a memorandum.

Agendas and minutes

Agendas and minutes of meetings are closely linked. Assuming that there has been an ongoing series of meetings, the minutes of the prior meeting are always circulated before the next meeting is called, or at the very least they are attached to the agenda of the next meeting. The minutes of the meeting are not a verbatim report of what was said at the meeting, but merely a summary of it. The minutes pay particular attention to points that were raised by individuals and tasks that were subsequently allocated to them. An agenda summarises what will be discussed at the next meeting.

Agendas and minutes have a fairly rigid format, which must always include the date, time and venue of the meeting. There is a strict order in which agenda items are placed. Prior to the agenda being sent out, those attending the meeting will be asked whether they wish to add anything to the list for discussion. Any last-minute items can be brought up in the 'any other business' section of the meeting.

Business forms

Business forms have to be well designed, as the whole purpose of the form is to ensure that the individual completes it as accurately as possible. Confusing forms asking for unnecessary detail in an odd order can prove problematic. Forms need to be as simple as possible, leave sufficient space and, wherever possible, provide multiple options. This makes it easier for the individual completing the form and for processing the information received from them.

One of an administrator's jobs may be to design a form for the business to use in order to record information. There are several key considerations when thinking about designing forms:

- make a rough copy first – you can then check the form for layout and whether or not it appears well presented
- make sure you have included all the necessary headings or questions
- make sure the headings make sense and are clearly understood
- leave space under each heading so that the respondents have sufficient room to complete their responses
- get someone to check the form – sometimes others can see mistakes which you have missed
- make sure the form looks as attractive as possible and that its layout is consistent. This means that the headings should all look the same and the font and font size should be used consistently
- make sure you are happy with the form before you do your final version – it

is better to change something slightly now than have to see it every day containing something you do not feel completely happy about.

A business would want its forms to be under its control. This means that it would want its employees to use the form at the right time, with the right procedures in place to ensure that the form gets completed and ends up in the right place. The business would want to be sure:

- the form is really needed

- the form is simple to understand and complete

- the form is the right size, regarding both the number of questions and in terms of being able to store it for future reference

- the questions are logical and asked in the correct order

- the questions are up to date or whether they need to be amended in some way

- the form is appropriate – in other words, does it serve the purpose for which it was produced in the first place?

Note taking

Note taking is a valuable skill to learn. Notes are taken in a variety of situations and not just at meetings, but also during conversations. This is done to remind you what has been discussed. It is good practice to take notes wherever possible, as you may always be asked to try to recall decisions that may have been made or points that have been put across. Develop your own style of note taking, perhaps using headings or underlining important parts. Try to keep the notes in a book, but leave gaps so you can add information if necessary. Try to concentrate on the main points, always read what you have written, use abbreviations or initials for people. You may also wish to type up the notes regularly, particularly if you are required to recall a conversation or a meeting for an absent employee.

Company newsletters

Many businesses have their own company newsletters. These are used as a way of passing on information to employees, so they are designed to be read only by people who work for the business. You may become involved in having to prepare, write, print and distribute a company newsletter. This will contain a number of short articles, with perhaps photographs or illustrations, in order to tell employees various bits and pieces of news, updates, changes in policies and procedures or simply news about other employees.

One of the most useful tools in preparing articles for company newsletters is a desktop publishing program, such as Microsoft Publisher. This type of software has the advantage of offering you a number of formats, or templates, to choose from. You can replace the text, pictures, logos and headings on the templates with your business's own images and text.

Preparing an article for a publication such as a company newsletter obviously involves some research and, of course, note taking. Articles can be of various lengths, but usually they are kept fairly short and to the point. Any article is always improved by a picture or a diagram or illustration. These help draw the reader's attention to the article and give them something to remember the article by, rather than having to remember everything that has been written.

Here is an example of a short article and the notes which were taken to prepare that article.

Frederick (Fred) Keeble is 66 next month.

He is retiring at the end of this month from the marketing department.

He has worked for the company for 23 years.

He is going to live in Spain with his wife, Glynis.

His son, Brian, and his two children and wife will visit frequently.

Fred started out in the warehouse and has worked in virtually every department.

Fred's current job is head of the marketing department.

Next Tuesday Fred will be presented with an engraved watch and some new luggage from a collection among other employees.

GOODBYE FRED

Fred Keeble, our Head of Marketing, will be retiring after over 20 years of service. Fred has worked for us in virtually every area of the business and at 66 has finally decided to retire to a home in the sun. As grandparents, Fred and Glynis are looking forward to a peaceful retirement and frequent visits from their grandchildren to their new home in Spain.

Although Fred will be leaving us this coming Friday, a special presentation will take place at 1700 on Tuesday to present him with an engraved gold watch and gifts purchased from the collection made by his friends and colleagues.

Give it a go

Read the following passage. Your manager wants this text summarised. Try to reduce the length of the text but ensure that you include the facts. Highlight the key points as bold italic.

Recruitment procedures

From next month we will use our own human resources department for all recruitment. In the past we have used external employment agencies, but we have now realised that the calibre of candidates is relatively low and that we are required to pay them, as a finding fee, 50 per cent of their first year's salary. The new arrangements will require each department to initiate recruitment by filling in an employee request form, which will then be passed to the HRM recruitment committee. The committee will then approve or disapprove of the suggestion. The department will then provide a job description and person specification, liaising with HRM. HRM will then circulate the job description and person specification to internal candidates first. If there are no suitable candidates then advertisements will be placed in the local or regional press. If no suitable candidates are found then national advertising will be considered. Short-listing of candidates following their completion of application forms and covering letters will be carried out by the department and HRM. The two areas will then invite no more than ten shortlisted candidates for each job post to interview. The organisation will reimburse reasonable travel and subsistence costs for candidates. Appointment is to be made on the day, with the successful candidate being contacted first. In the event that they decline the second ranked candidate will be offered the post and so on. If no suitable candidates are found then the post will be reviewed and re-advertised after a month.

Tables

Converting a mass of facts and figures into table format makes it far easier to understand and appreciate the importance of some of that information. It is not always possible to obtain information in an easy-to-read and understandable format. In many cases you will be asked to extract and adapt information which may appear to be hidden among lots of other information which is not necessarily relevant.

Designing a table requires you to think carefully about how you will present the information and whether the information you have is suitable for conversion into a table. Provided you have the same type of information, converting it into a table should not prove too difficult.

Give it a go

Prepare a table for the six months' sales figures using the information in the paragraph below:

> Last month's sales figures proved to be better than expected. Overall our sales figures for last month were 25% up on the previous month. The £40,000 for last month was twice that of 3 months ago. Four months ago the sales figures were just £10,000, but that was twice the month before. Our first month, the month before, saw just £2,000 in sales so this last month's £40,000 total is a great result.

Create your table with the following headings:

MONTH   SALES FIGURES

The column headings should be in capitals and emboldened and you should also highlight the £40,000 total so that it is the first thing that someone will look at when reading the communication.

Messages

When other people in the business or outside callers wish to talk to someone, it is not always the case that they are available. One of the many tasks in administration is to accurately note down messages from other people which you can leave on the relevant person's desk for them to look at when they return. In many cases you will need to summarise in the message the important information that needs to be passed on, which may include telephone numbers, names, dates or details about orders. Unlike a summary of written material, you do not have the benefit of being able to look back at the information and

Figure 212.3

make a judgement about what is important and what is not – you will have to summarise as you listen to the message. You can always ask the person to repeat certain things, such as telephone numbers.

Give it a go

Imagine you have just picked up the telephone and the caller wants to speak to Katie Walsh, but she is at lunch. Note down, as a message, the most important parts of the following conversation:

'Hello, my name is Suzannah Burman. I'd like to leave a message for Katie Walsh please. I should have phoned earlier, but I've been a bit busy doing my shopping and when I got to the car to drive home I found I had a flat tyre, so it took me longer than expected. Would you tell Katie that Alex has called me and his cold is a lot better now? He phoned to say that he will be back in work tomorrow. He can't remember what shift he is on tomorrow, perhaps she would be good enough to find that out for me. He tells me that he must visit the doctor tomorrow at 9.15 so in any case he won't be able to get into work until at least 10.30 and he hopes that is alright. Thanks very much and will you tell Katie that Alex would like to thank her for sending the get well card, bye for now.'

It is important to pass on messages quickly and accurately. It would be frustrating to try to pass on a word-for-word message, so when taking a message for another individual you should remember the following points:

● listen very carefully to the message

● make notes as you listen

● your notes should contain key words and important information, including the date and time of the call and the name and details of the caller

● once you have taken the message, before you pass it on write it out in a form that can be easily understood

● do not include any unnecessary information

● make sure you mention names, addresses, telephone and fax numbers, order numbers and any deadlines which need to be met

● you can then pass on the message by telephone, or write it on paper or a form, or pass the message on face to face

● you should ensure that your tone and style are correct both when receiving and passing on the message.

Give it a go

Before you try the next two messages, design a simple telephone message form. It should include the following:

- who the message is for
- who the message is from
- who they represent or what business or department they belong to
- their telephone number, fax number or email address
- the message itself
- any action needed
- who the message was taken by
- the date and time of the message.

Telephone message pads are often printed on brightly coloured paper and vary in the way in which they are formatted. But they have spaces to note down the most important details of the messages. Remember that accuracy and efficiency are essential. Make sure you produce the form so that it looks attractive, is easy to read and that you have left sufficient space for it to be used for a variety of messages.

Give it a go

Using your own telephone message form, now accurately and efficiently note down the most important information from the following two messages:

'I'd like to speak to Miss Doyle please. Oh, she isn't there, well, can I leave a message then? Can you tell her I was supposed to be coming in to see her next Friday? I think that's the 12th, no it's the 13th. Well, I can't come, I'm afraid, because I've got a dental appointment at 11 and then I have to go down to London. Could you tell her I can put it back a week and make it 11 o'clock if that's OK with her? Perhaps she could ring me to confirm? My name's Sally Scadding and I'm with Associated Electronics on 01244 505050. Oh and my extension is 279. Thanks very much.'

'Hello, can you put me through to Miss Smith please? Oh, she's not there. Is she likely to be back later on? It doesn't matter. My name is Ken Smith, no relation. I'd better leave a message, hadn't I? I need to speak to her urgently. We received your delivery this morning and I'm afraid I am very unhappy. One of the boxes has burst in transit and they are quite unusable. I ordered the three boxes two weeks ago. The order number is 12479 and they cost £555.39. I need you to send me out a replacement batch immediately. I've got customers waiting for these. I'm also very cross and I want to make a complaint as this is the second time this has happened. She really must ring me as soon as she gets back. If she's not at her desk by three then she will have missed me so she had better speak to Brian. His extension is 271 and mine is 248. I should have said we're Smith Communications and our number's 01256 0000.'

Leaflets and advertisements

Leaflets and advertisements should be simple and draw the reader's eye to the most important information. While leaflets can have more information, you should not be tempted to overload the reader with unnecessary detail. Leaflets need to look eye-catching and simply be a summary of what you want to put across.

Advertisements work best with the minimum number of words, so you need to think carefully about what you say and how you say it. Advertisements also benefit from the use of illustrations and different fonts in different sizes.

Give it a go

Following a meeting with other shop managers, Katie Walsh has just announced to all of the employees that the shop will now be open Monday to Saturday between 10 in the morning and 10 at night. One of the other shops will also be opening between 11 and 4 on a Sunday. In the past the other shop used to close at lunchtime on a Thursday and was open late only on a Wednesday and Friday night. It was closed on a Sunday. Some of the staff are unhappy but others are pleased that there will be more overtime.

Katie has asked you to design a leaflet which can be handed out to customers who come into the shop and she also wants the leaflet to be given out to people passing the shop. She also wants you to design an advertisement for the local newspaper to tell everyone about the new opening hours.

You may use a maximum of four different font styles. You can use whatever font size you wish and you should make use of bold, italic, underline and capitals.

Agendas

An agenda is used to inform people who are to attend a meeting about the nature of that meeting. The agenda will give the date, time and venue of the meeting and it also sets out the programme of business. Remember that all agendas will have the same first three items, namely Apologies for Absence, Minutes of the Last Meeting and Matters Arising from the minutes of the last meeting. The last two items on the agenda are also common, as they are Any Other Business and the Date of the Next Meeting.

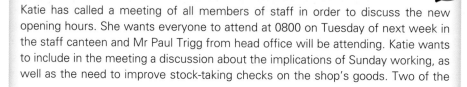

Give it a go

Katie has called a meeting of all members of staff in order to discuss the new opening hours. She wants everyone to attend at 0800 on Tuesday of next week in the staff canteen and Mr Paul Trigg from head office will be attending. Katie wants to include in the meeting a discussion about the implications of Sunday working, as well as the need to improve stock-taking checks on the shop's goods. Two of the other members of staff have asked you to add an item to the agenda you have been asked to draw up – Alex wants to discuss the increasing problem of shoplifting and Clare would like to have a discussion about staff uniforms.

Create your agenda and identify how many copies will have to be produced. Highlight what you consider to be the important parts of the agenda by using bold, italic, underscore or capitals.

Reports

Remember that reports can be short and informal, such as the memo-style report, or they can take a more formal form as in a business report format. Reports are usually written after some kind of research has taken place and are presented using a word processor. Reports can incorporate headings, sub-headings, numbered points and decimal-pointed headings or items.

Articles

Articles can be included in company newsletters or they can be sent as press releases to the media. Articles need to be informative and certainly in the case of press releases be interesting and eye-catching enough to grab the attention of the newspaper's editor.

Give it a go

Paul Trigg is very happy about the increased sales as a result of the new opening times. Katie is pleased too. She has asked you to encourage people to continue to visit the shop by placing an article in the local newspaper. In order to encourage people to visit the shop you have to think of something interesting and tempting. Base your article on what you think is important from the following information. This needs to be easy to read and must look professional and clear. You can use a maximum of two different fonts for this activity:

- sales figures are up 30 per cent
- more than 1,000 customers visit the store on an average Sunday
- evening sales now account for 20 per cent of the total sales
- Sunday sales account for 20 per cent of the total weekly sales
- staff are very happy; some take overtime or days off
- the shop will be offering a special 10 per cent discount to customers who visit the store after 7pm and the same discount on a Sunday
- customers spending more than £100 will be entered into a special raffle to win a meal for two at one of the leading restaurants in the city.

1.3 Explain the purpose and benefits of producing high quality and attractive documents

The appearance of a business's or organisation's documents has a direct impact on how people view the organisation. This means that the documents need to be easy to understand and well presented in order to help project a positive image of the organisation.

Now we have investigated the different types of business documents and formats and considered the different uses to which they will be put, it is important to remember that the way in which they are presented and laid out makes a big difference to the impression they give to the reader. All of the business documents and different formats need to be simple to use, which means they have to be easy to read and extract information from. Wherever possible you should try to use headings or sub-headings. These help break up long lengths of text and draw the reader's eye to the fact that you are making a new point.

Also, do not be tempted to try to say everything you need to say about a particular point in a single paragraph. Break up large chunks of text into convenient-to-read and logical paragraphs.

Above all, whatever business document or format you are using, the ideas need to be presented in a logical sequence. Pretend you are telling a story which has a beginning, a middle and an end:

● the beginning can be an introduction, because it tells the reader what you are about to say and why you are saying it

● the middle is often the largest part of any of these business documents or formats, because here you will put all the necessary information which supports what you have mentioned in the introduction

● the end may be a conclusion or conclusions, a series of recommendations, or simply ask the reader to now do something, having read what you have presented to them.

Providing you ensure that whatever document you are producing is easy to use and actually fits the purpose for which you are writing it, you are half-way there in producing a document which is useful. By adding in simple things, such as headings and sub-headings, breaking up the paragraphs and making sure that there is a logical sequence to your thoughts, you have transformed the document into something useful.

Give it a go

Go back to the article you wrote for the local newspaper. Evaluate the work you have done by asking yourself whether you could have made the presentation more effective, perhaps by using bulleted points, headings or sub-headings. If you think you could improve the presentation, go back to your computer-saved file and amend the layout of the document.

Think about all the different ways in which you talk or write to various people in your life. Do you speak the same way to your friends as you do to your parents, elders or teachers? Would you use the same language to your employer as you would to your closest friend? Probably not, and there are ways in which you are expected to use your tone and style of speaking and writing in different situations at work. The ways in which you could talk to someone you work with will differ enormously from the way you might be expected to talk to customers. This is what is meant by using the appropriate tone and style for different purposes.

The final thing to consider in terms of tone and style is how what is said, or written, is viewed by those outside the business. Clearly, rudeness or poorly chosen words can mean that the person gets a bad impression of both the writer and the business itself. All written material which will be seen by other people needs to be:

● tactful

● polite

● clear

● helpful

● informative

● offering a solution to a problem.

Here are various different approaches to dealing with people and the impressions they receive about the writer and the business:

Discourteous	Indifferent	Courteous	Special
Confrontational	Doesn't care	Polite	Very courteous
Rude	Bored	Friendly	Problem solver
Impolite	Uncaring	Positive	Adaptable
Aggressive	Avoiding	Good contact	Shows care

Think about the different impressions given and how they reflect on you as an employee and on the business as a whole. If people are handled correctly it can lead to:

● fewer customer complaints

● more time to spend on other things rather than dealing with problems

● a more positive working environment

● greater job satisfaction

● more business for the employer.

Give it a go

Which of the following sentences would not give the correct impression of yourself or the business if they were part of a letter to a customer? Why are they not appropriate? When you have identified the inappropriate sentences, reword them to make them acceptable.

1 We have considered your request for a refund and will not be giving you one.

2 We have decided to withdraw this product as we have designed a better one and therefore cannot repair your old one.

3 We have taken legal advice on this issue and will therefore not compensate you for your losses.

4 We have despatched the goods you have ordered, our apologies for the delay.

5 Rest assured we will not be supplying such poor quality goods on subsequent occasions; the replacement of them is a big hassle.

What is Evidence ?

Evidence can be reports, accounts, discussions and questioning.

■ 2. Know the resources and technology available and how to use them when producing documents in a business environment

2.1 Describe the types of resources available for producing high-quality and attractive documents
2.2 Outline ways of using different resources to produce documents

Businesses will use a wide variety of resources to produce high-quality and attractive documents. As we will see, the use of software packages can go a long way to ensuring this. However, photocopiers can be used to produce enlarged documents or very good copies of documents. Increasingly, businesses tend to use laser printers, not only because they are more economic than other forms of printers but also because their output is a better quality. Businesses will also use laminators to protect key documents that will be referred to on a regular basis and they will bind documents together to produce booklets. It is important that good quality paper is used. This can be achieved by using high-quality recycled paper.

The vast majority of businesses and organisations use the Microsoft Office suite of programs to produce a range of documents. The basic functions of Word, which is the word-processing package, provide a good start to ensuring that high-quality documents are produced, as the package allows you to:

- edit the text
- use the help screens
- use the spellchecker and thesaurus
- use a print preview to see what the document looks like before printing
- import text, images and tables from other applications
- use the mail-merge facility, to bring in addresses from a database.

This means that the Microsoft Office suite is a multi-purpose package, incorporating word processing, spreadsheets, databases and graphics. Effectively it allows you to do whatever you wish with a document. You can transfer information from one application to another.

The key advantages of using a software package such as Word are:

- text can be stored and edited later
- documents can be stored and printed

- mistakes can be edited

- documents are automatically laid out and professional-looking through the use of templates

- mistakes can be picked up before printing

- you can attach documents to emails.

Microsoft Excel is a spreadsheet package that allows number processing. It is also extremely valuable as you can present data in the form of tables, graphs, charts and other complicated forms of graphics.

Databases are also invaluable. Effectively they are like an electronic filing system. You are able to collect and store information in a series of records, structured into fields. The fields and the records can be searched and sorted. Reports can then be generated. The records are also valuable sources of contact details, such as addresses, which can be used for mail merging.

Over to you

What do you routinely use to generate documents either at work or in your centre? Are you aware that you can import material from one application to another? Can you merge documents? Do you regularly use images? How do you handle these?

2.3 Describe the different types of technology available for inputting, formatting and editing text, and their main features

We have already seen that the Microsoft Office suite provides many of the basic functions that are routinely needed for producing documents. It is important to note that businesses and organisations do not just use keyboards to input data. In fact, there is a wide variety of methods and collectively they are known as data input devices:

- keyboards and mice – standard input devices. The mouse uses a cursor and you can use one-click movements to highlight text for deletion or movement

- stylus – this works like a pen or a pencil. The movements appear on the screen

- touch pads – these are like a simple keyboard and are used for graphics and design

- scanner – this can read text and images, which you can then put into a Word document

- voice recognition – this can recognise speech and the words appear on the screen. It can then be edited

- bar code readers – these are found on almost every product. The bar code identifies the product and any associated information

- optical mark reader – this picks up pencil marks on documents and is ideal for multiple choice questionnaires

- optical character recognition – this is a feature of scanners. It reads the text characters and allows you to edit them on screen.

Businesses will use a variety of input devices. Credit cards and loyalty cards use magnetic strips; electronic point of sale used in shops reads bar codes.

In most normal situations you will find you will be using the keyboard and mouse as your primary means of inputting, formatting and editing text. In this way you can change font style and type, move around text, change the line spacing or alter the alignment of the text. You can also introduce headers and footers, text boxes or borders.

Give it a go

Imagine you work as an administrative assistant at a college. Part of your responsibility is organising travel arrangements for students, as some are bussed in from remote areas. In the past the service was paid for and provided by the local council. Due to cost cuts next year the council will only cover 75 per cent of the costs. They have warned you that in the following year this will drop to 50 per cent. The college has promised to cover any shortfall. One of the other major problems is that the county council has closed its college transport section and you will now have to carry out all the administrative functions.

Write a letter suitable for all students, telling them about the switchover. You should include a pledge from the college to cover the costs. You also need to include a tear-off slip, as you intend to take this opportunity for parents or guardians to inform you of the pickup point for their sons or daughters. They should be required to sign the tear-off slip.

Another major advantage of using application software such as Word is the ability to create templates. These can be standard versions of how particular documents should look. They will already incorporate addresses and other contact details. Some of them may be forms or specialised documents. Others are simple templates that can be used for memos or agendas. These templates will usually be blank for you to input information. The template will format that information into the correct style and layout.

One thing you will notice with most documents is the orientation and paper size. In Britain it is standard practice to use an A4 size page, although in other countries this can be different. The size of the page determines what you can fit onto it; you can see where text appears in the document by looking at the print preview. You can amend the way that the text or graphics fall if you feel the layout looks messy or cramped. In most cases you will be using portrait as your orientation. This will be standard for letters and agendas, for example. Some forms or complicated tables may need landscape orientation.

Other key issues to take into consideration include:

- column layout – you can determine how many columns will appear on each page, from one to several

- font – there are various designs and a variety of sizes. These can be used in combination with bold, italic or underlined

- headers and footers – some of these may appear in templates, but you can amend them or delete them. They will usually have a page number, date and perhaps the title of the document

- indent – this controls the space between the page margins and the paragraphs. You can set large left indents, which make it easier to pick out bulleted or numbered points, quotations, important points or even separate paragraphs

- justification – businesses have their own particular views about the right-hand margin of a document. Some like to see a justified right margin, which means each line of text finishes at the same point, giving you a straight right margin. This gives slightly irregular spacing. An unjustified right margin gives a more ragged look because each of the lines will end at a different place

- line spacing – template documents may already be set up for single or double line spacing, which are the two most common. This can easily be changed if required. Double line spacing makes it easier for people to read the text.

Give it a go

Following on from the previous activity, you have now been asked to create a timetable for the pickups and drop-offs of the buses for the college. You will have to work out the exact pickup times based on the assumption that the bus has to arrive at the college no later than 0840. The bus will leave the college at 1640. Use the following data:

Start point	Yardley Lane
5 minutes later	Neath Street
10 minutes later	Heath Road
10 minutes later	Getsford
5 minutes later	Trimfleet
5 minutes later	Offland
10 minutes later	Ugsford
5 minutes later	Swanhead
5 minutes later	Ilkeshall
5 minutes later	Spexham
Finish point	College

Remember to design the timetable so that it is easy to read. Make sure you work through the pickups and drop-offs, taking into account the time it takes to get from one place to the next.

What is Evidence ?

Evidence can be reports, accounts, discussions and questioning.

■ 3. Understand the purpose of following procedures when producing documents in a business environment

3.1 Explain the benefits of agreeing the purpose, content, style, and deadlines for producing documents

In agreeing the purpose, content, style and deadline for a document the individual creating that document is fully aware of the requirements of the user. This will help ensure that the document meets with the approval of the user. It is very important that finished documents meet those needs, so agreement before the document is produced is essential.

In many cases you will be given clear instructions as to the purpose of particular business documents. You will also be following the business's or organisation's style, or formats. What may be more difficult is that in many cases you will have a limited amount of time to produce the document. This may mean making sure that you get the document as close to perfection the first time as possible.

As we have seen, many businesses and organisations use templates. These ensure that the house style, or preferred appearance of documents, is followed. The house styles ensure that each document is presented and formatted in a specified way. This can include:

- paper size and orientation
- margins and spacing
- font type, style and size
- alignment of text
- use of headers, footers and page numbers
- preferred ways of formatting tables.

If templates are not provided by your organisation you will be required to follow a set of house style guidelines. This may mean:

- amending the page setup – this could involve changing the margins, page orientation and page size and whether you are applying the changes to one or all of the pages in the document
- modifying the text – you may have to change the formatting of the text by amending the font and its size
- modifying or creating headings – some businesses will prefer them to be bold, while others require them to be underlined. You can again change the styles and formatting of these and set them to be implemented whenever you start a new paragraph, or for every heading

- adding headers or footers – different organisations prefer page numbers, dates, company names or logos or other information to appear at the top or bottom of each page. They will also state what font to use

- using lists – there is a wide range of lists you could use. Broadly, they are bulleted or numbered, but each has a different style. There may well be a preferred standard

- using the spellchecker – your organisation may prefer to use English (UK) or English (US). This will determine whether the spellchecker picks up on the incorrect spelling of particular words. There are of course hundreds of other languages that can be set as the default language for the document

- using special symbols and characters – you can access different symbols and characters that can then be inserted into the document. You can in fact use some of these special symbols to customise bulleted lists

- creating tables – this can be done in a number of ways, such as using the toolbar, or you can insert a table and then choose from a range of styles. The organisation may have specified styles, including table column widths and the way the table headers are displayed

- using borders and gridlines – these are particularly relevant if you are designing forms, where different types of lines can be used to break up the page, either as a series of boxes or perhaps as a tear-off slip

- shading – whole documents and tables can be shaded with different colours. Again the organisation may have preferred colours and styles.

It is important to keep a list of tasks and their deadlines. You should always ask when a particular document needs to be presented and give yourself some additional time. You need to focus on the document and give it adequate time. Try to start and complete it in a series of easy steps. If it is looking as if the document will not be ready, you need to negotiate a new deadline at the earliest possible point. One way of avoiding missing deadlines is to listen carefully to what is being asked of you and then to produce your best attempt at the ideal document the first time. Make sure you clarify what is needed by asking relevant questions at the start of the task.

Give it a go

Do you routinely keep your own to-do list? What do you include on this to-do list? Do you regularly reorganise it?

3.2 Outline different ways of organising content needed for documents
3.3 Outline ways of integrating and layout text and non-text

We have already looked at many of the ways in which different documents are routinely formatted. For many documents there is not an internationally accepted style, but there are some common ways to organise the content for particular types of documents. We have looked at these in some detail in *Unit 206: Communicate in a Business Environment* and the first learning outcome of this unit.

In order to give a document a professional appearance you can combine text and graphics. These can highlight key points, such as figures or facts. You do not have to restrict your use of graphics to Clipart, shapes or charts; you can combine tables and diagrams into a text-based document.

Word can help you to combine these so that the page does not look too cluttered, while at the same time valuable space is not wasted. Document templates use this approach, as they will already have symbols, logos or names. Some will even have a lightly shaded watermark, which will appear under the text of the letter.

It is worth bearing in mind that the majority of documents are actually printed in simple black and white, rather than colour. So it is a good idea to get into the habit of using shades of grey rather than bright colours.

Other application software, such as Microsoft Publisher, presents you with a number of readymade templates. In these templates you can replace whole sections of text, pictures, diagrams or graphics with your own material. Publisher is ideal for creating fliers, leaflets, newsletters and brochures.

It is important to learn how to position graphics, as you can place them behind or in front of the text, in line with the text, square to the text or tight to the text. You can also text wrap, which means you can put text around the whole of the graphic or diagram in whatever manner you think looks the most effective.

Typical non-text items include:

- callouts
- WordArt
- pictures
- drawings
- diagrams
- charts, graphs and tables imported from either Excel or Access.

Give it a go

Go back to the activity where you created the letter with the tear-off slip for the college bus service. Using either Clipart or the internet, find a picture of a college bus or coach and insert it into the document. Rework the layout of your text to accommodate the picture.

3.4 Describe ways of checking finished documents for accuracy – including spelling, grammar and punctuation – and correctness, and the purpose of doing so

Microsoft Word automatically highlights spelling mistakes and grammatical errors. Be aware, however, that it is not foolproof. It will not pick up the fact that you have typed 'their' instead of 'there'. Word will underline incorrectly spelled words in red. It will underline sentences that do not make grammatical sense in green. Punctuation errors or additional spaces between words are also underlined in green.

It is important that you set the spelling and grammar checker for the right language, which in the majority of cases will be English (UK). Word will automatically highlight any spelling or grammatical mistakes as you type and usually offer you a series of suggestions. All you need to do is to choose the one you want from a list and click 'change'. Even if it does not pick up on any mistakes, make sure that you spellcheck when you have finished documents as something may have been missed.

It is important to remember that if you have typed in the wrong word, but it is still a proper word and the sentence makes grammatical sense, Word will not pick it up.

Word's spellchecker has thousands of words, but it will not have many proper names or abbreviations, for example. You can always add these to the Word dictionary, which means that the next time you type that word or abbreviation it will not be highlighted.

Always make sure that you proofread your document before you print it. Carefully check each sentence to make sure it makes sense. If it is a long and complicated document, get someone else to check if for you too. The purpose of making sure that your spelling, grammar and punctuation are correct is to ensure that every document you create is professional looking and reflects well on the business or the organisation.

Give it a go

Type up the following section of text, exactly as it appears below, and using the spellchecker correct all the mistakes.

Once upon a time chopping was a labor. Sleeves were rolled up, ther was huffing and puffing, as the cook set to wielding a cleaver to reduce the size of a large joint of meet. She would pound sugar or spices to a powder with a pestle and morter and rub fruits through a clothe to make a puree.

It is little wonder that labour-saving devises were greeted so enthusisticly. Some were weird, some were particle, but they mostly helped lightan the load of the cooks what used them.

Now we have electric servents, with blades to chop, grind and great, and I, for one, appreciate them, but we must be careful that this does not make for boreing meels.

3.5 Explain the purpose of storing documents safely and securely, and ways of doing so

In *Unit 219: Store and Retrieve Information* there is considerable information on the storage and retrieval of information and why this is important. However, documents are not stored just in a paper format but also electronically. This brings with it its own problems as the documents are extremely portable and original versions can easily be lost.

Documents are stored for a variety of reasons. Certain documents, such as contracts of employment or agreements with suppliers and customers, will have to be stored for legal purposes. Other documents will be stored as a result of the need to refer to them from time to time. It is usual for businesses and organisations to store documents for at least five years. In some cases documents are stored for longer, but the older documents are often removed and archived but not destroyed.

The vast majority of businesses will make sure that documents are stored on hard drives in different locations. This is known as backing up and it is done to protect the documents should there be a major problem at the main site, which means that the documents could become either lost or corrupted. Copies of documents can be put onto flash drives, memory sticks, zip disks, CDs or CD-ROMs. Some businesses use these to store archived copies of documents rather than allowing them to clutter their hard drives and electronic filing systems.

Businesses will store documents for a considerable period of time in case they need to be referred to at a later date. In order to protect the documents, archived material may be write protected (read only). This means that nobody can edit the original documents.

The access to the documents will be limited to only those who have authorisation to view them. A series of passwords, allowing access to different levels of document storage, is often used by businesses. This restricts the number of people who can look at specific types of documents and helps ensure that the documents remain safe and secure.

Give it a go

What kind of access restrictions are there on documents either at your place of work or at your centre? How do you organise your documents? Do you use folder systems? Are there common folder names? Who else has access to documents stored in your folders? Are the documents backed up and who is responsible for this process?

3.6 Explain the purpose of confidentiality and data protection when preparing documents

On some occasions you may be required to prepare documents that may contain confidential or sensitive data. Particular care needs to be exercised and any confidential or sensitive information needs to be secured while it is being used to prepare the documents.

Personal information in particular needs to be kept confidential. A duty of confidentiality falls on all businesses and organisations. Under the terms of the Data Protection Act the processing and disclosure of information is important, as are the rights of access to that information. It is important to remember that data refers to anything that is either processed by a computer or recorded as part of a filing system, so this includes hard copies.

All businesses and organisations process data; they organise it, alter it, retrieve it, use it and may eventually destroy it. Each major business or organisation will have a data controller who determines the way in which information is processed.

All information held by a business or organisation should be considered to be confidential, unless you are told otherwise. A business or organisation should not pass on information about an individual or another business without permission. There are exceptions, however, when there are legal requirements to do so, such as under the Social Security Fraud Act.

For more information about confidentiality and security of data you could refer to *Unit 219: Store and Retrieve Information* and *Unit 256: Meet and Welcome Visitors*.

Give it a go

What information do you think your employer or centre holds about you? Why do you think they need this information? Who would you approach to see this data? What could you do if the data was incorrect?

3.7 Explain the purpose and benefits of meeting deadlines

All businesses and organisations will set deadlines for tasks, activities or documents to be completed. For businesses, a failure to meet a deadline could mean that valuable business is lost. For the individual, meeting deadlines can mean a less stressful working environment. It can also improve self-confidence, and meeting deadlines rather than rushing to meet them will mean that the work produced will be of a higher quality.

Businesses and organisations rely on a number of people all being able to complete specific tasks on time. It is rare that a particular task that you will be asked to complete is an isolated task. It may be part of a far bigger task and you have been allocated part of it. It is very easy to underestimate how long a task will take. You only really know how long it will take when you start to work on it. It is always a good idea to take a close look at the task as a whole and see what is involved before you agree a deadline.

Often you will be relying on other people to complete part of the task, or provide you with information beforehand. If they have not done this then it may be impossible for you to complete the task. It is not always possible for others to be able to respond to your needs. Your task may not be their ultimate responsibility and they may have other calls on their time. Always try to tell them when you will need the necessary information and let them know when your deadline has been set.

You need to build in time to make revisions and corrections. It is rare for a task to be completed correctly at the first attempt. You may need to make changes or updates. This may not help a great deal, because whoever has allocated you the task will only be interested in when you have completed the task and not just when you have provided a draft version of it.

Give it a go

Whether you are in work or studying this course at a centre, you will have been given a series of deadlines to complete specific tasks. How often are you reliant on others before you can complete the task yourself? Has this caused you any problems? How have you dealt with situations when you have a clear deadline but someone you are relying on does not?

What is Evidence ?

Evidence can be reports, accounts, discussions and questioning.

■ 4. Be able to prepare for tasks

4.1 Confirm the purpose, content, style and deadlines for documents

Refer to 1.1–1.3 and then attempt the following activity.

Give it a go

You work for Universal Paints and Solvents Ltd as an administrative assistant. You have a variety of jobs to carry out over the course of any given day. The first job is to write a covering letter for customers who are going to be invited to a launch event, as your business has just signed a deal to distribute new American paints. Your company has agreed the details that are included in a letter from the hotel, regarding the catering and function room. You will need to draft a letter to customers that can later be mail merged. You also will need to attach a return form, so that customers can confirm their attendance and any specific catering needs. Use the following letter for information:

STAMFORD BRIDGE HOTEL

Harrison Lane, Aybridge, Essex, AB1 4AN

Miss S Bryant
Universal Paints and Solvents Ltd
Marchmont Industrial Estate
Aybridge
Essex

24 April 201-

Dear Miss Bryant

Further to your enquiry of 19 April I can confirm the following arrangements for your event to be held on 1 May at this hotel.

I can confirm that both the Buckingham Suite and the Cheshire Suite have been reserved for your exclusive use, and that we have set aside twenty rooms for your guests. The two suites offer you ample space for both the presentation and the static displays you described.

Our head chef, Mr Favier, has confirmed that we are able to cater for the provisional figure of fifty guests plus your own staff of twelve. We can, of course, cater for vegetarians or those with special dietary needs. Welcome drinks and appetisers will be available from 1.30pm as requested, with the buffet at 2.45pm, directly after your presentations. Our staff will be on hand for your guests and your own needs until 6pm. I would be grateful for confirmation of the number of guests, particularly those who wish to stay overnight at the hotel.

I look forward to hearing from you.

Yours sincerely

Paul Evans
General Manager

You need to confirm the purpose, content, style and suggest a deadline to complete the documents you have been asked to prepare. You have been given two hours to complete the tasks.

What is Evidence ?

Evidence can be reports, accounts, discussions and questioning. Evidence can also be witness testimony, observation and work products, including letters, emails and memos.

5. Be able to produce documents to agreed specifications

5.1 Prepare resources needed to produce documents
5.2 Organise the content required to produce documents

Refer to 2.1–2.3 and 3.1–3.7 and then attempt the following activity.

Give it a go

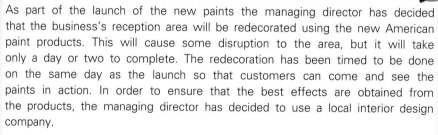

As part of the launch of the new paints the managing director has decided that the business's reception area will be redecorated using the new American paint products. This will cause some disruption to the area, but it will take only a day or two to complete. The redecoration has been timed to be done on the same day as the launch so that customers can come and see the paints in action. In order to ensure that the best effects are obtained from the products, the managing director has decided to use a local interior design company.

You will need to write a confirmation letter to the company and produce a memorandum for circulation to all employees. The memo should inform employees about the redecoration. The interior design company is called Graham Hobb Interiors and the address is 47 High Street, Aybridge, Essex, AB19 7AG. Your contact name for the company is Laurence Hobb.

The product development manager has also left you with a draft of a press release that he wants to send out to the local press to coincide with the launch of the new paint products. He assumes that you know the format for a press release and he wants you to prepare a draft for his approval. The information he has given you is:

Paintastik Effeks

Exciting new paint range designed in the USA and manufactured in the UK

Launch date May 1

20 colours available

Paints are not quick drying – they are designed to be mixed and matched on the wall for new paint effects

Paints manufactured by Universal Paints and Solvents, the leading UK paint specialist.

Available in 1, 2 and 5ltr tins

Brand new range of paint effect brushes and pads

Universal Paints and Solvents' own reception area will be redesigned with the new paints on the launch day. Work will be carried out by award winning company Graham Hobb Interiors.

5.3 Make use of technology, as required
5.4 Format and produce documents to an agreed style
5.5 Integrate non-text objects into an agreed layout, if required

Refer to 2.1–2.3 and 3.1–3.7 and then attempt the following activity.

Give it a go

Having prepared your resources and organised the content, you now need to use a software package and then format and produce the documents according to your brief. You should make use of any non-text objects if you feel this is necessary.

5.6 Check texts for accuracy
5.7 Edit and correct texts, as required
5.8 Clarify document requirements, when necessary

Refer to 2.1–2.3 and 3.1–3.7 and then attempt the following activity.

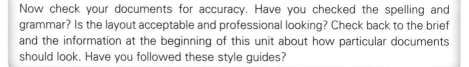

Give it a go

Now check your documents for accuracy. Have you checked the spelling and grammar? Is the layout acceptable and professional looking? Check back to the brief and the information at the beginning of this unit about how particular documents should look. Have you followed these style guides?

5.9 Store documents safely and securely following organisational procedures

Refer to 2.1–2.3 and 3.1–3.7 and then attempt the following activity.

Give it a go

What name have you given each of the documents? Think about who has access to these documents and whether they are able to amend them without your permission. If there was commercially sensitive information contained in any of the documents you have created, how might a business seek to protect this information from unauthorised access? You could do a screen print of your documents to show where they have been filed.

5.10 Present documents to the required format and within the agreed deadlines

Refer to 2.1–2.3 and 3.1–3.7 and then attempt the following activity.

Give it a go

If you are happy with the look of your documents, checked for accuracy and made any necessary edits and corrections, as well as clarified that your documents are fit for their purpose, you can print a hard copy. Print one of each of the documents and present them to your tutor or assessor. Did you complete the task in two hours? If at any stage it appeared that you would not meet the deadline, what actions did you take?

What is Evidence ?

Evidence can be reports, accounts, discussions and questioning. Evidence can also be witness testimony, observation and work products, including letters, emails and memos, or any other relevant documents produced.

Pull it together

There is a wide range of evidence that can be gathered to cover each of the learning outcomes and assessment criteria. Your tutor and/or assessor will be able to help you to identify which assessment methods are the most appropriate for you. These will differ according to your personal circumstances.

The range of assessment methods can include:

- observation of performance in the working environment
- examination of work products
- questioning
- discussions
- witness testimony
- examining your own statements
- recognising any prior learning.

Specific evidence can include:

- work instructions
- work plans, including resources and deadlines
- draft documents
- completed documents that meet organisational requirements
- screen prints
- records of where clarification was sought.

Store and Retrieve Information

■ Purpose of the unit

This unit is about securely storing and retrieving information and meeting the requirements of the organisation regarding confidential information.

■ Assessment requirements

To meet the assessment criteria for this unit, learners ideally need to have access to a working environment with associated equipment and resources. There is one major knowledge-based learning outcome and the remainder of the unit requires learners to show their ability to store and retrieve information. There are three main parts to the unit:

1 Understand processes and procedures for storing and retrieving information – why information needs to be stored and retrieved, the different systems used, legal issues including security and confidentiality, the importance of accuracy, providing information to agreed formats and timescales, deleting information and identifying problems that can occur with information systems.

2 Be able to store information – identifying, confirming and collecting information, following legal and organisational procedures, storing information in the right location, checking, updating and deleting stored information, dealing with or referring problems.

3 Be able to retrieve information – confirming and identifying information that needs to be retrieved, following legal and organisational procedures, locating and retrieving information, checking and updating information, providing information in the correct format and timescales, dealing with or referring problems.

■ 1. Understand processes and procedures for storing and retrieving information

1.1 Explain the purpose of storing and retrieving required information

Businesses and organisations need information. It is vital that their records are carefully organised and systematically maintained. This means working out an efficient way in which to store information so that when a search for that information is made, it is straightforward to retrieve it.

Increasingly, records and information are kept on shared drives or computer networks. But businesses and organisations still keep an enormous number of paper-based records. This means there have to be principles applied to daily filing tasks. Managing paper records and documents is a major job.

Even though computers have taken over many of the functions of more traditional forms of office equipment and can store information electronically, it is easy to create, print and copy documents. Businesses and organisations that claim to be paperless are often nothing of the kind.

Filing is still important and the management of those files is critical. Standard procedures have to be brought in to classify, sort, store and then easily retrieve files. The safe and secure storage of information and the easy access or retrieval of that information are imperative if an organisation is to function successfully and efficiently.

The purpose of filing anything is to be able to find it at a later date when it is needed. A good filing and retrieval system makes this easier. Businesses will often need access to information, which needs to be complete, accurate and up to date, in order to make proper decisions. Businesses that do not take filing seriously will be unable to find paper or electronic documents. At worst they become lost, but at best they are hard to find and this can be costly to the organisation.

The words 'storage and retrieval' can often be confusing when one has not worked in an office. In fact, they mean 'filing'. This word can also cause a reaction – often one of groans and moans! Filing is often thought to be boring and routine, and in essence it is. Nowadays, however, storage and retrieval includes the computerised systems of storing and retrieving information.

Another word for filing is 'indexing'. Obviously this involves a logical and effective way of recording documents and storing them in an efficient system which will allow the easy retrieval of that information when required.

Filing is the basis of record-keeping and entails the processing, arranging and storing of documents so that they can be found when they are required. The documents are placed in consecutive order and preserved in that system until they are required for reference. This can be carried out in any number of locations – a telephone directory is an index of alphabetical names and addresses. Your own address book is also a method of indexing in alphabetical order.

1.2 Describe different information systems and their main features

Businesses and organisations will use one of two main types of information system. However, they may in fact use both types of system. The traditional information system is manual or paper based. This system involves filing, storing and retrieving physical documents, which are organised into files and cross-referenced with an index system for easy retrieval. Businesses may choose to retain a manual or paper-based system, as it best suits their purposes, or they have chosen not to go to the expense of digitising all their existing records even if they have moved over to the second main type of information system, which is electronic.

Essentially, electronic information systems work in a similar way to a manual or paper-based system. The system needs to have a clear file structure and electronic or digitised versions of documents need to be stored in the correct place on a database system. Obviously one of the big advantages with an electronic system is that multiple users can access the same information at the same time. The other key advantage is that a lot less space is taken up by filing cabinets.

It may not always be possible for a business to switch over to an entirely electronic information system. As we have seen, they may already have many years' worth of paper-based documentation. They may also feel that legally or for backup purposes it is advisable to retain some of their paper-based materials.

So what are the basic techniques required to ensure that the storage and retrieval of information and documents are efficient? Let's look at this in some detail by considering the following points that will help you adopt good filing practice:

- ensure that the papers which have been passed for filing have been marked in some way to indicate that they are ready for storing
- sort the papers into order so that they are grouped in the required way
- remove any paperclips and staple multi-page documents together – this will ensure that they do not get separated during the filing process
- each individual file should be in date order, with the most recent documents at the top or front
- be neat with the documents – curled edges can easily become torn
- file daily if possible – this makes it less of a chore and also ensures that the files are up to date
- follow organisational procedure regarding 'out' or 'absent' cards. These are cards which are inserted into a file if the paperwork contained in the file has been removed by a member of staff. The card will indicate who has the file, when they took it and when they should return it to the filing cabinet
- follow up all overdue files regularly when they have been borrowed by another member of staff or department and have not been returned on time
- use a cross-reference system whenever a file is known by more than one name. It is often necessary to update files, for example when an organisation changes its name, or when a personnel file changes name because the member of staff marries. This could cause confusion as some people may still refer to the file, or look for it, under the old name. For this reason a system

has to be in place which enables the person searching to find it without too much difficulty. The cross-reference slip would be placed either in the old or in the new file, directing the person seeking the file to the correct place

- thin out the files when necessary – there will be an organisational procedure regarding the length of time documents are held in the system. When they become obsolete or out of date, they may be transferred to the 'archives'. This is an additional storage area where files are stored in boxes in case they are required for reference. The archives could be in another room or even in another building. We look at archiving in more detail a little later in this unit

- be aware of health and safety regarding filing cabinets. For example, always close drawers after you have used them and lock drawers and cabinets before leaving the office at night

- always ask for help if you are unsure where something should be filed, and do not be afraid to offer ideas if you think the system could be more efficient with some improvements.

Using classification methods

When documents are filed, it could be that they are done so using any of the following systems. Different methods will prove suitable for different circumstances. The following can be found in any type of organisation and are known as the different classification methods of filing.

Figure 219.1

Alphabetic

This method refers to the filing of documents according to the first letter of the surname or organisation. It is the most common method of classification used in businesses. This is normally the first letter of the surname of the correspondent,

- VAT records – they need to be kept for at least six years, although HMRC may allow a shorter period if it is impractical to keep the records

- PAYE – HMRC recommends that they should be kept for at least three years after the income tax year to which they relate

- other tax documentation – HMRC can reassess any time up to six years after the tax year, so it is advisable to keep business records for six years

- company records – corporation tax and accounting records should be kept for six years after the tax year. Details of company directors should be kept for at least five years

- government grants – these should be kept for four years after the grant has been received.

Electronic documents are easy to modify, therefore if they are used as evidence in court they are often not viewed with the same level of confidence as paper documents. One way of ensuring that electronic documents are protected from being tampered with is to write protect the originals.

Some organisations have industry-specific legislation to consider. The Access to Medical Reports Act 1988 and the updated version in 2009 allow individuals the right to request access to their medical reports. These can be supplied to their employer or to an insurance company by their doctor. Individuals need to be told about the information that is being passed on and to have access to the report before it is passed on. The doctor has to keep the report for a minimum of six months from the date that it has been disclosed.

It is therefore important for organisations to create procedures to make sure that employees are fully aware of the requirements to protect confidential information and of the retention periods necessary before the disposal of sensitive or confidential information.

1.4 Explain the purpose of confirming information to be stored and retrieved

The main purpose of filing paperwork is being able to find it again when it is needed, either by yourself or by someone else. Being able to find the right information from a filing system is known as retrieving information and this job would be carried out in order to:

- add information to the contents of the file

- obtain some information from the contents of the file.

But giving away information can prove complicated. If someone takes individual documents from a file, they may go missing for ever. You should never allow just one or two pages to be taken from a file unless:

- most of the information contained in the file is confidential and the person needing the one or two documents cannot see the rest of the confidential information

● the information contained in the file is much too large to take away.

The golden rules for making sure that information from a file does not get lost or filed back in the wrong place are:

● record the fact that information has been taken from the filing cabinet by inserting an 'out' or 'absent' card in its place

● use a log sheet to record the fact that the file has been borrowed, when the person took it, where they have taken it to and when they have agreed to return it

● keep information on the log sheet up to date and chase up any files that are not returned when they were agreed to be returned.

In many cases it will be obvious where the information will need to be stored. If the information relates to a particular customer or project, for example, it would have to be stored with existing data about that customer or project. Other documents may not be as obvious and may contain information that might need to be accessed by a variety of people at a later date. Nonetheless, the information has to be stored in a particular location, although it may need to be cross-referenced to other parts of the filing system so that it is easier to find if someone is searching for it using slightly different search criteria.

All of this is designed in order to not only put the information in the right location but also make it as straightforward as possible for authorised individuals to be able to retrieve that information. Therefore the purpose of storing the information in the first place needs to be established to make sure that it is filed in the right place.

1.5 Describe ways of checking information for accuracy
1.6 Explain the purpose of checking information for accuracy

Accurate information is essential. If a business or organisation is working from faulty or inaccurate information, it may make the wrong decisions. Accuracy should always be a major concern, rather than the speed of filing or storing the information. Information needs to be checked, corrections need to be made and it is always wise to compare information that already exists with the new information and highlight any key changes.

There are some handy tips to consider when checking information for accuracy:

● check the source of the information – who provided the information and is it accurate?

2.2 Follow legal and organisational procedures for security and confidentiality of information to be stored

Refer to 1.3 and then carry out the following activity.

Give it a go

One of the peculiarities of the filing system used by the accounts department is that customers and suppliers are all filed within the same system. This has grown up as a procedure over a number of years. In the past only a handful of filing cabinets was used and it made sense for all the information to be stored in one location. The system has now outgrown itself. There are at least 3,000 individual customer files and nearly 700 supplier files. Your manager would like you to review the procedures and to broaden your investigation by considering:

● any legal procedures relating to security and confidentiality

● a new and improved organisational procedure that not only makes the system more efficient but also ensures security and confidentiality.

You should provide a brief memorandum or email outlining your thoughts.

2.3 Store information in approved locations

Refer to 1.4 and then carry out the following activity.

Give it a go

The manager is in agreement with your proposals. Outline a memorandum that can be handed out to all staff. It should summarise the new filing procedures. Make sure you have put in checks to ensure that once the system has been updated, all of the information within the files is stored in the new, approved locations in the information system.

2.4 Check and update stored information, if required

Refer to 1.5 and 1.6 and then carry out the following activity.

Give it a go

The business has just bought a smaller competitor. From an initial look at the customers and suppliers, over half are existing customers and suppliers of your business; all the others are new to your business. Your manager wants you to bring the two sets of records together and incorporate them as one filing system. You need to think about how this is going to be achieved and what steps would have to be taken and in what order. Write down all of the steps necessary and then order them. Also note how you would check and update duplicate files to make sure that the information is correct.

2.5 Delete stored information, if required

Figure 219.3

Refer to 1.8 and then carry out the following activity.

Give it a go

As part of your work on the filing system you have identified a number of files that fall into three categories. These are:

- empty files – with no paperwork, only a customer or supplier name on the folder
- customers who have not made a purchase from the business for more than five years
- business customers and suppliers who have gone out of business and are no longer trading.

Importantly, all of the files have been checked to make sure that there are no outstanding payments to be received or to be paid out to these customers or suppliers.

Your manager wants you to suggest how to deal with these 'dormant' files. What is your advice as to how they should be either disposed of or archived?

2.6 Deal with or refer problems, if required

Refer to 1.9 and then carry out the following activity.

Give it a go

You have reorganised the filing system, but there are still some significant problems, including:

- files are still being removed from the system and going missing
- file users do not reorder the contents of the files after use and the date order is jumbled
- some users are refiling records incorrectly. This is particularly the case with customers or businesses whose names have changed
- people are taking documents from files, rather than taking the whole file out of the system.

Briefly suggest how you should tackle each of these problems. State what procedures you think should be put in place in order to ensure that the information system remains reliable and intact.

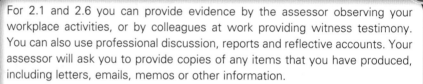

What is Evidence ?

For 2.1 and 2.6 you can provide evidence by the assessor observing your workplace activities, or by colleagues at work providing witness testimony. You can also use professional discussion, reports and reflective accounts. Your assessor will ask you to provide copies of any items that you have produced, including letters, emails, memos or other information.

For 2.2–2.5 it may be difficult to provide physical evidence, but much of it can be collected through workplace observation, witness testimony, professional discussions and reports or reflective accounts.

3. Be able to retrieve information

3.1 Confirm and identify information to be retrieved

Refer to 1.1 and then carry out the following activity.

Give it a go

Your manager has suggested that it is a good idea to identify key accounts. From your manager's description these are customers who order products from the business on more than one occasion per month. For suppliers it is those that make deliveries to the business on a monthly basis.

How would you go about identifying these key accounts? Where would you look in the files to identify the information that you need to class them as key accounts? Would it be advisable to have a separate filing system for these key accounts? How would this system be managed if changes take place, such as a customer ordering less frequently or a supplier not delivering products every month?

Write your suggestions as a memo to your manager.

3.2 Follow legal and organisational procedures for security and confidentiality of information

Refer to 1.3 and then carry out the following activity.

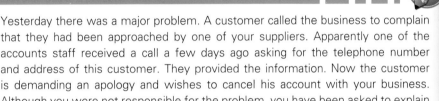

Give it a go

Yesterday there was a major problem. A customer called the business to complain that they had been approached by one of your suppliers. Apparently one of the accounts staff received a call a few days ago asking for the telephone number and address of this customer. They provided the information. Now the customer is demanding an apology and wishes to cancel his account with your business. Although you were not responsible for the problem, you have been asked to explain how this could have happened. Your manager also wants you to issue a list of legal and organisational procedures that all staff should follow in the future to ensure that secure and confidential information is not leaked out of the business.

3.3 Locate and retrieve the required information

Refer to 1.4 and then carry out the following activity.

Give it a go

Your business has a number of area sales representatives. They make routine visits to customers and show them new products and services, as well as taking orders from them to be passed onto the business. At the sales conference some of the representatives have complained about the time it takes for members of the accounts staff to find customer records relating to customers in their area. They have suggested that the files be stored geographically rather than alphabetically or any other system. Your manager has asked you to comment on your reactions to this suggestion.

Do you think this is a better way of organising the filing system? What might be the benefits? What might be the problems? Prepare an email to be sent to all sales representatives. Is there a way in which their suggestions can be incorporated into a filing system to speed up location and retrieval?

Unit 221

Use Office Equipment

■ Purpose of the unit

This unit is about using a variety of office equipment, following the manufacturers' and the organisation's own guidelines for use.

■ Assessment requirements

To meet the assessment criteria for this unit, learners need to know about a range of office equipment and demonstrate their ability to use that equipment. There are seven parts to the unit:

1 Know about different types of office equipment and their uses – identifying the main types, describing their features and when they are used for particular tasks.

2 Understand the purpose of following instructions and health and safety procedures – why it is important to follow manufacturers' and organisational instructions, identifying health and safety procedures and the purpose in following these when using equipment, plus the importance of keeping equipment clean and hygienic.

3 Understand how to use equipment in a way that minimises waste – examples of waste, ways to reduce waste and the purpose of minimising waste.

4 Know about the different types of problems that may occur when using equipment and how to deal with them – examples of equipment problems, following manufacturers' and organisational instructions and procedures when dealing with problems, providing examples of how to deal with problems.

5 Understand the purpose of meeting work standards and deadlines – explaining the purpose of meeting work standards and deadlines when using equipment.

6 Understand the purpose of leaving equipment and the work area ready for the next user.

7 Be able to use office equipment – locating and selecting equipment, following manufacturers' and organisational guidelines, minimising waste, keeping equipment clean and hygienic, dealing with equipment problems, referring problems when necessary, ensuring final work product meets agreed requirements and is delivered to agreed timescale and making sure that equipment, resources and work areas are ready for the next user.

1. Know about different types of office equipment and its uses

1.1 Identify different types of equipment and their uses

Businesses and organisations use a standard range of office equipment. Some businesses have specific requirements related to the type of work being carried out in the office.

Office equipment may be multifunctional, such as a printer that can also scan or fax documents, or it can be a single-use piece of equipment, such as a shredder, which is designed to destroy confidential documents before disposal.

Many pieces of office equipment are directly related to communications or the creation or sharing of information. A computer, for example, is often part of a larger network of computers, which allows the sharing of documents, information and software applications. Linked to the computer network will be another range of office equipment, the most common being the printer. This, of course, is designed to produce hard copies of documents, spread-sheets, reports, etc. The network may also have scanners, which are designed to digitise paper documents and in some cases they use **optical character recognition** in order to read and digitise documents.

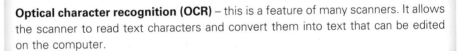

Don't forget

Optical character recognition (OCR) – this is a feature of many scanners. It allows the scanner to read text characters and convert them into text that can be edited on the computer.

Although the specification does not state exactly which types of office equipment need to be identified, other common types of office equipment include:

- photocopier
- laminator
- binder
- fax machine
- telephone
- franking machine
- shredder.

Figure 221.1

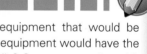

Give it a go

Write down a list of the minimum pieces of office equipment that would be necessary to run a small office. Which of these types of equipment would have the greatest use? Which ones would be used only occasionally? Compare your list with that of other members of your group, or discuss your choice with your assessor.

1.2 Describe the different features of different types of office equipment

Computer

Increasingly the most important piece of office equipment is the computer. This can be a standalone machine, which has its own software and is linked to a printer or scanner. More commonly, however, computers tend to be linked to a larger network of computers with a separate hard drive, which is used to store the data. Printers and scanners are shared by a number of computers.

Keyboards, mice, scanners, digital cameras, webcams and other pieces of equipment are all used to input information onto computers. Some businesses will also use:

- voice recognition software
- bar code readers
- optical mark readers

- magnetic strips

- optical character recognition.

Linked to all of the computers is what are known as output devices. These are pieces of equipment that allow the user to see information, or have access to that information, which is held on the computer network. The most common are monitors and printers. These come in a variety of types. Monitors tend to be flat screen, with a good screen resolution and a sharp image, making it easier for users to look at the screen for extended periods of time. Many small businesses use multifunction printers. These are scanners, photocopiers, fax machines, and may have slots for memory sticks or compact flashcards. Some small businesses will use inkjet printers, but increasingly popular are laser printers, either a mono or colour version, as they are faster and quieter.

Photocopier

Larger businesses and organisations in particular will use sophisticated photo-copiers. These can:

- copy whole documents, putting each page in order

- staple documents

- print on both sides of the paper

- sort separate sheets or sets of sheets for multiple distribution

- print black and white or colour

- print on paper from A5 to A3 (some specialist photocopiers will print up to A1)

- enlarge or reduce original documents

- automatically debit the user's budget when a code is inserted.

Binding machine and laminator

Occasionally there may be a need to use a binding machine. This piece of office equipment punches a series of holes in a document and then allows the user to bind together the pages.

Businesses will use a variety of binding machines. Effectively they allow pages to be fixed together to form a basic book. The comb binder uses round, plastic spines with between 19 and 21 rings. The binding machine punches rectangular holes and then allows the spine to slot into place.

A wire binder allows the documents to lie flat on a desk and binds the documents together with a double loop wire. The binding machine creates the holes and then the pages of the document are hung onto the wire spines. The machine then squeezes the spine together to secure the document.

Thermal binding machines melt an adhesive in a steel binding cover to fix documents together with hard or paperback covers. They can bind multiple documents at a time.

The simplest form of binding is to use a slide binder. This is a simple u-shaped plastic sleeve that you slide over the edge of the documents to create a basic bound document.

Alternatively, key documents can be protected using a laminator. Covers of bound documents are often laminated in order to protect them.

Fax machine

Although many businesses have multifunction printers and make use of email, fax machines are still used. The whole idea behind the fax machine is that a copy of an original document is transmitted from one location to another. This is used particularly when documents require signatures or exact copies of original documents are required.

Franking machine

Businesses will also use franking machines. These are designed to allow the business to create its own postal labels or postage impression and thus reduce the need for postage stamps. The business will use a set of scales to weigh the envelope or parcel, select the correct amount of postage and print the postage impression or a postage label. Businesses have to buy credit for their franking machines and top up the credit as it is used.

Telephone

One of the other most common types of office equipment is the telephone. In many businesses each employee has their own dedicated telephone extension. This system has become more and more sophisticated, as it allows each user to leave a personal voicemail message. Any messages left for that telephone extension are digital recordings with the date and time of the call logged.

Different telephone systems offer a range of functions. Typically they have the ability to be able to transfer calls, to switch unanswered calls from one extension to another and to be able to talk to several people on the same telephone network at the same time.

Shredder

Paper shredders are mechanical devices that cut paper either into strips or particles. They are ideal for destroying confidential or sensitive documents. The most common is the strip cut shredder, which has rotating knives that cut narrow strips. Cross-cut or confetti shredders cut the paper into rectangles or other shapes and are considered to be more effective in destroying documents. Some businesses use particle cut shredders, which reduce the documents to small squares or circles. Some large businesses might use disintegrators or granulators, which reduce the paper into particles tiny enough to go through a mesh.

Give it a go

How are wireless computers and printers connected to a network? How are the computers linked to external hard drives that hold data? Why might a business still use cables?

1.3 Explain why different types of equipment are chosen for tasks

It is important to think about what type of equipment you might need for a task and whether or not it is readily available to use. Basic equipment, such as printers and photocopiers, should be readily available, but more specialist equipment may need to be booked in advance, as it may be a joint resource and stored in a different location.

Even though modern multifunction printers and sophisticated photocopiers can carry out a number of different tasks, there is still a need for specialist equipment. In some businesses communication is now no longer carried out using telephones but by using headsets connected to the computer network.

Each piece of office equipment requires a considerable amount of thought and investment, in order to make sure that it can cope with a broad range of tasks required by the business or the organisation. Although it is often better to buy a large printer rather than have small printers on every desk, there can be difficulties in sharing the equipment, particularly at busy times.

Increasingly, though, businesses are looking for machines that are multifunctional. These save on maintenance and operating costs. They are also looking for machines that are more environmentally friendly. These are ones that consume less energy, or have environmentally friendly consumables, such as refillable toners.

Each specific task may require the use of one or more pieces of office equipment. Producing a letter, for example, requires the use of a keyboard, mouse, monitor, computer hard drive, and modem in the case of wireless or cables in the case of wired networks. To output the letter a printer is needed and a franking machine may be necessary in order to add a postage label to the envelope.

Give it a go

You have been asked to word process a 20-page document. Forty copies of the document are needed and they need to have sturdy covers, as they will be used for some time. They also need to be posted out to 25 different locations around the country. List all of the office equipment you would need in order to carry out this task.

What is Evidence ?

Evidence can consist of reports, reflective accounts, professional discussions and questioning.

■ 2. Understand the purpose of following instructions and health and safety procedures

2.1 Explain the purpose of following manufacturers' instructions when using equipment
2.2 Explain the purpose of following organisational instructions when using equipment

There are various reasons for always following manufacturers' guidelines about using equipment. This is from initial installation and use of the equipment through to its daily use and maintenance. Some manufacturers' instructions are complicated and they stress the importance of carefully following the guidelines for use and being consistent in how you use them. Sometimes this is related to health and safety. It is important to understand not only why guidelines have to be followed but also how they have to be followed.

Usually when new pieces of office equipment are introduced to the office an individual, perhaps from the manufacturer or supplier, will install that equipment. They will explain exactly how it functions. They will explain not only what it can do but also what it is not designed to do. For a printer, for example, there may be a limit to the thickness of card or paper that can pass through its rollers. For a shredder there may be a limited number of sheets that it can process at any one time.

Manufacturers' instructions do not always provide you with the answer to a specific problem – they tend to focus on the normal use of the product and try to anticipate common problems that may occur. In not following the instructions, not only may the piece of equipment fail but the business or organisation may find that any right to get it replaced or repaired has become invalidated.

Organisations will also have specific guidelines or instructions on the use of the office equipment. Even the most innocent piece of equipment will have a potential series of hazards. Users could suffer from an electric shock, they could damage their hands or eyes or they could contaminate the office with fumes or dust. Organisations may produce specific manuals for particular pieces of office equipment. They may also provide training on its use. Many office equipment suppliers provide basic training, which can then be passed on to other users, as part of their installation package. This will usually include:

- the basic operating instructions for the piece of equipment
- safety hints and tips and safe working practices
- procedures for simple faults
- reporting methods for more serious faults
- recommended servicing and maintenance.

Businesses and organisations carry out regular safety audits and health checks on office equipment. This is to make sure that it is maintained and that any particular problems are highlighted and dealt with at the earliest possible opportunity. A prime example is the monitor or display screen. An organisation would be alerted to particular problems and take into account the following:

- the screen should not produce excessive heat, noise or vibration
- anti-glare screens can be fitted
- wrist rests should be used to eliminate inappropriate keyboard techniques – this is related to ergonomics. Ergonomics is about designing equipment or aids that aim to reduce the likelihood of injury and illness, or reduce accidents
- the screen size should be large enough for routine word processing (minimum height of characters on the screen should be around 3mm).

It is a legal requirement for all British businesses and organisations to use Portable Appliance Testing (PAT) on a regular basis. Essentially it is an electrical safety measure. According to the Health and Safety Executive, at least 1,000 people suffer from electric shocks or burns in offices each year, of which 30 are fatal. The level of inspection and testing depends on the risk of the appliance becoming faulty, so the frequency of tests depends on the type of equipment involved. Testing should take place on any portable appliance, handheld appliance, fixed equipment or appliance and other electrical business equipment, including computers, computer screens, photocopiers and mail processing machines.

Give it a go

A business is about to install a large multifunction photocopier. It has already identified that when the toner needs changing this must be done in accordance with the manufacturer's instructions. It also recognises that as the photocopier will be in heavy use, it should be located in a well-ventilated area. What other sensible precautions should be taken?

2.3 Identify health and safety procedures for using different types of equipment
2.4 Explain the purpose of following health and safety procedures when using equipment

It is important to understand that all businesses, organisations and employees need to comply with health and safety legislation. This is designed to reduce the number of accidents.

There are many laws that directly affect working in an office environment. Clearly some of them apply to office equipment that uses electricity, or is a potential fire hazard, while others relate to equipment that could injure the user or poison them in some way. The laws that affect those working in an office environment are:

● *The Health and Safety at Work Act, 1974 (HASAW)* – this is probably the most well-known and important Act and it applies to all work premises, whatever the size of the business or number of employees. The employer's duties are based on the principle of 'so far as is reasonably practicable'. This means that risks need to be balanced against the costs and other difficulties of reducing a risk. The Act requires employers to use common sense and implement suitable measures to tackle potential risks and employees to take reasonable steps to ensure their own safety and that of others.

● *Workplace (Health, Safety and Welfare) Regulations 1992* – these regulations cover a wide range of health, safety and welfare issues, including heating, lighting, seating, and ventilation, welfare and workstations.

● *Offices, Shops and Railway Premises Act, 1963* – this Act concentrates on shops and offices and provides a number of clear guidelines to the employer on the provision of facilities to employees, including temperature, fresh air supply, toilet and washing facilities, lighting and area of working space.

● *Fire Precautions Act 1971, the Fire Precautions (Factories, Offices, Shops and Railway Premises) Order 1989, the Fire Precautions (Workplace) Regulations 1997, the Fire Precautions (Workplace) (Amendment) Regulations 1999* – this series of Acts and subsequent amendments and additions requires employers to have a valid fire certificate, specifically in the case of hotels and boarding houses and factories, offices, shops or railway premises. In the second case a certificate is needed if more than 20 employees are working in the building or more than 10 employees are working on a floor other than the ground floor.

● *Employers' Liability (Compulsory Insurance) Regulations, 1969* – these regulations require employers to have necessary insurance in the event of their employees having an accident or suffering from ill health as a result of their work.

● *Health and Safety (First Aid) Regulations 1981* – these regulations address the requirements of an employer to provide first-aid cover and trained personnel.

- *Health and Safety (Safety Signs and Signals) Regulations 1996* – these regulations came into effect following a European Union Directive. They require employers to provide safety signs where there is a risk that has not been avoided or controlled by other means. The safety signs are aimed at reducing risks, such as the regulation of traffic, the marking of dangerous substances or areas, and incorporating fire safety signs, including directions to exits.

- *Reporting of Injuries, Diseases and Dangerous Occurrences Regulations, 1992 (RIDDOR)* – a revised version of these regulations came into force in 1996, requiring employers to notify the Health and Safety Executive of occupational injuries, diseases and dangerous events in the workplace.

- *Health and Safety (Display Screen Equipment) Regulations, 1992* – these regulations are specifically related to work with visual display units (VDUs) or computer screens.

- *The Control of Substances Hazardous to Health Regulations, 2002 (COSHH)* – these regulations require employers to make regular assessments of the risks from hazardous substances and to ensure that precautions are taken to reduce these risks.

- *Provision and Use of Work Equipment Regulations, 1998 (PUWER)* – these regulations aim to ensure that all equipment, including machinery, used by employees is safe.

- *Manual Handling Operations Regulations, 1992* – these regulations cover the movement of objects in the workplace, either by hand or by force.

- *The Electricity at Work Regulations, 1989* – these regulations require employers to ensure that all electrical systems are safe and regularly maintained.

- *The Noise at Work Regulations, 1989* – these regulations require employers to ensure that their employees are protected from hearing damage as a result of their work.

- *Personal Protective Equipment (PPR) Regulations, 1992* – these regulations require employers to ensure that their employees have the appropriate protective clothing and equipment for their work.

- *Management of Health and Safety at Work Regulations, 1999* – these regulations require employers to carry out risk assessments and to make the arrangements to implement any necessary measures. Competent individuals should also be identified to pass on information to other employees and to carry out the necessary training.

- *Health and Safety Information for Employees Regulations, 1989* – these regulations require an employer to display a poster informing their employees what they should know about health and safety.

Businesses and organisations will identify procedures for using equipment in order to ensure that their employees follow not only the health and safety legislation but also the user guidelines produced by the manufacturer.

Give it a go

Most offices use a variety of electrical equipment on a regular basis. All electrical equipment could be a potential hazard and there are varying degrees of risk involved. Make a list of the office equipment you use on a regular basis. Beside each piece of equipment, write down whether you think this machine or piece of equipment is safe or harmful, and why.

2.5 Explain the purpose of keeping equipment clean and hygienic

Making sure that office equipment is kept clean and hygienic not only means that the equipment will often function better but also reduces the spread of bugs, viruses and other germs. This is particularly true of pieces of office equipment that are shared by a number of people.

Clean and hygienic office equipment can lead to a big reduction in cross-contamination. Dirty computer screens have been shown to cause headaches, nausea and eye strain. Dust and dirt cause machines to overheat and, perhaps, break down. Even small problems such as a mouse that has stopped rolling properly or a sticky keyboard can slow down work and lose valuable time. Another example is marks or scratches on the glass of a photocopier. If these are not dealt with, they will produce poor quality copies, which will not only mean a loss of time but will also produce avoidable waste.

The major cause of accidents within the workplace tends to be attributed to employees working in an untidy and careless manner. Having said that, the employer has to take responsibility for ensuring that employees have all

Figure 221.2

the information they need to work in a safe manner and eliminate the risks to themselves, their colleagues and visitors to the organisation. This information could take several forms:

● ensure staff are familiar with all equipment being used

● ensure staff are trained in health and safety matters

● ensure staff have access to manuals or handbooks relating to equipment or machinery being used

● ensure staff are clear about safe working practices

● ensure staff are familiar with the health and safety policy of the business.

Give it a go

Using the following facts, create a poster that could be placed on a notice board in the office:

● an office desk can have 10 million microbes

● telephones, keyboards and mice can have up to 25,000 microbes

● cold and flu viruses live on surfaces for 72 hours

● sufficient skin falls off the average human every day to fill a teacup

● one in three men and 17 per cent of women admit to not washing their hands after visiting the toilet.

What is Evidence ?

Evidence can consist of reports, reflective accounts, professional discussions and questioning.

■ 3. Understand how to use equipment in a way that minimises waste

3.1 Give examples of waste when using equipment

In offices and businesses up and down the country, thousands of tons of paper are thrown into wastepaper baskets every day. Many businesses have begun to encourage their employees to recycle paper. Every sheet which you waste costs the business money. But a fraction of this can be saved by placing waste paper in a recycling bin. Recycling companies collect the paper and pay the business by weight.

You should try to avoid wasting paper as much as you can. Some people have difficulty in noticing mistakes in documents when they are on the computer screen. Therefore they print out draft documents to check them. Try to avoid doing this unless it is absolutely necessary, because each draft, if there is a mistake, will simply go into the bin.

Although printers are far more reliable than in the past, there is still always the chance that the paper will feed in crooked, or that you will put headed paper in back to front, or upside down. Try to remember how the paper should go in and this will cut down this type of waste. You could put a note above the printer to remind you.

Paper, envelopes and other documents which are stacked up by a window may discolour in the sun. Try to make sure that any stocks of paper are in boxes and put away in a cupboard.

Although your business may have its own policies about waste, the following list gives you some tips on how you can minimise waste yourself:

- why not photocopy on both sides of the paper?
- why not reuse folders by putting sticky labels over old labels?
- any out-of-date headed paper can be used as scrap paper
- store paper away from sunlight and heat
- check your documents before you print them out
- try a single photocopy for quality before you do a long photocopy run
- don't make extra copies of documents unless you absolutely need them
- try to reuse external envelopes for internal mail
- think before you write on anything – you may make a mistake or not leave enough room and waste the paper or card
- use recycled printer refill cartridges if you can
- use shredded paper for packaging
- don't rip open padded envelopes – if you open them carefully they can be reused.

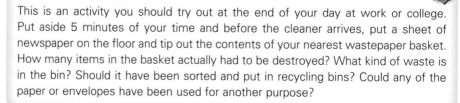

Over to you

This is an activity you should try out at the end of your day at work or college. Put aside 5 minutes of your time and before the cleaner arrives, put a sheet of newspaper on the floor and tip out the contents of your nearest wastepaper basket. How many items in the basket actually had to be destroyed? What kind of waste is in the bin? Should it have been sorted and put in recycling bins? Could any of the paper or envelopes have been used for another purpose?

3.2 Give examples of ways to reduce waste

Probably the best way to reduce waste is not to create it in the first place. Items should be used as many times as possible and everything should be recycled if appropriate because waste disposal costs can be high. Recycling can minimise the impact the business or organisation has on the environment.

Suppliers can be asked to use less heavily packaged products when they deliver. Paper could be reused or recycled, as should printer toner and ink cartridges. Printers should be set to print double-sided and internal documents can be printed in draft quality.

Businesses should use email wherever possible, as this cuts down on the amount of printing and faxing necessary. Emails and documents do not need to always be printed out. Paper that has been printed on one side only could be reused as scrap paper. Envelopes can be reused for internal mail.

There are other savings to be made, such as not leaving office equipment on standby but turning it off after use.

Reducing or minimising the amount of paper wastage within a business is important to an organisation because it helps it to reduce running costs. Because paper is wasted so much, there are a number of ways you can contribute to the minimising of waste paper when photocopying, including:

- make sure the original document is clean
- make sure the glass on the photocopier is clean
- make sure you put the original document in the right way up and that it is straight
- make sure you key in the right number of copies required
- take a draft copy first, before doing multiple copies, to make sure the copy is of an acceptable standard
- print only the number of copies you need
- photocopy on both sides of the paper whenever possible
- check that the cartridge has toner before starting
- check that nobody has requested more copies than they need.

Over to you

Over the course of a day or week, honestly write down each time you print or copy a document. Also note down how many copies are substandard and not suitable for use. If you write down how much you have wasted it may encourage you to be more careful.

Give it a go

Write down a list of all the equipment you use regularly. For each item of equipment, keep a log of the times you have encountered even a simple problem with it and identify what you did to rectify the problem.

4.2 Explain the purpose of following manufacturers' instructions and organisational procedures when dealing with problems

Manufacturers' instruction booklets will have a list of common problems that users encounter, with troubleshooting solutions. These are usually fairly straightforward explanations of how to deal with the common problems, such as paper jams, replacement of batteries and trouble with cabling or connections.

The business or organisation may also have a policy with regard to office equipment. It may not want users to try to fix problems themselves and may have dedicated support in order to deal with equipment problems in a more systematic and efficient way. Simple problems such as paper jams may appear to be relatively straightforward, but trying to fix the problem yourself could mean creating a bigger problem. It could also mean that the machine is out of action for longer, as you may have caused more damage to the machine while trying to deal with the problem.

It is worth bearing in mind that many pieces of larger office equipment are not owned by the organisation or business. They may be leased or rented and part of the arrangement with the owner of the office equipment is that they carry out all repairs. Also, attempts to mend equipment that is still in the warranty or guarantee period could cause difficulties, as unsupervised repairs may invalidate the warranty or guarantee terms. All repairs in these situations should be carried out by the manufacturer or supplier of the office equipment.

Over to you

Write down at least five pieces of office equipment that you use regularly, either at college or at work. How old is the machine? Does the business own the equipment or is it leased or rented? Who is responsible for repairs and are users encouraged to troubleshoot and deal with minor problems themselves?

4.3 Give examples of how to deal with problems

A wide variety of things can go wrong with office equipment. A photocopier, for example, could suffer from a major problem that may need to be resolved if an urgent job needs to be completed. In this instance here are some issues that you could consider:

- is the photocopier producing any copies at all? Or is it crumpling or tearing paper?

- does the machine sound different to you?

- if the copier is jamming only one size of paper, it means that the trouble could lie in one of the paper cassettes. By switching the position of the cassette, the problem may be solved

- if the cassettes all seem to be jamming, then the rollers may be worn out

- if the machine is jamming and crumpled paper is being produced, there must be something inside that is causing the paper to stop somewhere.

Simple problems can be solved, but in other situations the problem may be more serious and maintenance people may have to attend to fix the equipment.

Figure 221.3

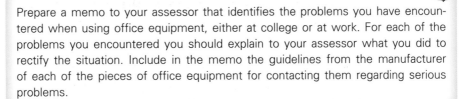

Over to you

Prepare a memo to your assessor that identifies the problems you have encountered when using office equipment, either at college or at work. For each of the problems you encountered you should explain to your assessor what you did to rectify the situation. Include in the memo the guidelines from the manufacturer of each of the pieces of office equipment for contacting them regarding serious problems.

5. Understand the purpose of meeting work standards and deadlines when using equipment

5.1 Explain the purpose of meeting work standards and deadlines when using equipment

All businesses and organisations rely on their employees to carry out tasks to an acceptable standard as well as in a timely manner. Poor work and missed deadlines can cost the organisation money. It can also have a negative effect on the business because customers, suppliers and other businesses may question how efficient they are at carrying out tasks.

Employees are key resources for any business or organisation and the efficient use of equipment is a vital skill that all users need to be able to achieve consistently. They need to be shown an acceptable work standard, both in terms of product and the amount of time that should be used to accomplish this. The equipment is there in order to allow users to complete tasks in a more efficient way, as well as to produce work products that conform to standards.

It is very important to meet deadlines. It is also vital to find out why there are delays, particularly if this is a problem that crops up on a regular basis. It may have a great deal to do with the workload, or it may be that the equipment being used is not effective. Solutions need to be identified to deal with problems, so solutions and options need to be considered. If deadlines are missed then whoever will be affected by the delay needs to be informed. Necessary steps need to be taken to complete the task as soon as possible, even if this means putting extra employees on to the task.

Over to you

Imagine that you have been asked to print off 200 copies of a newsletter, which has to be mailed out today. The printer has no cartridge and there are none in stock. Also, there are only 150 suitable envelopes and again there were none in stock. First, suggest how you would deal with the situation in order to meet today's deadline. Second, can you identify either at your college or workplace whose responsibility it is to ensure that there are sufficient printer cartridges and envelopes in stock?

What is Evidence ?

Evidence can consist of reports, reflective accounts, professional discussions and questioning.

■ 6. Understand the purpose of leaving equipment and the work area ready for the next user

6.1 Explain the purpose of leaving equipment and the work area ready for the next user

Shared work areas in particular are often the messiest in an office environment. Very few people clean up after themselves. Most businesses will have waste paper baskets placed around the office for unwanted copies of documents. However, it is often the case that particularly around photocopiers, fax machines and printers there are discarded documents on work surfaces and floors.

Not all office environments are open to the general public, such as customers or suppliers, and thus the office workers see no particular reason to tidy up after themselves. However, shared work areas are, of course, used by a wide variety of office workers. Also, if the offices are open for extended hours, those workers who start later in the day will find the environment already cluttered with mess.

It is good practice to get into the habit of leaving shared work areas as you found them. Not only is this good manners, it also has health and safety implications. An office environment, like any other work space, needs to be safe for people to carry out their duties. Cleanliness is a major factor. Some useful tips include:

● office equipment and consumables should be kept in their place at all times. This means that problems such as losing equipment or cluttering up shared work areas are cut down

● being able to find the office equipment ready for use and any consumables close at hand improves efficiency

● leaving equipment in a poor state after use can mean that dust, dirt and bugs are spread around the office space. A clean environment contributes to workplace safety

● hazardous materials should be dealt with in an appropriate way. If photocopier or printer cartridges have been replaced, they should be disposed of immediately and not left beside the machine. Spillages should also be dealt with immediately. These items can be dangerous to health and can pose a risk

- never leave the copier when it has run out of paper or toner without replacing it.

Many businesses appoint occupational health and safety officers to make sure that people comply with safe working practices. A clean working environment is a vital part of all of this.

Give it a go

Choose a shared work area and monitor it over the course of a few days. Note down every time you see mess, clutter, discarded equipment or consumables. What should have been done with these items? Are there waste bins or recycling bins close to the equipment? How can your college or business ensure that these areas remain safe and clean and ready for all users?

What is Evidence ?

Evidence can consist of reports, reflective accounts, professional discussions and questioning.

7. Be able to use office equipment

7.1 Locate and select equipment needed for a task

Refer to 1.1–1.3 and then try the activity below.

Give it a go

Choose a typical routine task that you carry out at college, in your real work environment, or at your place of work. Now create a simple log or list using the following headings:

- name of office equipment
- location of equipment
- location of consumables
- key uses of equipment.

Also add another column entitled 'ready for the next user'. You will need to use this log for your 7.9 evidence.

7.2 Use equipment following manufacturers' and organisational guidelines

Refer to 2.1 and 2.2 and then try the activity below.

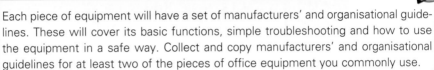

Give it a go

Each piece of equipment will have a set of manufacturers' and organisational guidelines. These will cover its basic functions, simple troubleshooting and how to use the equipment in a safe way. Collect and copy manufacturers' and organisational guidelines for at least two of the pieces of office equipment you commonly use.

7.3 Use equipment minimising waste

Refer to 3.1–3.3 and then try the activity below.

Give it a go

Create a simple log using the following headings:

- equipment used
- date
- waste created
- reason for waste
- disposal of waste.

Use this log, ideally over the course of a week, to keep a record of your use of equipment and how much waste you have generated.

7.4 Keep equipment clean and hygienic

Refer to 2.3–2.5 and 6.1 and then try the activity below.

Give it a go

Look at your copies of manufacturers' and organisational guidelines. Are there any tips about how to keep the equipment clean and hygienic? Does the college or organisation provide cleaning products suitable for commonly used office equipment? Do the office cleaners routinely clean the office equipment? Are specialist cleaners used to clean computers and keyboards? Is a cleaning routine a part of the general maintenance of major machinery such as photocopiers? Whose responsibility is it to ensure that shared equipment is kept clean and hygienic?

7.5 Deal with equipment problems following manufacturers' and organisational procedures
7.6 Refer problems, if required

Refer to 4.1–4.3 and then try the activity below.

Give it a go

Again refer to your manufacturers' and organisational guidelines and procedures. What are the most common problems associated with your chosen office equipment? Do the guidelines recommend that a general user of the equipment should tackle the problem? Or do they suggest that specialist assistance is required? In your college or workplace environment, how are routine problems handled? If the problem is more serious, who becomes involved? Does one individual have the responsibility of handling problems? Is this person internal or external to the organisation?

7.7 Make sure final work product meets agreed requirements
7.8 Make sure that product is delivered to agreed timescale

Refer to 5.1 and then try the activity below.

Give it a go

Create another log, which should ideally be used over the course of a week. Use the following headings:

- task
- date
- final work product required
- deadline
- completion date.

Make sure that you log all work you have carried out that required a final work product, such as a letter, email or memo. Make sure you attach a copy of your final work product to your log as evidence that you have completed the task. How many times have you met the deadline and produced the work to agreed requirements? How many times have you had to do more work or missed the deadline?

7.9 Make sure equipment, resources and work area are ready for the next user

Refer to 2.5 and 6.1 and then try the activity below.

Give it a go

Use the log that you created for 7.1. Put a tick alongside the piece of equipment each time you use it. In the final column, which reads 'ready for the next user', tick to confirm that you have left the equipment, resources and work area in a reasonable state. You should ensure that either your assessor or workplace supervisor countersigns this log to confirm that you have used the equipment and have left the surrounding area ready for the next user.

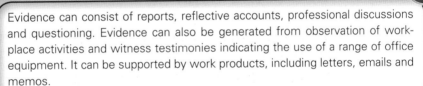

What is Evidence ?

Evidence can consist of reports, reflective accounts, professional discussions and questioning. Evidence can also be generated from observation of workplace activities and witness testimonies indicating the use of a range of office equipment. It can be supported by work products, including letters, emails and memos.

Pull it together

The best way to gather evidence for this unit is to begin by providing confirmation that you can identify the range of typical office equipment and know how it should be used. You also need to focus on the features of the equipment and good practice related to its use and location in the work area.

For the seventh learning outcome, evidence is best gathered by demonstrating your use of office equipment. This can best be achieved by the assessor observing your use of the equipment, or gathering witness testimony from colleagues that confirms your ability to use the office equipment.

Remember to be systematic about this. Not only do you have to locate and select equipment for specific tasks, you also need to be aware of any guidelines about its use, the minimising of waste, routine maintenance and cleaning of the machinery, and dealing with common problems. You need to make sure you use the most appropriate equipment to carry out specific tasks within specified timescales.

Remember to always leave equipment, resources and the work area in a tidy and considerate state, ready for the next user.

Meet and Welcome Visitors

■ Purpose of the unit

This unit covers the procedures to follow and hospitality to offer when meeting and welcoming visitors to business premises.

■ Assessment requirements

To meet the assessment criteria for this unit, learners will not only have to understand the organisation's procedures for meeting and welcoming visitors but also be able to demonstrate their ability to carry out this role. There are two parts to this unit:

1 Understand procedures for meeting and welcoming visitors – reasons for people visiting a business, their requirements and how their needs can be met, dealing with visitors in a prompt and courteous manner, presenting a positive image of self and organisation, following health, safety and security procedures, describing problems that could occur, dealing with them or referring them when appropriate, the purpose of communicating with visitors and the organisational structures and communication channels within the organisation.

2 Be able to meet and welcome visitors – greet visitors and make them feel welcome, identify visitors and the reason for their visit, use organisational systems to receive and record visitors, ensure visitors' needs are met, present a positive image, follow health, safety and security procedures, use appropriate communication channels, deal with problems or refer them, follow procedures for departing visitors.

■ 1. Understand procedures for meeting and welcoming visitors

1.1 Describe different reasons for people visiting a business, their requirements and how their needs may be met

A visitor's first point of contact with a business or an organisation is usually in the reception area. The duty of greeting visitors to the business or organisation usually then falls on the receptionist.

Whatever the type of organisation and regardless of its size, a number of visitors are likely to call during the course of a working day. It is important that the receptionist always projects a good image to the visitor, regardless of their reason for calling.

Visitors can arrive at the business for a variety of reasons:

- they may have an appointment with a member of staff
- they may be a courier or a postman delivering something
- they may require a signature for a delivery
- they may be visiting to collect a parcel or documents
- they may have arranged to meet a member of staff in order to attend a meeting elsewhere
- they may be attending an interview for a job within the organisation
- they may be a customer of the business
- they may be a supplier to the business
- they may be enquiring as to the name and availability of a member of staff to arrange a meeting
- they may be dropping off sales literature or information that may be of use to the business
- they may be a government representative, such as someone from HM Revenue and Customs or the Health and Safety Executive.

The first thing that needs to be done is to find out who they are and their purpose for the visit. The receptionist can then make a judgement as to how their needs can best be met. For example, if a visitor arrives and wishes to see a member of staff and has an appointment, the receptionist will simply call that member of staff's extension and inform them that their visitor has arrived.

Figure 256.1

279

It is common practice for the receptionist to record the arrival of visitors or the time and date of a delivery. This is particularly important if the visitor is going to be allowed access to the building, in which case a visitor's badge may have to be issued.

Give it a go

Write down as many different reasons for people visiting your business, organisation or centre as you can think of. What are their main requirements? How are their needs met when they are welcomed to the premises?

1.2 Explain the purpose of dealing with visitors promptly and courteously

Whether the visitor is a first-time or a regular caller, it is important that the impression this person receives is a good one – the visitor always needs to be left with a positive impression of the business or organisation. This begins with the first contact that the visitor has when entering the business's or organisation's premises. Projecting a professional image, regardless of the purpose of the visit, is an essential reception role.

The receptionist needs to be able to deal with any enquiry in the following way:

● the visitor needs to be greeted promptly and in a polite and courteous manner

● the receptionist needs to identify the best person to deal with the visitor

● the receptionist then has to contact the person concerned to find out whether they are free

● if the person is free, the receptionist should direct the caller to the appropriate place in a clear and accurate manner, or arrange for the member of staff to come down and collect them

● if the person is not free, the receptionist should ask the visitor if it is possible for them to wait and direct them to suitable seating and, perhaps, offer refreshment

● if the person they wish to see is not in the building, the receptionist should try to arrange for an appointment at another time. Alternatively, they should ask the visitor whether there is someone else they would prefer to see and the receptionist should contact that person.

As we will see, it is important for any visitor staying on the premises to be logged into the visitors' book. It is also good practice, particularly if the visitor is likely to call on a regular basis, that the receptionist takes a note of their name so that they can be greeted personally the next time without having to introduce themselves.

Ideally, reception areas should be staffed at all times. There should be cover for lunch and breaks, as well as for holiday and sickness periods. Some larger organisations employ people whose specific role it is to allow or deny access to the building for visitors before they even reach reception.

The receptionist should be aware of expected visitors. This means that when a visitor arrives for an appointment they will be able to look for their name in the appointments book. This will allow the receptionist to be able to greet the caller by name. They will then be able to contact the member of staff and receive instructions as to whether the visitor should wait to be collected or sent up to the office. It is also an opportunity if there is any documentation required to be completed or passed onto the visitor before the appointment begins.

Even if the visitor is unexpected and does not have an appointment, the receptionist has several alternatives:

● Are they prepared to wait to see the person they want to see?

● Is there another individual who can help them?

● Would they prefer to call back at another time or day?

● Could the receptionist pass a message on for the caller?

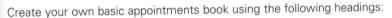

Give it a go

Create your own basic appointments book using the following headings:

● Name of caller

● Company

● Time of arrival

● To see

● Time of departure

Now complete the book with the following information:

● Mr Thompson is expecting Mr Kane to visit at 1115 and then Miss Jennings will see Mr Kane at half past 12

● after Miss Jennings has left, Mr Thompson wants to see Mr Kane again at quarter past 4

● the personnel manager is expecting to see Miss Dunn at half past 2, Miss Jackson at quarter past 10, Mrs Hollingsworth at quarter past 12, Miss Smith at 25 to 4 and Mr Fortescue at 5 past 4.

Fill in your appointments book so that the appointments appear in the correct order and use the 24-hour clock.

1.3 Explain the purpose of presenting a positive image of self and the organisation

For organisations whose employees have direct contact with their customers, it is important that the staff look presentable. If wishing to represent a company in the best way, an employee would have to think about the following:

- the way they dress for work

- their personal hygiene

- the way they behave when they are at work

- their personality – whether or not they are often grumpy or sometimes a bit too loud

- their general attitude when they are at work – whether or not they look as if they are approachable and how they treat other people.

Some employees are issued with a uniform for work. Some organisations prefer uniforms for a number of reasons, including:

- they form part of the company image in that the uniforms may have the company logo printed on them

- the employees will always be easy for the customer to find because they will all be wearing the same clothes

- it avoids having to pay employees an allowance for their work clothing

- it means all employees will turn up for work in the appropriate clothes and, hopefully, they will all look smart and well presented.

If an individual doesn't work for an organisation that issues a uniform, they will be expected to dress in clothes appropriate to the job. This means as smartly and as tidily as possible. Very often organisations insist on certain dress codes. These are rules about what can or cannot be worn for work. Some of them are based on health and safety reasons. These are:

- long hair needs to be tied back if the job involves working with food or equipment

- no nail varnish can be worn when food is being handled or prepared

- dangling jewellery should not be worn in case it gets tangled in equipment or machinery.

As well as wearing suitable clothing and using protective equipment, sometimes organisations insist that their employees wear their name tags on their clothing or wear their pass. These name tags and passes are worn for security reasons, to try to make sure that only authorised people get into certain areas of the organisation. But they are also worn so that visitors to the organisation can recognise the member of staff and call them by name.

Over to you

Work dress codes can range from formal to relatively casual. The dress code is usually determined by the amount of contact an employee will have with customers or visitors. Why would a business establish a dress code? Why would a business think that dressing in a particular way projects a particular image? What might that image be? Try to give at least two examples of different dress codes.

1.4 Explain the purpose of following health, safety and security procedures when dealing with visitors, including own responsibilities

Health, safety and security procedures need to be followed in order to prevent unauthorised access to the building. It is also important that the organisation and the emergency services know who is in the building in the case of a fire or other reasons for evacuating the premises.

When you began working for your employer, or started your course of study at the centre, hopefully you received an induction into the organisation's procedures and policies. During this induction programme you were probably made aware of several issues regarding the business's health and safety policies, including some of the following:

● the name(s) of key employees within the business who have been designated as health and safety representatives

● what the business's procedures are for ensuring that health and safety standards are met

● where the Health and Safety at Work Act is displayed within the business premises

● what the business's procedures are for identifying and reporting health and safety hazards and risks

● what the business's procedures are for reporting accidents

● what the business's procedures are for employee behaviour during an emergency situation

● what the business's procedures are for the use of equipment, machinery, products and materials from a health and safety point of view.

By law, an organisation has to have a safety policy in place which must state the ways in which the business intends to protect its employees, customers and visitors from health and safety problems. This policy will be revised and updated on a regular basis by senior management and from these revisions the employees will be made aware of the business's codes of practice. The safety policy will be a written account of how the business intends to train and instruct its employees on health and safety matters and how it will keep a record of its procedures for reporting accidents and emergencies.

Depending on the size and complexity of the organisation, the codes of practice will be a detailed account of:

- how employees should act in the event of an emergency
- how employees should act in the event of an accident
- trained first-aid personnel within the business
- the location of the first-aid room
- named safety representatives or members of a safety committee.

In larger organisations a safety committee is set up and in smaller businesses a safety officer or safety representatives are designated. These individuals will keep the management of the business informed of any changes in government legislation regarding health and safety and inform them of any problems within the business that could mean it is not complying with these laws. In addition, they will strive to prevent or reduce risks by:

- ensuring all relevant employees are issued with and are using personal protective equipment. This would be issued to anyone dealing with toxic or otherwise dangerous materials or substances
- ensuring all machinery and equipment is being used in accordance with the manufacturers' safety instructions. This is particularly relevant when the use of safety guards is recommended
- ensuring the premises are adequately ventilated. This is particularly important when hazardous fumes or smoke are involved in the business's activity. Extractor fans and machinery to circulate the air can ensure that sufficiently good air quality is maintained at all times
- ensuring suitable fire extinguishers and/or fire blankets are available throughout the business's premises
- ensuring safety warning signs are clearly marked. These need to be displayed prominently so that they can easily be seen by employees, customers and visitors
- ensuring sufficient individuals are trained to deal with first-aid situations. Under the Health and Safety at Work Act, the employer is required by law to make sure that qualified individuals are available
- ensuring employees are adhering to the business's safety policy by carrying out safe working practices. It's no good having a safety policy in place if the employees are not working safely.

Security alerts are a little more detailed in nature and, unfortunately, more common than they used to be. Security alerts and threats to an organisation's premises can come from both inside and outside the company. Those coming from the inside can include the theft of goods by one of the employees and could result in evacuation in order that all staff can be searched. Threats from outside the organisation can be listed as follows:

● robberies or burglaries – often result in some form of violence to those working within the organisation

● bomb threats – often carried out in order to either threaten a company or make a political statement

● activists and spies – who are capable of entering the premises in order to do damage, tamper with the site or steal information.

The emergency procedures implemented and practice evacuations will aim to make sure that in the event of a real emergency, quick, clear thinking is the key to safe evacuation of a building or the vicinity of a potential accident. There are a number of things to try to remember should you find yourself involved in an emergency situation:

● move swiftly to get out of the building or at least out of immediate danger and try not to panic

● if you are the last person to leave a room, close the door behind you. This is a way of double-checking that a room has been cleared of personnel and if a fire is the emergency, it will help to stop it from spreading

● make sure you are aware of notices that give you the location of the fire assembly points and fire exits

● follow the emergency procedures in operation in your workplace.

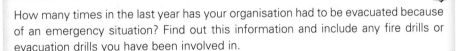

Over to you

How many times in the last year has your organisation had to be evacuated because of an emergency situation? Find out this information and include any fire drills or evacuation drills you have been involved in.

1.5 Describe different types of problems that may occur with visitors, including conflict and aggression
1.6 Describe ways of dealing with different problems and when to refer them to an appropriate colleague

It is difficult to give you definite advice regarding the use of organisational procedures to resolve difficulties as organisational procedures differ from business to business. You will have a distinct advantage if you are in work as you will at least be able to learn what the organisational procedures are. If you are studying this course at college, you may have to adopt the college's organisational procedures in order to provide evidence for this assessment objective.

Customers may have a number of special requirements. These can relate to any of the following:

- they may have special needs as a result of their personal circumstances
- they may have a physical or mental impairment (they may be in a wheel-chair, be hard of hearing or have an eyesight problem)
- they may not be able to speak or read English very well
- they may have special needs that are dictated by their culture or religion
- they may have an unusual request
- they may want to complain
- they may want some advice, information or guidance.

The staff should always be able to deal with complaints and respond positively to the customer. As you already know, employees should:

- listen carefully to what is being said
- ask questions to make sure they understand exactly what the complaint is about
- explain to the customer what they can do to help them with their problem
- get help from someone else if it is a problem they can't deal with themselves
- keep the customer informed of what is being done at all times.

There also needs to be clear procedures in order to account for visitors and ensure that they are evacuated if there is an emergency in the building.

Internal communication can be an issue when visitors arrive at the building. Sometimes when an individual arrives for an appointment the person they are expecting to see has not informed the reception, so there is no record of their meeting. It is important in cases such as this that the individual they are due to see is contacted immediately and that the visitor is politely asked to wait. On other occasions visitors may have arrived too early or too late for their appointment. Again, the individual who is expecting them should be contacted to check whether it is convenient to see them now.

Sometimes customers get angry. If this happens while you are on reception, you should make sure you remain calm and do not argue back. The old saying may claim 'the customer is always right', but this is not always the case. Sometimes customers get angry because they know they are wrong. But this doesn't mean an employee has the right to be rude to a customer, even if they do become abusive.

Anyone dealing with an abusive customer should:

- apologise for the fact that they are upset about something to do with the organisation
- show sympathy – for example, tell them they understand why they are so upset
- ask the right questions to get to the bottom of what they are complaining about
- let the customer see they are going to try to do something about their problem
- get someone to deal with the situation as quickly as possible
- try to explain to the customer what is being done at every stage
- try to explain why the problem may have arisen in the first place
- not put the blame on someone else
- try to agree with the customer what would be best for them
- promise the customer that they will do all they can to make sure that the solution actually happens
- keep their promise.

Sometimes customers may need help and assistance. Sometimes wheelchair users or others with a disability of some kind may require assistance to gain access to a particular part of the organisation. Whatever the nature of the request, employees should always be polite and show the customer that they are happy to help them. It is important that however small the request for assistance may be, the customer feels they are valued and that the staff actually care about them.

A customer may have a query about any of the organisation's products and services. You should make sure you are clear about what the customer wants. It may be that they need information or advice about the price of the product or it could be that you have to give them additional information in order to convince them to buy the product. If this is the case, you will require information about the different methods of paying for the products or services offered by the organisation.

In either your business or the college the regular staff who deal with customers will face situations when it will be impossible for them to cope with certain people with complex problems. While most of the staff are trained to deal with routine problems and other matters, your business or your college will have specialists who know far more than other employees about the area in which the customer is having difficulties. In these cases you will have to take down the basic information about the customer's difficulty, promise to pass on the information and ensure that the appropriate member of staff to whom the difficulty is to be referred follows it up. Remember, even when you have referred, or passed on, a problem, the customer will remember you as being the person they approached in the first place and if the difficulty is not resolved, there is every likelihood that they will ask for you again to enquire about the progress of their difficulty.

If it is appropriate that you apologise on behalf of the business, you should do so. However, there are many situations when making an apology infers that the business accepts responsibility for something that has occurred. This may cause problems for the business as the customer may want to claim compensation (money) from the business as a result of any losses or damages which they have suffered.

Under most circumstances, however, a simple apology in relation to a late delivery, or not calling a customer when promised, is reasonable. But in more complicated situations, when the customer is blaming the organisation for a problem which they are experiencing, it would be best simply to give a basic apology and promise to refer the issue to a more senior member of staff.

Give it a go

Here are some statements from customers. Write down what you would say in response to them:

1 'I paid express delivery and you promised me that it would be delivered this morning. It is now 2 o'clock. Where is it?'

2 'So, you are out of stock. I've got five customers waiting for these. Now that's your problem. What are you going to do about it?'

3 'Not faxing that information through to me in time has cost me a lot of money. I have a good mind to take your business to court.'

4 'When I got the box home it was supposed to have batteries and it didn't. My son was really disappointed.'

5 'What do you mean she is off sick? She arranged for me to call her this morning.'

1.7 Explain the purpose of communicating with visitors

Any visitor to the business or organisation is important, whether it is a customer, a supplier or a delivery man. Effective communication with all individuals is extremely important as you will have to understand their message or requirement and they will have to understand your responses.

Communication is the life blood of any business or organisation, as it:

● helps build relationships

● gives specific instructions

- passes on information

- shares ideas and values

- helps negotiations

- allows discussion

- stimulates interest

- creates awareness of the business or organisation.

Above all, communication is a two-way process. All messages need to be received and understood. By gauging the response of the visitor you can assess whether they have understood what you have told them and whether they need additional information.

Good communication with visitors is all about creating a good impression of the business or organisation. In a reception environment communication is both verbal and non-verbal. You will have to be able to read communication signals and also be aware of the fact that your body language gives non-verbal signals to the visitor. This means making sure that you:

- are careful with your facial expressions – we send almost hidden messages by our facial expressions, for example your eyes can widen with surprise or narrow with anger

- use gestures – you can nod in agreement or shake your head in disagreement. Bear in mind that some gestures can appear threatening or aggressive

- are aware of your posture – the positioning of your hands, feet and shoulders can mean different things. Sitting back in a chair shows relaxation and confidence; sitting on the edge of the seat could show that you are tense or anxious

- maintain eye contact – this is a very powerful form of non-verbal communication. You should look at the person you are talking to, but not stare at them. By giving the visitor eye contact you are showing that they have your undivided attention.

Give it a go

Try having a conversation with someone without using your hands, changing your facial expression or even looking at them. How much more difficult is it to get points of view across, or even to have a proper conversation? You may notice that you use non-verbal communication far more than you had ever thought.

1.8 Describe organisation structures and communication channels within the organisation

The easiest way to visualise an organisation's structure is to think about a pyramid. At the top of the pyramid there are few people making the most important and the biggest decisions about the business. As you go down the pyramid there are various layers of managers. After the managers are team leaders or supervisors. At the broadest part of the pyramid, the base, are the rest of the employees.

Now think about the pyramid with an arrow running from the top to the bottom. This represents instructions or orders being passed down the various layers of the organisation, until they reach the employees at the bottom. If you were to then put another arrow pointing in the opposite direction, this would represent the information provided by employees to their team leaders or supervisors, who then check that information and pass it on to the various layers of management. The management then passes on this information to the owners of the organisation. Armed with this information the business's owners can now make their decisions and create the orders and instructions to be passed back down in order to ensure that the business continues to run successfully. The following diagram illustrates these issues:

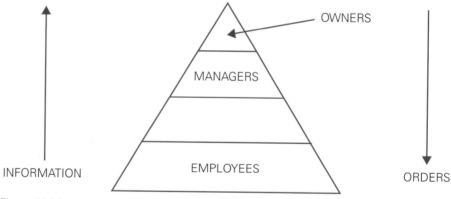

Figure 256.2

The way in which an organisation chooses the structure it adopts will depend on a number of issues, including:

- the size and nature of the market in which it operates
- the type of business in which it is involved
- the need for good communication throughout the organisation
- the size of the organisation itself
- the number of different branches or sites owned by the organisation
- the type and number of customers the organisation has

● how much the organisation is affected by government laws

● how much the organisation is affected by new technologies

● the responsibilities and obligations the organisation has

● the way it was structured in the past

● the way it is presently structured

● what the organisation's plans are for the future

● how complex the organisation's activities are.

A functionally based organisational structure is usually designed around the different parts of the organisation that produce, market and sell the product or service. In other words, the different departments or functions will all be controlled by a board of directors, who elect or appoint a managing director. The managing director is supported by a range of senior managers, each of which has the responsibility for one particular function of the organisation. The following illustration explains a functional structure:

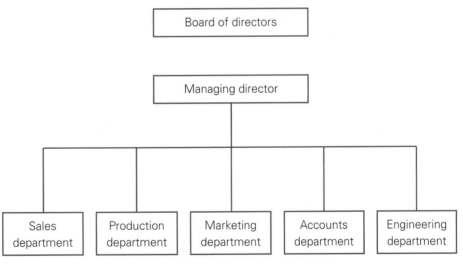

Figure 256.3

Give it a go

Think about either the college in which you are studying this course, or your place of work. You may also have a part-time, Saturday job with an organisation you could think about for the purposes of this activity. See if you can draw up an organisation chart (as shown in the diagram above) for your business or college. Instead of worrying about people's titles, put in the names of those people you know if that makes the task easier.

Many organisations, particularly large ones, use a functional organisational structure. These functions are, in fact, the different areas or departments of the business. The business needs to be organised in the best possible way in order to meet the objectives that have been set for it. This helps to define what individuals do and precisely what departments are responsible for.

Using this type of organisational structure, a business can group certain functions that it carries out logically under a particular manager. There are usually four ways of grouping employees, or grouping what the business does:

- by what they produce, known as the product

- by their function, or what they do for the organisation

- by process, which means how they do it, for example by having various regional offices

- by type of customer, for example if they deal with other business organisations, or with retail outlets (shops).

The functional areas of an organisation, often otherwise known as the departments of an organisation, all have their own specific jobs to do. In order that you understand fully what this can involve, we need to look at each of the departments separately.

It is important for the receptionist to be familiar with the structure of the organisation. They need to know to which department, section or branch of the business to direct visitors or callers. The receptionist will also need to know who is employed in each of these areas, or at least the main contacts, as well as the best way to contact those people. They will have their extension number, mobile number or bleeper on their contacts list.

Finance/accounting

The finance or accounts department of an organisation supervises all matters involving money. Computers and calculators are used extensively. Sometimes the finance department is split up into two further sections:

1 The day-to-day accounting procedures are handled by the financial accounting section. The staff here keep track of all money coming into the business and all money going out of the business.

2 The management accounting section concentrates on analysing the financial figures and trying to predict, or forecast, how much the business will earn, and how much the business will have to pay out, in the future.

The information the finance department calculates is needed by the directors, shareholders and senior managers of the business. The finance department gives this information to them in written documents, including those called balance sheets and profit and loss accounts. By law, the finance department has to keep written records of all financial decisions taken by the business, including records of all sales made and items purchased.

Give it a go

We have mentioned that the finance department deals with wages and salaries. From your business or from your college, see if you can find out the following:

1 What information would the finance department need to keep about each of its employees?

2 Does the finance department of your business or college do all the tasks we have discussed, or does it employ another business to do some of them?

3 By law, what information does the finance department have to provide about employees for the Inland Revenue, which is a government department that collects tax?

4 What information does the finance department keep about each of the employees regarding their pensions?

Human resources

The main function of the human resources department is to recruit the right new employees and organise them so that they provide the right type of work the organisation needs in order to meet its objectives. The human resources department is also sometimes known as the 'personnel department'.

The staff here closely monitor the selection of new employees. But this is not the end of the function of the human resources department. They also try to ensure that suitable employees are trained and developed adequately and, if particular employees are suitable, they try to ensure that they are given higher and often better paid jobs (promotion) within the business.

Close contact is kept with all the other departments of the business to make sure that the employees are receiving the right kind of training by organising:

● the induction of new employees – telling them about the organisation when they start

● training – perhaps to cover how to use new technology

● retraining – perhaps when an employee's job has been moved from one department to another.

The human resources department is also responsible for keeping all employee records, including details of:

● holiday entitlements – days of holiday already taken and the number of days the employee has left to take

● sickness records – the number of days the employee has taken off due to illness

● qualifications of each employee

● experience of each employee, both before joining the business and while working for the business

- wage or salary of each employee
- pension details for each employee
- confidential reports from the employees' line managers or supervisors
- details of the training each employee has undertaken.

Give it a go

Human resources department employees often have the pleasant task of informing the most suitable candidate that they have got the job they applied for. However, they also have to tell the unsuccessful candidates that they have not been accepted for the job. They would want to do this as tactfully as possible and this obviously involves using the right tone and style in the business letter.

Imagine that you work in the human resources department and have the task of writing to three unsuccessful candidates. Compose a standard letter that could be sent to all the unsuccessful candidates.

Production

The production department is involved in all functions which revolve around actually producing the products or services for the customer. This department will monitor levels of wastage to ensure the most efficient use of resources. It will also check the cost of raw materials and parts purchased to make sure that profit margins are maintained.

As new products are developed, and technology changes, the production department will be responsible for purchasing all the necessary machinery and equipment required, as well as organising the production process.

In close contact with the sales department, the production department must make sure that it can manufacture or supply customers with the quantity required, at the time it is needed. The tight monitoring of production levels means that the production department should know how long it would take to produce enough products to fill a particular order. Planning in advance and close contact with the sales department is vital as deadlines must be met.

The production department is also responsible for the quality of the business's products. Each product must meet a number of strict quality standards and must be exactly the same every time. Products will be selected from the production line and tested by either the research and development department or, if the business has one, the quality assurance department.

The production department will communicate and work closely with most of the other departments within the organisation. It would also communicate with the business's suppliers. The production department would not necessarily communicate directly with the business's customers.

Give it a go

Look at the following list of other departments the production department might work closely with:

- Sales
- Marketing
- Purchasing
- Research and development
- Finance
- Human resources
- Administration.

Use each of these departments as a heading on a table. Under each heading give the reasons why you think the production department might need to communicate with that department. What information would the production department need to give each of these other departments? What information would the production department need to obtain from each of these other departments?

Research and development (R&D)

Working closely with the marketing department (which is keeping a close eye on competitors' products and services), the research and development department would attempt to come up with new products for the business.

The main function of the research and development department is not just to come up with new products or services but also to come up with the most efficient and effective way of producing them. It will, after carrying out lots of tests, pass on its designs and proposed ways of producing the product to the production department. The production department will then take over the responsibility of putting the new products into production.

Give it a go

As you will see from the sub-heading used for the research and development department, this department is often known as just R&D. Using a dictionary, see whether you can find out what these other initials or acronyms represent:

ABTA

E&OE

COHSE

PABX

LAN

WAN

CAM

CAD

Purchasing

The purchasing department is responsible for assisting the business's other departments in ordering and buying the goods and services required. Whatever the purchasing department is ordering from the suppliers, they would need to ensure that they are receiving the best possible price, as well as ensuring that the goods will be received when they are required by the other departments. The purchasing department would keep a stock of catalogues and price lists from suppliers. When the purchasing department's employees receive a purchase requisition (a request to purchase) from one of the other departments, or individuals, within the organisation, they would research the various suppliers until they find the right product, at the right price, with the right delivery time.

Give it a go

See if you can obtain a copy of a catalogue from an office equipment business and one from an office stationery business.

You work in the purchasing department of a business and have received a purchase requisition for the following:

2 reams of A4 white photocopy paper

2 pine desks

1 typist's chair

Have a look through the catalogue and see if you can find out:

● the cost of each of these items

● the total cost of the order

● details of how long it would take to receive the order.

Now write a memo to your tutor, informing him/her what you have researched.

Sales

The sales department's main responsibility is to create orders for the business's products or services. Many organisations employ a large sales force, which may be based either on a local level, in the case of retail outlets (shops), or in the case of organisations which supply other organisations, on a regional basis.

The greater the emphasis is on selling to individual customers, the larger the sales force. Those businesses that rely on large amounts of advertising to gain interest in the products or service can have quite a small sales force.

Much of the information that the sales department provides is analysed by the marketing department. Often the sales department will also develop what is known as point-of-sale materials. These include posters, leaflets, brochures, pamphlets and catalogues.

Give it a go

Sales force employees often have to work out their own schedule or timetable for the week. Imagine that you are a sales representative of your business and you have the following information and commitments lined up for next week:

1 You have to be present at head office for only two hours during the week.

2 You have a total of over 200 customers on your customer list.

3 Your sales area covers one-tenth of the UK.

4 You usually spend at least 20 hours per week in the car, travelling to visit customers.

5 You usually spend on average 20 minutes with each of your customers.

6 Keeping your paperwork up to date takes at least one and a half hours each day.

7 Telephone calls (including those made on your car phone or mobile) take up at least one hour each day.

See if you can draw up a timetable that would allow you to include all these items in a normal Monday–Friday, 8-hour-day working week.

Marketing

The main function of the marketing department is to try to meet the business's customers' needs and to predict what they may need in the future. Working closely with the sales department, the marketing department carries out a great deal of research to try to discover what customers want, where they want to be able to buy what they want and how much they are prepared to pay for it. They also try to design the best way to inform customers about what it is the business is offering for sale.

The marketing department also has the responsibility of advertising the business's products and ideas through marketing campaigns. They will work on the design and development of these campaigns in close cooperation with the sales department and other interested areas within the business.

Give it a go

You have been asked by your business to contact several hundred possible new customers about a new service the business is offering. The business does not wish to spend too much money on postage, so they want you to design something which can be delivered with the free local newspaper that everyone in the area receives through their letterbox. Here is the information you have been given:

We are planning to expand the services we currently offer by now offering a delivery service. The sandwich take-away shop is doing very well, but we think we can increase our customer numbers by offering a delivery service too. All the local office blocks might want to have sandwiches delivered at lunch times and we think there may be some people who would like us to prepare sandwiches for them if they have guests or are holding parties.

Distribution

The effective and efficient distribution of the business's products is the responsibility of the distribution department. Very often this one department can be split into two distinct sections. These are:

● the stores or warehouse – this is where the products are safely stored. These may be the products that are ready to be sold on to customers. It could also be where all packaging or raw materials or part-finished products are stored before being required by the production department. This section of the department would need to keep a careful check on the stock levels of all items for which it has overall responsibility and should inform the relevant department should stocks begin to approach their 'minimum stock levels' as they would need to be re-ordered from the supplier

● the distribution or transportation – the main function of this section is to coordinate the business's transport needs. This will include the purchasing, or hiring, of company cars, lorries and trucks, as well as ensuring they are frequently serviced and maintained. The department will have to maintain records such as insurance, vehicle registration, road tax, service records and hiring or purchasing agreements regarding each of the business's delivery vehicles.

In situations when an organisation provides a delivery service to the customer, it is essential that the most efficient and cost-effective (cheapest) routes are used. This task is often carried out using computer software.

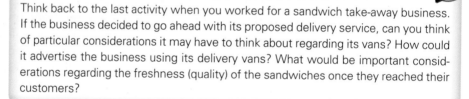

Give it a go

Think back to the last activity when you worked for a sandwich take-away business. If the business decided to go ahead with its proposed delivery service, can you think of particular considerations it may have to think about regarding its vans? How could it advertise the business using its delivery vans? What would be important considerations regarding the freshness (quality) of the sandwiches once they reached their customers?

Administration

Some organisations have what is known as a central administration department. The main function of this department is to control the paperwork and to support all the other departments by providing them with secretarial or administrative work, for example:

● word processing or data input

● filing of paperwork

● making telephone calls

● dealing with the mail, both incoming and letters going out of the business

- gathering information or collecting data for another department to use

- sending fax and email messages.

The administration department will deal with a variety of information from a variety of places. They will have to process that information in order to make it useful to others, including doing the following tasks:

- research and obtain information – this may involve searching for information on the Internet, or from libraries, from catalogues or reference books

- summarise the information – this could take the form of reading something and then presenting it in a different, shortened format

- present the information – the administration employees will have to be knowledgeable about the ways in which the business prefers to present its information. Information can be presented in a number of ways, including memos, letters, reports, articles or notices.

Give it a go

You work in the administration department of a primary school in your local area. The headmistress is expecting four visitors on Tuesday of next week at 11.00. They are inspectors who will be touring round the school before they come back to spend three days inspecting the school's staff and students. The headmistress has left this note on your desk:

Can you do two things please:

Write to the inspectors (do a standard letter first and I'll check it through before you send it). I want them to know that I will expect them at 11.00 and I have reserved car parking spaces for each of them. We'll have coffee at 11.00 and then I've arranged lunch in the staff restaurant at 1.00. I don't know what else they want me to do, but I assume they will get in touch again if they want anything special.

I also need you to let all the teachers know about the date, and the time of the visits. Can you do a memo to all staff giving them the details?

Customer services

Without customers, a business is unable to survive. However large or small a business may be, it will always want to make sure that its customers are happy. Because the customers' needs, wants and requirements change all the time, the business will have to think ahead of its customers to make sure it always gives them exactly what they require to keep them satisfied.

The customer service department is the main point of contact that customers have with a business. It could be that the customer has a complaint to make, or that they require more detailed information from the department.

Give it a go

If you worked in the customer service department of a business and were asked to design a special form to log customer complaints, what headings would you include? First of all draft out a form that you think would be suitable for this purpose and once you are happy that you have included all that is needed, word process and print out a copy of the form.

IT services

The information technology (IT) or computer services department will have responsibility for the hardware and the software that a business uses. It will also be responsible for maintaining the business's databases, telecommunications systems and other office technology. As most organisations now incorporate computers into many of their routine activities, this department would need to be up to date on any developments in the technologies used and know how to use new software. Once the IT staff have mastered the use of this new software, they would then assist in training employees from other departments who are going to use it on a regular basis. Sometimes an organisation will employ the services of another business or an individual (consultant) to carry out the work done by an IT department.

Give it a go

Why do you think some businesses prefer to use a computer services consultant, rather than keep a department of their own for this purpose? Have a look on the Internet and see if you can find a computer services consultant or business. What services do they offer a business? Why would a business find it more useful to pay them to help?

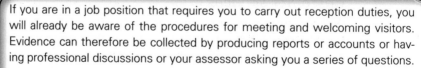

What is Evidence ?

If you are in a job position that requires you to carry out reception duties, you will already be aware of the procedures for meeting and welcoming visitors. Evidence can therefore be collected by producing reports or accounts or having professional discussions or your assessor asking you a series of questions.

If you are carrying out this unit at a centre, you will need to experience reception duties, perhaps by shadowing the receptionist and helping out when meeting and welcoming visitors to the centre. Again, this can be supported by reports, accounts, discussions and questioning. Your assessor will be able to help you assemble the necessary evidence.

■ 2. Be able to meet and welcome visitors

Although nothing would replace actually doing reception work for real and dealing with real visitors to a business or organisation, role play can be useful to provide evidence. The following nine role plays and activities are designed to allow you to show that you are able to meet and welcome visitors.

Figure 256.4

2.1 Greet visitor(s) and make them feel welcome
2.2 Identify visitors and the reason for their visit

Refer to 1.1 and 1.2 and then attempt the following activity.

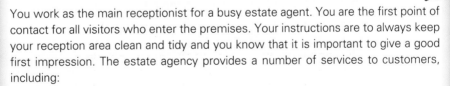

Give it a go

You work as the main receptionist for a busy estate agent. You are the first point of contact for all visitors who enter the premises. Your instructions are to always keep your reception area clean and tidy and you know that it is important to give a good first impression. The estate agency provides a number of services to customers, including:

● residential sales

● sales, leases and renting of commercial premises

● private renting of residential properties

● insurance advice

● mortgage advice

● valuations of properties.

In a discussion with your assessor, explain how you would greet visitors and make them feel welcome. What questions would you ask in order to identify the purpose of their visit and who you should direct them to? Make sure that you consider the following:

- the visitor should be greeted immediately and made to feel welcome
- you should ask for the visitor's name and/or the company they represent if appropriate
- you should ask the reason for their visit and/or whether they have an appointment
- you should watch their body language
- you should be prepared to answer questions
- you should deal with them if they need to wait
- you should deal with any problems that may arise
- you should know when and to whom to pass on problems.

Role play

Welcome a visitor and find out the purpose of their visit. The visitor has an appointment. They will need to sign the visitors' book but they do not need a security badge.

What is Evidence ?

For 2.1 and 2.2 evidence can be supplied through observation, witness testimony, discussion, reports and accounts and inspection of products such as visitor logs.

2.3 Use the organisation's systems to receive and record visitors, as appropriate

Refer to 1.4 and then attempt the following activity.

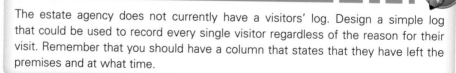

Give it a go

The estate agency does not currently have a visitors' log. Design a simple log that could be used to record every single visitor regardless of the reason for their visit. Remember that you should have a column that states that they have left the premises and at what time.

What is Evidence ?

For 2.3, evidence can be supplied through observation, witness testimony, discussion, reports and accounts and inspection of products such as visitor logs. Visitor books are the primary source of evidence.

2.4 Make sure visitors' needs are met

Refer to 1.1 and then attempt the following activity.

Give it a go

Using your log book designed in the previous activity, complete it by putting in the following entries, noting which member of staff you have directed each of the visitors to see.

Staff members and duties:

Brian Jones	–	Residential sales
Louise Greenwood	–	Mortgages and insurance
Tony Philpott	–	Rentals
Barry White	–	Commercial

Visitors:

Mrs Fredericks 1030	–	interested in selling her house
Mr Franks 1015	–	wants to rent a shop
Miss Greenway 1125	–	looking for a flat to rent with friends
Mr Cuthbert 1210	–	has seen a house for sale he likes
Mrs Bultitude 1310	–	wants to insure her house
Mr Smythe 1340	–	has seen a house he likes in one of your adverts but not sure if he can afford to buy it
Mr Long 1645	–	has sold his house through you and is dropping off the keys.

2.5 Present positive image of self and the organisation

Refer to 1.3 and then attempt the following activity.

Give it a go

Even visitors with appointments may have to wait for a short period before seeing the individual they had arranged to meet. What steps should you take in order to ensure that you present a positive image of yourself and the estate agency if this is the case? What should be present in the reception area? What should you offer the visitors? How might your actions have a positive or negative effect on the estate agency?

2.6 Follow health, safety and security procedures, as required

Refer to 1.4 and then attempt the following activity.

Give it a go

The estate agency is in a busy high street. The door opens inwards straight into the reception area. The waiting area for visitors is underneath the staircase to the first floor. All the offices of the other staff are on the first floor, as is the toilet. Although no security badges are required for visitors, you should have security procedures. Consider the following and how you would deal with them:

- the head room under the stairs where the seating is for visitors is restricted
- the nearest seat for visitors is very close to the front door
- a visitor wants to use the toilet
- an electrician is at work on the ground floor and there are a number of cables lying on the floor, along with his toolbox
- the stairs to the offices have just had the banister repainted and the paint is still tacky
- the doormat just inside the front door is curled in one corner.

2.7 Inform others of visitors' arrival, as required, in line with appropriate communication channels

Refer to 1.8 and then attempt the following activity.

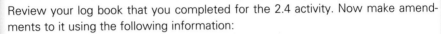

Give it a go

Review your log book that you completed for the 2.4 activity. Now make amendments to it using the following information:

Brian Jones is not available to see anyone all morning as he is out visiting properties. He will not be back in the office until 1300. In his absence Barry White will deal with his work.

Louise Greenwood is at lunch between 1200 and 1300.

Tony Philpott is not in the office between 1400 and 1600.

Barry White is not to be disturbed between 1300 and 1500 as he has paperwork to catch up on.

If suitable members of staff are not available, you should book customers in to see the appropriate member of staff the following day from 0930. Amend your log book to take into consideration these changes and complete one for the following day.

2.8 Deal with any problems that may occur, or refer problems to the appropriate person

Refer to 1.5 and then attempt the following activity.

Give it a go

A delivery man arrives at the estate agency with 5,000 copies of your brochure, which is to be inserted into the local free newspaper. The brochures should have been delivered to the newspaper's printer, but the delivery man is insistent that having carried them from his van he is going to leave them in your reception area. He is assertive and aggressive. How would you deal with the situation? What would you do if the delivery man insisted on leaving the boxes near the front door, cluttering up the reception area? Could you deal with this situation alone or would you have to pass it on to someone in a more senior position? The brochures were ordered by Brian Jones but he will not be back for at least another half an hour.

What is Evidence ?

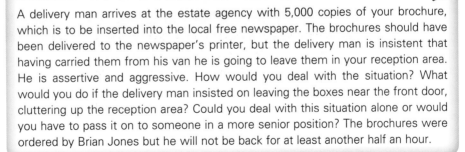

For 2.4–2.8 evidence can be supplied through observation, witness testimony, discussion, reports and accounts and inspection of products such as visitor logs.

2.9 Follow procedures for departing visitors, as required

Refer to 1.4 and then attempt the following activity.

Give it a go

Using the original log book (before amendments were made), complete the column for departing visitors from the following information:

Mrs Fredericks left after 40 minutes

Mr Franks was in the building for 15 minutes

Miss Greenway took several brochures and left after 5 minutes

Mr Cuthbert was in a meeting for an hour

Mrs Bultitude's business took 35 minutes

Mr Smythe received mortgage advice and left after 45 minutes

Mr Long left the keys with you.

Update your log book. In a discussion with your assessor, identify what you might say to each of the visitors as they departed the premises.

What is Evidence ?

For 2.9, evidence can be supplied through observation, witness testimony, discussion, reports and accounts and inspection of products such as visitor logs. Visitor books are the primary source of evidence.

Pull it together

A number of assessment methods can be used in order to cover the learning outcomes and assessment criteria. These will include:

● observation of performance in the working environment

● examination of work products

● questioning

● discussions

● witness testimony

● statements

● recognising prior learning.

In terms of evidence there are a number of documents that would prove to be useful. These include:

● visitors' signing-in book

- your notes on the health and safety procedure
- minutes of one-to-one discussions or team meetings
- records of training related to reception work
- appraisals and reviews
- personal development plans
- notes on problems encountered and actions that you took.

Index